FOLLOWING
THE
SANTA FE
TRAIL

FOLLOWING

A GUIDE FOR

THE SANTA FE TRAIL

MODERN TRAVELERS

Marc Simmons

ANCIENT CITY PRESS
SANTA FE, NEW MEXICO

International Standard Book Number:
0-941270-39-4 Clothbound
0-941270-38-6 Paperbound

Library of Congress Catalogue Number:
86-071417

Title page photo: Fort Union, looking south. (Neg. No. 1835, courtesy U. S. Army Signal Corps Collections in the Museum of New Mexico.)

Second Edition

Designed by Mary Powell
Maps by Mary Powell ©
Cover design by Stephen Tongier

Printed in the United States of America

10 9 8 7 6 5 4

To the members of
THE FORT LARNED HISTORICAL SOCIETY
(Kansas)
and the
CAVE SPRING ASSOCIATION
(Missouri)
who are working to preserve
America's heritage

and to
the memory of
ART CLARK, outdoorsman
who personified our pioneer spirit
in the Modern Age

TABLE OF CONTENTS

LIST OF MAPS

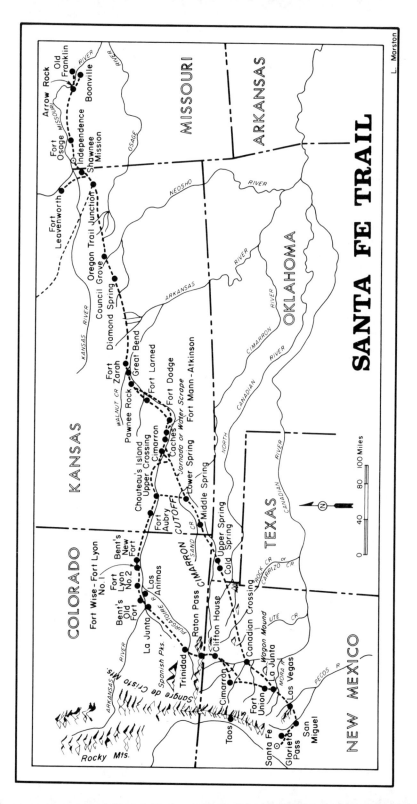

From Larry M. Beachum, *William Becknell: Father of the Santa Fe Trade* (El Paso: Texas Western Press, 1982). Used with permission.

PREFACE

The aim of this book is to assist contemporary travelers in finding their way over the Santa Fe Trail. Modern paved highways parallel much of the old wagon route, but in some places graded county roads must be followed for short stretches. With the directions I have provided anyone should be able to retrace large sections of the trail with comparative ease, although I have not tried to describe the route precisely mile by mile.

I made my first trip over the Santa Fe Trail in 1978 on assignment for the *National Geographic*. Even though I had studied trail history for years that was my first opportunity to travel its entire length and see the country firsthand from Franklin, Missouri, to Santa Fe, New Mexico. Since I live near the end of the trail my drive by necessity went from west to east. That proved a bit of a disadvantage because the early Santa Fe traders whose journals I was reading and using had made the journey from the other direction. So in following their accounts from campsite to campsite and landmark to landmark I had to keep reversing their order of things. As most of the country was new to me I found myself frequently disoriented.

A more serious problem proved to be the lack of any adequate guide that could lead me to major points of trail interest via modern roads. My time was limited, and I wasted a great deal of it in fruitless searches for some important sites that I regretted not finding. Several persons who had been over the trail before me told me about places not to be missed, but their directions were usually so vague and inaccurate that I ended up hopelessly lost. Unfortunately, more often than not, local residents are of little help since most of them are unaware of historical sites and monuments in their own communities.

Two older trail guides were of some help, at least in alerting me to points I should look for. In *The Santa Fe Trail*, a highway log published in 1954, Margaret Long concentrates her attention on the nearly two hundred granite markers placed along the trail by the Daughters of the American Revolution and in the process neglects much else of interest. Since her book appeared, the Interstate Highway System has been built and many secondary highways have been rerouted. As a result, Long's road directions to numerous markers are no longer accurate.

Hobart E. Stocking's *The Road to Santa Fe* was written in 1971. The author, a trail buff and geologist, gives much that is useful and entertaining but it is quite impossible to find many of the places he describes owing to the sketchy nature or total lack of road directions. Even so, I was glad to have his book.

By the conclusion of my first round-trip tour of the trail to Missouri and back to Santa Fe I had become a confirmed Santa Fe Trail addict. My reading and my own experience had convinced me that some mysterious force laid hold of travelers' affections and drew them back again and again to that historic old wagon road. Of Eliza Sloan, who made ten or more crossings of the prairies in the 1850s and 1860s, her daughter wrote years afterward: "My mother, on one pretext or another, would join a new caravan, for she was never happier than when passing to and fro over the Santa Fe Trail." Eliza's case was somewhat unique, but persons who became enamoured of trail life and remained wedded to it for much of their lives were fairly common.

The "force" leading to addiction curiously has persisted to the present day. More and more I encounter people best described as "trail junkies," persons who still find excitement and adventure in exploring today's remains of the Santa Fe Trail. Perhaps some of the explanation lies in traveling with a purpose, which offers a stimulating and fulfilling experience in contrast to random sightseeing. And then, of course, one must take into account the magic and beauty that persists in much of the landscape through which the Santa Fe Trail passes.

Many individuals make a voyage on the trail without ending up as hopeless junkies, but in the majority of such cases I suspect their travels are undertaken in a rather casual manner. For those who bone up on the subject beforehand, who master trail history in some depth and then strike out by automobile, foot, muleback, horseback, covered wagon or bicycle (and I have met persons who have traveled by all these methods), the chances are excellent that they will succumb to the spell of the trail.

But such an undertaking can be enjoyed in a variety of ways. So my guide is addressed to the addicts as well as to everyone else who may be interested in embarking upon a long or short excursion on the Santa Fe Trail.

In the introduction to this guide I have provided several categories of information that persons planning a trip should take into account. Something is said about road conditions and the best times of the year for trail travel. Suggestions are made concerning maps and books required for a successful tour. The types of markers that will be encountered are also discussed in this introduction.

With only a few exceptions I have not attempted to make recommendations with regard to lodging and meals. That sort of information is easily obtained from standard guides and tourist brochures. Requests for this type of material can be addressed to the Chamber of Commerce in larger places like Independence, Kansas City, Fort Leavenworth, Council Grove, Dodge City, Trinidad, Raton, Las Vegas and Santa Fe. Travelers should keep in mind that smaller towns may offer very limited accommodations. Council Grove, for example, a focal point on the trail, has only two motels, but it does have a splendid restaurant, the historic Hays House, dating from covered wagon days.

The main body of the text briefly describes the chief points of interest along the Santa Fe Trail and gives precise directions for finding them while using standard road maps. I have tried to provide the kind of detail that I needed but could not readily obtain on my first trip. Use of this guide should help in avoiding wild goose chases and leave more time to spend at those sites deserving of a prolonged visit.

The appendix offers a schedule of annual history-related special activities and celebrations that should be considered when planning a trail tour. I have also included a list of all trail sites that appear on the Registry of National Historic Landmarks.

Historic pioneer trails serve as some of the most interesting and colorful links to our nation's past. Retracing them can be an exhilarating and educational experience. An added pleasure I have found in exploring the Santa Fe Trail comes from meeting people all along the way who are dedicated history buffs and know many obscure details of the trail story in their localities. I have found them unfailingly friendly and eager to share information. This includes most private owners of trail sites. They like to talk to persons who are retracing the old wagon road. If you are open, receptive and courteous you will have a splendid opportunity to become acquainted with America at its grassroots. I think you will also find that traveling with a purpose, pursuing a single theme like the Santa Fe Trail, is far more rewarding than the usual vacation spent visiting popular and much-frequented tourist spots.

In compiling this guide I have incurred many debts over the years. Numerous people went out of their way to provide me with trail data and in some cases to guide me to elusive sites. I must first acknowledge the help of photographer Joan Myers of Santa Fe, a trail junkie of first rank. Together we have explored various segments of the western quarter of the trail, and she has called my attention to hard-to-find places that I would otherwise have missed.

No less deserving of my thanks is Pauline (Polly) Fowler of Independence. Every scholar and writer seriously interested in the starting point of the Santa Fe, Oregon and California trails eventually finds his or her way to Polly's door, which appropriately bears an address on the street called "Santa Fe Trail." Polly, the leading authority on Independence history and the Sibley trail survey, has given me hospitality, informed conversation and patient guide service. So too has William A. Goff (and his wife Virginia) in Kansas City. Bill is the foremost expert on old Westport and the route of the trail through the surrounding metropolitan area.

Also in Missouri, deserving of thanks, are Bertha Carson Amick (a descendant of one of Kit Carson's brothers), Franklin; Dr. Richard Forry, Arrow Rock; Marguerite Simpson and Pat O'Brien, Independence; and Jan Johnson of the Convention and Visitors Bureau of Kansas City. All were of assistance. I am especially indebted to Roberta L. Bonnewitz of Raytown for reviewing my entries on her area and to Sylvia Mooney and Whit Kirk, spearheads behind the flourishing Cave Spring Association, also in Raytown. My thanks too go to Sharon Fleming of Columbia.

In Kansas I am grateful to Michael E. Duncan, manager of the Mahaffie House and Farmstead, Olathe; Mary Jo O'Brien of the Olathe Public Library; Amelia J. Betts and Katharine Kelley, stalwart promoters of trail history in Baldwin City; George E. Strunk of Burlingame; Roe Groom and the staff of the Hays House Restaurant in Council Grove; Galland and Della Ellwood of Windom; Claude Unruh, Durham; Robert Nelson, who took time from his farming to show me the sites at the Little Arkansas Crossing; and Clyde Ernst at the Rice County Historical Museum, Lyons. Others in Kansas who must be mentioned are the late Jane Robison, Dodge City; David A. Dary, Lawrence; Joseph Snell and James H. Nottage, Kansas State Historical Society, Topeka; Don Coldsmith, Emporia; Leo Oliva, Hays; Jerry Jacobs, Wichita; Dave Brownlee, Syracuse; the staff of the Hugoton Public Library (who gave me shelter during a snowstorm); and in Garden City Brian F. Bergheger, director of the Finney County Historical Society, and Jesse Scott, Jr., accomplished trail hound who directed me to the site of Chouteau's Island on the Arkansas.

In Larned I have received many courtesies at the Santa Fe Trail Center administered by the Fort Larned Historical Society. My thanks go to its president, Mrs. H. C. Campbell, former director Bill Pitts, the current director Ruth Olson and to tireless archeologist Earl Monger, who has charted the route of the Santa Fe Trail through Pawnee County. Bill Henry, historian at the neighboring Fort Larned National Monument answered a number of my questions.

In the Oklahoma Panhandle I am pleased to acknowledge the help of Norma Gene Young, Boise City, and Truman Tucker, Kenton. Coloradans who lent aid include: John Patterson, former superintendent of Bent's Old Fort National Historic Site; John Graves, owner of the Iron Springs Stage Station site; Anthony Johnson and historian Janet Lecompte, both of Colorado Springs; Evelyn Vinogradov, Denver; the late Morris Taylor, Trinidad, who hiked with me to the summit of Raton Pass shortly before his untimely death; and the late Viola Russell of Stonewall, the last daughter-in-law of trail traveler Marian Russell.

Among those in New Mexico deserving of recognition are Mary P. Gaskin, owner of Willow Springs in Raton; William Wheatley and Billie Mock of Clayton (the latter the owner of McNees Crossing on the North Canadian); Steven Zimmer and the Buddy Morse's of Cimarron; Dr. and Mrs. Joe H. Knowles, owners of the Rock Crossing on the Canadian; Homer Hastings, former superintendent of the Fort Union National Monument; Joe and Diana Stein, Las Vegas; and Linda and Cindy Frye, former owners of Pigeon's Ranch Stage Station. In Santa Fe my thanks go to Dan Murphy, Earl Kubicek, Liz Dear, Orlando Romero, Sherry Smith-Gonzales and Alyce Weaver.

Finally, I would like to note the aid of Dr. David Weber, Dallas; Aaron and Ethel Armstrong, Roswell; Howard Bryan, Albuquerque; Octavia M. Glasgow, El Paso (a Magoffin descendant); Professor W. H. Timmons, also of El Paso; Dewey Tidwell, Las Cruces; Allan Maybee, Riverton, Wyoming; and Drs. James and Dolores Gunnerson, Lincoln, Nebraska.

Not to be overlooked is my typist Susie Henderson, who was responsible for the preparation of the final manuscript.

January 1984   Marc Simmons
                                                Cerrillos, New Mexico

PREFACE TO THE SECOND EDITION

The warm reception accorded the first edition of *Following the Santa Fe Trail* by travelers, general readers, and reviewers has encouraged both author and publisher to expend considerable effort in the improvement of the second edition. The entire text has been set in new type; more illustrations and maps have been included, and an index added. In a number of cases, directions have been clarified or expanded.

During April of 1985, I retraced the entire route of the trail taking note of recent changes that required additions or deletions in the guide. I especially benefited from information supplied by Les Vilda and David and Denise Fikar who the previous summer had hiked the trail from Fort Osage to Santa Fe. Among other things, they called my attention to several fine sets of wagon ruts that I had failed to discover on earlier trips.

Others who provided notable assistance in the process of revision were Ralph Hathaway, Roe Groom, Lloyd Burns, Katharine Kelley, Ava Betz, Aaron and Ethel Armstrong, Ruth Olson, Earl Monger, Betsy Crawford, Mary Jean Cook, Jesse Scott, Jr., Gregory Franzwa, Darlene Smith, Jeanie Covalt, Wilmer Ekholm, Polly Fowler, Prof. Stanley B. Kimball, and particularly Paul Bentrup of Deerfield, Kansas.

At this writing, sentiment is growing for the formation of a new Santa Fe Trail Association that could assist in preserving and interpreting the historic old caravan route. In the meanwhile, readers are encouraged to join the vigorous Oregon-California Trails Association (Box 42, Gerald, Missouri 63037), which has set both the pace and the standard for such organizations.

The purpose of a book like the present guide is to serve as a vehicle for entry into a fascinating and exciting world now vanished. All of the sites, landmarks, and monuments described in the following pages become touchstones to yesterday, giving access to a period of history brimming with color and adventure. After a few days spent under the open sky, retracing the Santa Fe Trail, it often happens that the modern age seems to withdraw to the back of the stage while the nineteenth century moves into the floodlights. At such times, one can catch the pulse and spirit of the trail era, so that arriving at last on the Santa Fe plaza, it is possible to proclaim, "Yes! Through experience and my own imagination I've forged a link with the past and I know in a small but authentic way what it was all about."

September 1985

Marc Simmons
Cerrillos, New Mexico

INTRODUCTION

The Santa Fe Trail was the first and most exotic of America's great trans-Mississippi pathways to the West. Its opening in 1821 preceded by two decades the birth of the Oregon and California trails. Unlike them, the Santa Fe Trail began in the United States and ended in a foreign country, Mexico, at least for the first quarter-century of its existence. The strange customs, unfamiliar language and breath-taking scenery found at the foot of the trail exerted a strong appeal and filled overlanders bound for New Mexico with a special excitement.

The trail to Santa Fe was first and last a highway of commerce. In that, it differed markedly from trails farther north whose traffic was composed mainly of pioneer settlers, ranchers, farmers and miners pushing toward the Pacific in quest of new homes and opportunities to be won from the land. The Santa Fe Trail was opened by a merchant, William Becknell, who foresaw profits to be made in transporting American goods across the southern prairies to eager Hispanic customers in the Republic of Mexico's far north. The merchants who followed him with mighty caravans of Murphy freight wagons merely enlarged upon a commercial opportunity that Becknell first brought to public attention. Within a short time the Santa Fe trade ballooned into a million-dollar-a-year business, pouring Mexican silver coin and raw products into the state of Missouri and precipitating a minor economic boom in what heretofore had been a depressed area on the American frontier.

The twenty-five years in which Mexico controlled the western end of the trade are generally regarded as the heyday of the Santa Fe Trail. In that period occurred many of the most dramatic events associated with trail history, including noted Indian fights, weather disasters that befell several caravans, the survey of the route in 1825, the first experimentation with military patrols, rocky diplomatic negotiations with Mexico and, of course, the travels of Josiah Gregg, whose classic book on the subject, *Commerce of the Prairies*, first publicized this chapter in America's far western adventure.

After General Stephen Watts Kearny led a conquering army over the Mountain Branch of the Santa Fe Trail in 1846, the first year of the Mexican War, and brought the Southwest under United States rule the character of overland commerce changed. With both ends of the trail in American hands, the traffic was no longer of international scope. Forts were added along the route to guard against Indian attack, and the freighting of military supplies became a new business. Stagecoach and mail services were inaugurated. More varied types of travelers put in an appearance. Where once the trail had been frequented only by merchants, their wagonmasters and ox drovers, by the late 1840s one could begin to meet, besides U. S. Army soldiers, newly appointed government officials, gold seekers bound for California, Catholic priests and nuns, a sprinkling of Protestant missionaries and even a few emigrant families.

The last phase of the trail story unfolded during the 1870s as railroads pushed across Kansas and into the Southwest, creating a new railhead with each advance and progressively shortening the Santa Fe Trail. When the train reached Las Vegas in the summer of 1879, only sixty-five miles remained of the original wagon route to Santa Fe. In February of 1880, with that last gap closed by rails, newspapers in New Mexico's capital proclaimed in bold headlines: "The Santa Fe Trail Passes Into Oblivion."

The subsections that follow are aimed at assisting modern travelers in enlarging their understanding of the trail and increasing the enjoyment that comes with retracing the wagon tracks of the pioneer merchantmen from Missouri. Recommended background readings, maps and travel tips are discussed. Markers, monuments and trail ruts are also described.

RECOMMENDED READINGS

The literature on the Santa Fe Trail is vast, almost overwhelming for the beginner. Basic for anyone doing serious research on the subject is Jack D. Rittenhouse's *The Santa Fe Trail, A Historical Bibliography.* Published in 1971 to commemorate the 150th anniversary of the opening of the trail by Becknell, it contains an annotated listing of 718 titles. Since its publication, of course, new works have appeared, so the number of books relating to the trail now must number around 800.

The titles I am recommending here comprise a basic reading list that should be consulted by all those planning a trip over the trail. Everyone should read at least one general Santa Fe Trail history chosen from among the several I have suggested. Failure to do so will seriously diminish the value and pleasure of a tour. Also read as many of the firsthand accounts as time permits. Primary journals or diaries and recollections of trail life by individual participants impart a taste and feel for the past like nothing else and give a sense of what caravan travel was like.

Whenever I am on the trail I carry a small library of my own books in the back seat of the car. At each historic stop I have only to reach behind, pluck an appropriate volume and read the words of a traveler who preceded me to that place by 150 years. How remarkable it is, for example, to stand in Independence Square and read Matt Field's lively description of a noisy and colorful wagon caravan preparing to depart for Santa Fe; or to climb Pawnee Rock with Susan Magoffin's diary in hand and to consult the entry for July 4, 1846, recounting her experiences and emotions there; or to reach the eastern limits of Santa Fe and turn to Josiah Gregg's vivid recital of the arrival of an ox train at the trail's end. With such books we are able to look backward as through a prism and make the entire, grand Santa Fe Trail adventure part of our own experience.

Bookstores located on or near the trail often have many of the following titles in stock. Elsewhere, you will have to ask your bookseller to order what you need from the publisher. Although they will not be available for background reading before starting, many items can be purchased along the way. Indeed, a number of specialized books and pamphlets will be available only at the historic sites they describe. At places like Arrow Rock, Council Grove and Santa Fe, for example, keep a lookout for small historical publications that are of value to trail buffs.

National Sites or Monuments such as Fort Union, Fort Larned, Bent's Fort and Pecos sell pertinent books in their visitors' centers. So too does the Santa Fe Trail Center at Larned. Los Artesanos Bookshop on the plaza in Las Vegas, New Mexico; the Taos Bookshop across the street from Kit Carson's house; and the Museum Shop at the Palace of the Governors, Santa Fe, all carry a large selection of in-print trail titles. The first two shops also stock many out-of-print books on the Santa Fe Trail.

Items marked with an asterisk (*) in the listing below are available in paperback. "OP" indicates that a book is out-of-print. Unless you can find a copy in a rare bookstore you will have to consult it in a library.

GENERAL HISTORIES

* Robert L. Duffus, *The Santa Fe Trail* (Albuquerque: University of New Mexico Press, 1979). First published in 1930 and thus a bit outdated, this is still the best survey of the trail for the general reader.

Stanley Vestal, *The Old Santa Fe Trail* (Boston: Houghton Mifflin,

1939; reissued as a Bantam paperback, 1957; both now OP). A highly readable account of the main incidents in trail history. A fifty-page summary was printed separately as a pamphlet with the title *Wagons Southwest: Story of Old Trail to Santa Fe* (New York: American Pioneer Trails Association, 1946). This is a handy little item and someone needs to reissue it.

Henry Inman, *The Old Santa Fe Trail* (reprint, Minneapolis: Ross & Haines, 1966). First published in 1897, Colonel Inman's account, based partly on his own experiences, is filled with color and excitement. Though not always reliable, the book is still a useful introduction to the trail. Recently OP.

* Seymour V. Connor and Jimmy M. Skaggs, *Broadcloth and Britches, The Santa Fe Trade* (College Station: Texas A & M University Press, 1977). A scholars' treatment of the trail, it is also the most recent and up-to-date survey of the subject.

Max L. Moorhead, *New Mexico's Royal Road, Trade and Travel on the Chihuahua Trail* (Norman: University of Oklahoma Press, 1958; OP). In spite of its title, this book is mainly on the commercial aspects of the Santa Fe Trail prior to 1848.

* Josiah Gregg, *Commerce of the Prairies* (Lincoln: University of Nebraska Press, 1969). This classic account of the Santa Fe trade, 1831-44, is here abridged and includes only those chapters devoted to Gregg's experiences. Still, because of its accessibility as a paperback, it is a book you should carry with you.

TRAIL GUIDES

In the past there has been a shortage of competent guides to the Santa Fe Trail. Even now there is nothing in that category to equal the several excellent Oregon Trail guides that have appeared recently. Those books can be used with profit because the first thirty or so miles of the Oregon Trail, beginning at Independence, followed the route of the Santa Fe Trail. The three titles listed here are all published by The Patrice Press, Box 42, Gerald, Missouri 63037. The prices given (plus postage) are those that held in 1985. You may wish to write the Patrice Press for an updated list.

* Gregory M. Franzwa, *The Oregon Trail Revisited* (3rd ed., 1983; $6.95 + $1.35). This book is especially valuable in following the Santa Fe Trail through Independence and metropolitan Kansas City.

* Aubrey L. Haines, *Historic Sites Along the Oregon Trail* (1981; $12.95 + $1.75). In 439 pages this volume catalogues all important

historic sites. Those listed as far as Gardiner, Kansas, will be of interest to Santa Fe Trail travelers.

* Gregory M. Franzwa, *Maps of the Oregon Trail* (1982; $14.95 + $1.75). Only the first thirteen maps relate to the Santa Fe Trail.

(The above are model studies and may well inspire the reader to undertake a retracing of the Oregon Trail.)

Margaret Long, M.D., *The Santa Fe Trail* (Denver: Kistler Company, 1954; OP), is the most complete auto log ever published. However, its road directions are in many cases no longer accurate owing to changes in the Federal highway system. Still, for anyone interested in tracking down the many DAR markers it is indispensable. Only one edition was published, and if you can locate a copy in a rare bookstore it may be priced as high as fifty dollars. You will do better to consult it in a library.

Hobart E. Stocking, *The Road to Santa Fe* (New York: Hastings House, 1971; OP). In print until recently, copies of this volume may still be found on some bookstore shelves. Its road directions are poor and it skips some important places, yet it is good on history and geology along the trail and has superb maps. Recommended.

* Gene and Mary Martin, *Trail Dust, A Quick Picture History of the Santa Fe Trail* (Boulder: Johnson Books, 1972). A dandy little guide as far as it goes, it makes a useful companion to Duffus. The pamphlet is sold at various points along the trail. The last information that I have indicates it can be purchased by mail from the publisher at 1880 South 57th Court, Boulder, Colorado 80301, for $2.95 + $1.00. Recommended.

William E. Brown, *The Santa Fe Trail* (Washington: National Park Service, 1963; OP). A photocopied typescript with maps and illustrations, this bound report was limited to one hundred copies issued by the National Park Service as part of the National Survey of Historic Sites and Buildings. The first section is a fine narrative history of the trail, and the second evaluates the development potential of major trail sites. A number of these reports were placed in libraries and if you can find one it is worth having it copied and bound. This is legal since it is a government document in the public domain.

MEMOIRS, JOURNALS AND BIOGRAPHIES

Books by and about individuals who traveled the Santa Fe Trail help us capture the spirit and flavor of those thrilling days. The titles mentioned here are the ones I consider most admirable. Check Rittenhouse's bibliography for others.

* Mrs. Hal Russell, ed., *Land of Enchantment, Memoirs of Marian Russell Along the Santa Fe Trail* (reprint edition, Albuquerque: University of New Mexico Press, 1981). This is my favorite. If you fail to read it beforehand and do not carry a copy on the trail your trip will suffer.

* Stella M. Drumm, ed., *Down the Santa Fe Trail and into Mexico: The Diary of Susan Shelby Magoffin* (Lincoln: University of Nebraska Press, 1982). Regarded as a classic of trail literature, this book should be read entry by entry as you move west on your tour.

* Howard Louis Conrad, *Uncle Dick Wootton* (Lincoln: University of Nebraska Press, 1979). This is the standard biography of a major trail figure.

* Kit Carson, *Autobiography* (Lincoln: University of Nebraska Press, 1966). Carson crossed the trail many times on his way west to further adventures.

* Lewis H. Garrard, *Wah-to-yah and the Taos Trail* (Norman: University of Oklahoma Press, 1974). An account by an observant seventeen-year-old, this book is engagingly written. Garrard participated in stirring events along the trail in 1846 and 1847.

* Larry M. Beachum, *William Becknell: Father of the Santa Fe Trade* (El Paso: Texas Western Press, 1982). A slim, well-written book representing the only biography of Becknell.

* W. W. H. Davis, *El Gringo: New Mexico and Her People* (Lincoln: University of Nebraska Press, 1982). The first chapters describe Davis's trip by stagecoach over the trail in 1853. The rest gives a picture of life in territorial New Mexico.

John E. Sunder, ed., *Matt Field on the Santa Fe Trail* (Norman: University of Oklahoma Press, 1960). Impressions of a trail trip in 1839 make this an entertaining and informative book.

* Robert W. Frazer, ed., *Over the Chihuahua and Santa Fe Trails, 1847-1848, George Rutledge Gibson's Journal* (Albuquerque: University of New Mexico Press, 1981). Soldiers' memoirs are fairly common, but Rutledge's is the only one currently available in paperback.

SPECIAL STUDIES

Scholars have produced authoritative studies on various phases of trail history. Some of the best are cited here.

Morris F. Taylor, *First Mail West: Stagecoach Lines on the Santa Fe Trail* (Albuquerque: University of New Mexico Press, 1971; OP). Taylor's volume is the only one on stagecoaching, and more still needs to be written on the subject.

George Walton, *Sentinel of the Plains: Fort Leavenworth and the American West* (Englewood Cliffs, New Jersey: Prentice-Hall, 1973; OP). A general history of the fort which also contains much on the military side of the trail.

Chris Emmett, *Fort Union and the Winning of the Southwest* (Norman: University of Oklahoma Press, 1965; OP). This is the most complete history of any army fort on the trail.

* David Lavender, *Bent's Fort* (Lincoln: University of Nebraska Press, 1954). Lavender's book is must reading for background on the Mountain Branch of the trail.

Leo E. Oliva, *Soldiers on the Santa Fe Trail* (Norman: University of Oklahoma Press, 1967; OP). A general survey of military operations.

* Robert W. Frazer, *Forts of the West* (Norman: University of Oklahoma Press, 1965). This compendium includes capsule histories of all the military posts established on the Santa Fe Trail.

Kate L. Gregg, ed., *The Road to Santa Fe* (Albuquerque: University of New Mexico Press, 1952). Although a later paperback edition was also issued, both are now OP. Containing accounts of the trail survey of 1825, the book is useful for those dedicated to finding every significant point of interest along the route.

MAPS

The guide you have in hand must be used in conjunction with standard highway maps. Those available at service stations vary in quality. Maps produced by Rand McNally (sold at Fina stations) and by the H. M. Gousha Company (sold at Phillips 66 and Conoco stations, among others) show the most back roads and other details a modern driver likes to have. Both state and city Rand McNally maps are sold in many newsstands and bookshops as well.

American Automobile Association maps are also quite good, particularly the one for the Kansas City/Independence area. Maps of the five individual trail states are issued by the respective Highway Departments or Tourist Bureaus in each state. While I find them less satisfactory than the maps recommended above, they are at least offered free through the mail or at tourist information centers.

There are some specialized maps that will benefit persons who are following the trail very closely. All state highway departments sell large-scale county maps clearly showing local road systems. Examples of these can be seen in Franzwa's *Maps of the Oregon Trail*, cited above. United States Geological Survey quadrangle maps depict the nature of the country in the clearest fashion. These can be consulted at some large libraries. To purchase copies write (if you live west of the Mississippi): Distribution Section, U.S. Geological Survey, Box 25286, Federal Center, Denver, Colorado 80225. Ask for the free Index to Topographic Maps for each of the five trail states. Ordering information will be included.

A book not mentioned in the bibliography above was privately printed by the late Kenyon Riddle and is entitled *Records and Maps of the Old Santa Fe Trail*. Occasionally copies can be found in used bookstores, and most good libraries have it. The text is a hodgepodge of trail facts. Of greater value is a series of eight maps inserted in a pocket at the back of the book. Riddle closely studied the western end of the trail, particularly Raton Pass and the area around Fort Union. His maps of those places are of greatest value. Good fold-out maps can also be found in Brown's already cited report for the National Park Service.

Hobart Stocking drew a series of fine maps for his book, *The Road to Santa Fe*. In addition to the trail and modern highways, they contain much historical information. He deposited the originals with the National Archives and copies can be purchased. To order, ask for the 7 Stocking Maps (Record Group 200) from *The Road to Santa Fe* by Hobart E. Stocking, Stillwater, Oklahoma, 1966. Specify "Oversize Xerox Copies." At last report they sold for $1.80 per sheet or $12.60 for the seven, but the prices may increase. (Note: Reduced 17" x 23" positive photostats at $7.25 per sheet are also sold, but the cheaper Xerox copies are almost as good and a better bargain.) Make checks or money orders payable to: Cashier, National Archives (GSA), Washington, D.C. 20408.

Valuable also is the series of maps based on U.S. Geological Survey quads to be found in Charles S. Peterson et al., *Mormon Battalion Trail Guide* (Salt Lake City: Utah State Historical Society, 1972; OP).

MARKERS AND MONUMENTS

Much of the excitement in following the Santa Fe Trail today comes from seeing actual physical remains like ruts, old forts or period artifacts preserved in museums. Natural landmarks like Pawnee Rock, the Cimarron River and the Wagon Mound, which were there when the merchant caravans passed by, are also exciting things to be seen.

By contrast, markers and monuments represent recent additions to the trail, since all were installed within this century and some inside the past few years. Because of this many travelers pay little attention to them. However, that is a mistake. The markers provide a sense of continuity, calling attention to the location of the trail on stretches where no original remains can be found. They serve as reminders that you are on the right course, and those with a text offer valuable historical information.

Some, like the monument paid for by Kansas school children at the Cottonwood Crossing, are one of a kind. Others occur in series placed by government agencies or private groups. In several instances, the programs initiated to raise money for markers have interesting stories and constitute part of the history of the modern trail. Some of the marker and monument groups that you will encounter are described below.

DAUGHTERS OF THE AMERICAN REVOLUTION (DAR) MARKERS

The DAR launched the earliest and still the most ambitious effort to commemorate the old Santa Fe Trail. Between 1902 and 1912, DAR chapters in all the trail states except Oklahoma re-located the fading route through research, raised funds from private and government sources and saw to the placement of handsome incised markers of red or gray granite. The precise number of markers placed by the organization has not been determined, since additions of which no record was kept have been made from time to time over the years.

Twenty-nine DAR markers were placed in Missouri. According to Mrs. T. A. Cordry's rare little book, *The Story of the Marking of the Santa Fe Trail* (Topeka: Crane & Co., 1915), ninety-six stones were distributed along the trail in Kansas. But others were added later, including the most recent (1979) at the Little Arkansas Crossing, so the actual figure must be over one hundred. Moreover, special DAR markers with a bronze plaque attached to granite were installed at various points between Kansas City and Santa Fe. Originally there were supposed to have been ten of these, but only six can be located now.

The Colorado chapters of the DAR placed twenty-seven markers in that state, most of them on the Mountain Branch. However, four were located on the north side of the Cimarron River where the Cimarron Cut-off angled for a few miles across the southeastern corner of Colorado. Several of these have now been moved to more accessible locations. A total of nineteen markers were placed in New Mexico, and three or four have since disappeared.

Changes in the highway system have caused some markers in all the states to be moved from the original sites. In her 1954 guide, *The Santa Fe Trail*, Dr. Long located most of them. Of those she noted, perhaps as many as one-quarter can no longer be found by her directions.

I have made no attempt to locate all the DAR markers along the Santa Fe Trail. Instead, in this guide I have tried to call attention to those that are particularly visible, especially ones at major sites. Many others are scattered almost at random along highways and back roads, often obscured by weeds or bushes. The majority of the markers bear a simple and quite similar text, but a few have special inscriptions and the location of these I have tried to include. After a few days on the trail, the DAR markers become familiar friends. By scanning the roadsides, new ones will be discovered in unexpected places.

PIONEER MOTHER STATUES

As an outgrowth of its success in marking the Santa Fe Trail, the DAR joined with other interested groups to provide monuments for the National Old Trails Road. Established by act of Congress in 1806 as the first Federal road, it began in Cumberland, Maryland, and eventually was extended to St. Louis. From there an extension across central Missouri known as the Boone's Lick Road led to a hook-up with the Santa Fe Trail, which was considered part of the system after the Federal survey of the trail was initiated in 1825. By 1837, with the boom in railroading, the government abandoned upkeep of the National Road.

In 1912 citizens in Kansas City formed the National Old Trails Road Association. Its purpose was not only to research and mark the historic route from coast to coast but also to encourage Congress to develop a national highway system with the advent of automobiles beginning to challenge the supremacy of railroads. The DAR became closely involved with the Association's program. Red, white and blue historical signs were adopted, and the same colors were painted in alternating stripes on telegraph and telephone poles along the National Road. The only evidence of this work that I can find today along the

The Pioneer Mother in Council Grove, Kansas.

Santa Fe Trail is one of the red, white and blue signs nailed to a tree at the Lanesfield School near Edgertown, Kansas.

More lasting was the installation of twelve statues of the Pioneer Mother placed in each of the states on the National Road from Maryland to California. This became a special project of the DAR. Four of the statues were intended for the Santa Fe Trail: one each at Lexington, Missouri; Council Grove, Kansas; Lamar, Colorado; and Santa Fe, New Mexico. For reasons explained later in this guide the last was installed at Albuquerque instead of Santa Fe. Standing ten feet high on a six-foot base, the statues are made of pink algonite stone. The figure, a mother in sunbonnet with two children, was executed by St. Louis sculptor August Leimbach. The four on the Santa Fe route have special trail inscriptions around their bases.

Unrelated to these statues are two other Pioneer Mother memorials in the Kansas City area. One is a heroic bronze statue in Penn Valley Park, the other a red stone monument at Old Westport. Women are also honored by the special DAR marker atop Pawnee Rock and the Plainswoman statue on the campus of Dodge City Community College.

AMERICAN PIONEER TRAIL ASSOCIATION MARKERS

In 1948 the American Pioneer Trail Association (successor to the Oregon Trail Memorial Association) arranged through its Kansas City Chapter to mark the route between Missouri and New Mexico with appropriate signs. The metal oval signs with white background were produced by the Independence Stove and Furnace Company of Independence, Missouri. They showed a teamster with a mule-drawn freight wagon and bore the words "Santa Fe Trail." These markers were placed with appropriate ceremony on schoolhouses along the entire route.

Almost all have been stolen or in a few cases moved to safer locations. Examples can be seen at the Hays House in Council Grove and at the Santa Fe Trail Center in Larned, Kansas. In 1950, under the leadership of attorney Dean Earl Wood, an additional twenty-seven signs were obtained and mounted on trees and light poles along what Wood had determined by careful research to be the precise trail route through Kansas City. A few of these remain. The original locations are listed by Wood in his book, *The Old Santa Fe Trail from the Missouri River* (Kansas City: Mendenhall Printers, 1951), pp. 267-69. Locations of several surviving examples are noted in this guide.

THE SANTA FE TRAIL ASSOCIATION MARKERS

Like other trail groups that preceded it, this association lasted only a few years. But while it was active during the early 1960s the group did good work to encourage people to retrace the Santa Fe Trail. It published maps and a small trail guide distributed free at businesses along the route. The Cimarron Cut-off was designated as "the official trail," and along the way from Kansas City to Santa Fe green covered-wagon signs were attached to US 56 signs as far as Springer, New Mexico, and thereafter to the old US 85 signs. A few of these attractive little signs are still in place.

OFFICIAL STATE HIGHWAY MARKERS

Each Highway Department or Tourist Bureau in the five trail states has placed attractive historical markers at major sites along the route. These contain some of the longest and most authoritative texts of any markers. Their locations have been carefully noted in this guide.

SPECIAL MARKER AND MONUMENT GROUPS

Several groups of associated markers and sites related to a particular individual or event are worth mentioning. In your background reading pay special attention to the stories behind them.

Charles and William Bent were closely identified with the saga of the Santa Fe Trail. Places of interest related to their careers include: William Bent's house, Kansas City; Bent's New Fort (ruins), west of Lamar, Colorado; Bent's Old Fort (reconstruction), near La Junta, Colorado; William Bent's grave, Las Animas, Colorado; Charles Bent's house, Taos; and Charles Bent's grave in the National Cemetery, Santa Fe, New Mexico.

Christopher (Kit) Carson is another famous name firmly linked to the trail's history. As a boy he left from the site of Old Franklin, Missouri, on his first trip to Santa Fe. The State Historical Marker near Pawnee Rock refers to his stopping at that renowned site. See the chapel marking the spot where he died in 1868 at Fort Lyon, Colorado, as well as the large equestrian statue in Kit Carson Park at Trinidad. A reconstruction of Kit's farm home is at Rayado, New Mexico, and his principal residence is preserved nearby in Taos, where his grave is. Santa

Fe too has a Kit Carson monument.

The name of William Becknell, Father of the Trail, is commemorated on markers at Franklin, Arrow Rock, Council Grove, Pawnee Rock, Dodge City, Cimarron and Wagon Mound. Strangely, Josiah Gregg who made such a large contribution to the trail story is badly neglected by markers. His name is mentioned in passing on only a few. However, a tall granite Josiah Gregg Memorial Monument is located on the campus of Palo Duro High School in Amarillo, Texas. It commemorates an alternate "Santa Fe Trail" that Gregg helped blaze in 1840 from Fort Smith, Arkansas, across Oklahoma and the Texas Panhandle to New Mexico. Ruts of that trail are said to be visible on the school grounds, but I cannot see them. However, there are some fine ruts adjacent to State Road 136 north of Amarillo and about thirty miles south of the town of Fritch. An official Texas Highway Marker, with reference to Gregg, marks the site.

Spanish explorer Francisco Vásquez de Coronado and his chief friar, Father Juan de Padilla, receive considerable attention along the although they traveled it some three hundred years before its formal establishment. Markers or monuments honoring them can be visited in Kansas at Council Grove, Herington, Lyons and Fort Dodge. There is a Coronado mural in Santa Fe's main post office. A little known monument to Father Padilla is at the west end of Ellwood Park in Amarillo, Texas.

Members of the Mormon Battalion, who marched over the trail to Santa Fe and on to California during the first year of the Mexican War (1846), are remembered by five new markers installed in 1983 at Fort Leavenworth, Council Grove, McPherson and Larned in Kansas and on the courthouse square at Boise City, Oklahoma. Two older Battalion markers are in New Mexico, the first at the Fort Union Rest Stop near Watrous and the second along I-25 between Santa Fe and Albuquerque. The latter was recently removed by highway expansion, but reports say it will be rebuilt in the same vicinity.

TRAIL RUTS

Among the most interesting features of the modern trail are the ruts or tracks of the original trace left by the heavy wheels of freight wagons. Most people can scarcely believe that such ruts are still to be seen after more than a hundred years. Of course, in many places agriculture or urban expansion has destroyed all sign of the trail. Yet, here and there from Missouri to New Mexico, Santa Fe Trail ruts have

Santa Fe Trail wagon ruts across the boundless plains. (New Mexico Department of Development, No. 25015.)

been preserved. Some are very short lengths, carefully protected in parks or lots. Others, particularly on the western third of the trail, run for miles where the land has remained largely undisturbed.

Ruts accessible to the visitor have been noted throughout this guide. A few, like those at Fort Leavenworth, Baldwin City, Fort Larned, Dodge City and Fort Union, are well marked. Most are not. Their appearance and character vary considerably, and it requires some practice to recognize them.

Usually ruts appear as wide depressions in the ground, heavily grassed over. When the wheels had churned a deep track through mud or dust, the trains moved over a few feet and began a new road. West of Fort Larned the wagons often traveled four abreast. The result is ruts of extensive width. Ascending a ridge coming out of a stream or river valley the wagons generally formed a single file so that in time a deep cut was made at the crest. Such a cut or swale, for instance, can be viewed at William Minor Park just west of the Blue River in Kansas City. At Fort Leavenworth and behind the Sibley Cemetery at Fort Osage the trail is represented by a grassy dirt ramp leading from the Missouri River landing to the top of the neighboring bluffs.

At the western end of the trail, many ruts have been badly eroded by weather. They form conspicuous gullies called arroyos. The Soil Conservation Service has placed small earth check dams across some of these.

TRAVEL TIPS

Josiah Gregg tells us that traders waited until the first green grass appeared in late April or May before setting out on the trail. They wanted to be sure of adequate feed for their draft animals, but, equally important, the greening signaled the end of the blizzard season. No man wanted to be caught on the open plains in a snowstorm. Stories of a few improvident ones who dared a winter crossing, suffering fearfully or even perishing in the attempt, were known to all.

The warning implied in those early stories is best heeded today. In his *Road to Santa Fe* Stocking speaks of a blinding snowstorm encountered while following the Cimarron Cut-off through the Oklahoma Panhandle. His car stalled on an icy highway and he had to be rescued. Except for short trips during which there is a near-term promise of good weather, travel on the Santa Fe Trail should be avoided in winter.

The best times of the year are late spring, early summer and early fall. The extreme heat of mid-summer, especially in Missouri and Kansas, discourages many people from sightseeing. On the other hand, cool Santa Fe (at 7000 feet altitude) offers an escape from the east in July and August.

A rainy spell can set in at any time during the warm season. Unpaved roads quickly turn to quagmires, making travel impossible. If in doubt, check locally about conditions before leaving the paved highway.

The majority of historic trail sites described in this guide are open and accessible to the public. However, a number are on private property. Many of these can be easily viewed from a nearby public road. Those wishing to enter must get permission from the owner, as at Diamond Spring, for example. (At last report, the owner there is hospitable to trail travelers.) In a few instances noted herein (McNees Crossing is a case in point), the rancher or farmer freely admits visitors without advance permission. Remember to close gates behind you upon entering and leaving. It goes without saying that visitors should respect all sites. If you observe unauthorized digging or vandalism report the matter to local authorities.

Modern-day exploration of the Santa Fe Trail will prove most profitable when it is preceded by careful planning. Study this guide, read your background sources, collect and carefully peruse your maps and lay out an itinerary that is tailored to your interests and needs. At that point you are ready to shout, as did the early wagonmasters, "Catch up! All's set! Ho, for Santa Fe!"

A NOTE TO READERS

The original starting point of the Santa Fe Trail was the little river town of Franklin, Missouri, in the central part of the state. That place is the logical beginning for this guide and for your tour. Following the trail to its fork in western Kansas, you can there take the Cimarron Cut-off to Santa Fe and then return by way of the Mountain Branch (or vice versa) so as not to miss any of the sites. Persons living near the western end of the Santa Fe Trail will also want to drive east on one of these routes and return via the other, but on the journey out they will have to follow the guide in reverse. For those unable to devote the several weeks required to cover all the trail at once, brief excursions of a few days can be made along convenient sections of the route.

In the pages that follow, no attempt has been made to recount the full histories of individual trail sites. That would have required a book many times larger than the present guide. Rather, a few summary details have been provided to place the point of interest in proper perspective and the traveler is left to learn more through collateral reading. However, in some places I have added unusual bits of information derived from my own primary research which are not available in the commonly used standard sources.

No guide of this kind is ever complete, and by the time it leaves the printer it is already out of date. Roads change, markers are added or removed, historical sites are altered and even destroyed by vandals. In my collection are many photographs and slides of landmarks and monuments that disappeared soon after I shot them.

Some of those on the lamented list include the Nebraska House Hotel on Independence Square, demolished to make way for a parking lot; the small but significant Point of Rocks a few miles west of Dodge City, destroyed when the highway was widened; and Uncle Dick Wootton's two-story adobe house in Raton Pass, torn down by its owner. The list of stolen markers would run to several pages. A beautiful new one placed and dedicated at the Wayne City Landing on the Missouri River in August 1983 was vandalized within two weeks, but has now been restored.

I have deliberately excluded several places on the trail because they are particularly vulnerable to damage, mainly from treasure hunters. Reference to two other places was deleted because they are on private property and the owners prefer not to have visitors.

In my eight complete trips over the Santa Fe Trail and many shorter jaunts on individual sections, I believe I have found all the major sites and most of the minor ones. However, I should admit that with every new trip I discover something of interest previously overlooked. By keeping a sharp watch readers will make their own finds and thus add to the fun of trail travel.

The author of this guide will be grateful to those who provide him with corrections and additions. Address correspondence to Ancient City Press, P. O. Box 5401, Santa Fe, New Mexico 87502.

Abbreviations Commonly Used in the Text:
DAR = Daughters of the American Revolution
I = Interstate Highway
MOT = *Maps of the Oregon Trail*
OTR = *Oregon Trail Revisited*
SFT = Santa Fe Trail
SR = State Road

-A Caravan Corraled-

MISSOURI

FRANKLIN

The original starting point of the SFT was Franklin. Platted in 1816 on a low flood plain on the north bank of the Missouri River, it was named in honor of Benjamin Franklin. From here William Becknell, the "Father of the Santa Fe Trail," departed for New Mexico in 1821, the year Missouri became a state. Franklin was also the home of the teenage Kit Carson, who ran away from his job as a saddler's apprentice in 1826 to join a wagon train headed for Santa Fe. As the first outfitting center for the infant Santa Fe trade, Franklin was also the residence of numerous other men closely identified with the trail, among them M. M. Marmaduke, the Coopers, William Workman (the saddler who employed Kit and later went to Santa Fe himself), and Dr. John Sappington.

Between 1826 and 1828 the Missouri encroached upon its own flood plain and by the later year Franklin had been washed into the river. Many residents moved to higher ground 2 miles away and started New Franklin.

Access to New Franklin is from I-70 (the main St. Louis to Kansas City highway). Exit at Boonville, drive north through the center of that town and cross the Missouri on a very high and narrow steel bridge. You are on US 40. Leaving the bridge, SR 87 intersects from the left (west). At this junction a DAR marker is on the right (east side of 40). It commemorates Old Franklin. Across the road from the marker is the Kit Carson Motel, the only reminder that this was once the young scout's home.

Here, go west ¼ mile on SR 87. Where the railroad tracks cross the highway is a large limestone monument, easily missed. It is on the left facing the tracks and very close to them. An inscription commemorates the *Missouri Intelligencer and Boon's Lick Advertiser*, the first weekly newspaper established (1819) west of St. Louis. Today the back files of this paper are a prime source for the history of the SFT. Its pages carried the first announcement of Becknell's initial trip to Santa Fe and, on October 12, 1826, a notice that the boy Christopher Carson had fled his apprenticeship. Soon after that the *Intelligencer* moved its offices 15 miles north to Fayette to escape the Missouri's flood waters. The monument notes that the original newspaper office was "500 feet west of this spot." That would be the center of Old Franklin. A flood in 1973 uncovered traces of the town here in the fields on both sides of SR 87.

At just under 2.5 miles from the *Intelligencer* monument, SR 87 curves to the right and climbs a hill. Paved State Road Z continues straight ahead. Follow it and at .8 mile from the junction is the historic home, Cedar Grove, on the right. It is on high ground behind a low stone wall with a DAR marker in front. (Margaret Long missed this marker in her listing.) The two-story Greek Revival house has green shutters and a white porch across the front. Builder of the main section in 1856 was a physician, Dr. Horace Kingsbury.

Attached to the left end of this structure is a small brick Federal-style house dating back to 1824. It was built by pioneer farmer Nicholas Amick and is one of the oldest area residences still standing. During its earliest years of occupation, the boy Kit Carson was working in the saddle shop at nearby Old Franklin, and Santa Fe-bound caravans passed in front, the present SR Z being the original SFT. (Private residence.)

Continue ahead on winding Z (known locally as the Old River Road) to the hamlet of Petersburg at 6.4 miles from Cedar Grove. Just past the church, Z turns to the right and becomes J. But here go straight ahead on a dirt road (weather permitting) .8 mile to a DAR marker (also missed by Long) next to a telephone pole on the left and just before a farm house made of gray blocks. The base of the marker reads "Cooper's Fort." The site of Cooper's Fort was directly across the road in an open field. In 1985 the Boonslick Historical Society placed a commemorative sign on the spot.

Cooper's Fort was built for protection of local settlers during the War of 1812 by brothers Benjamin and Sarshall Cooper. Benjamin led a party with pack mules to Santa Fe in 1822 at the same time Becknell was taking out the first wagon train. He returned to New Mexico the following year with traders headed by his nephew Steven. Fort Cooper was silted over by a flood in 1844, but another flood in 1903 revealed the location.

Return to Petersburg and continue on SR J, 3.5 miles to Boonesboro. There, turn left (north) on SR 87 and go 1.3 miles to the junction with SR 187 which enters from the left. Take SR 187 and drive 2.5 miles to Boone's Lick. Here are interpretive signs, DAR marker, and a path leading down to the salt springs.

This saline spring or "lick" was discovered in 1804 by Nathan Boone, youngest son of Daniel. The next year he and his older brother, Daniel Morgan Boone, returned to the site and began making salt by boiling the water in large kettles. The place soon became known as Boone's Lick and in time a large part of central Missouri was referred to as "Boone's Lick Country."

James and Jesse Morrison bought the lick from the Boones by 1811. Before his overland excursion to Santa Fe, Becknell worked for the Morrisons, perhaps as foreman of the large salt-making crew. He was living at the site in 1817, while owning property in nearby Franklin. Joseph L. Morrison, the sixteen-year-old son of James, fell into a kettle of boiling salt water and was scalded to death in 1833. Some years ago, a broken monument marking his grave was reported to be near the top of the curving hillside near the spring.

Just beyond the lick to the west is the Missouri River. Atop a bluff on the far side is the historic town of Arrow Rock which figured conspicuously in the early history of the SFT. Travelers from Franklin heading west crossed the river here by ferry. Becknell is known to have operated the ferry both before and after his Santa Fe venture.

Return via SR 87 to US 40 at the Boonville bridge. Here at the Old Franklin DAR marker a gravel road joins from the east. Follow it .2 mile to a large mansion on the left. This is "Rivercene," a National Registered Site. A sign on the two stone pillars at the gate reads:

"Steamboat Captain's House." It was built in the middle nineteenth century by a Captain Kinney who at various times owned nine steamboats on the Missouri River. (Private residence.)

Return to the junction of SR 87 and US 40 at the DAR "Old Franklin" marker. From that point continue northeast 1 mile on US 40 to the junction with SR 5 which enters from the left and is the road to New Franklin. Instead of turning off to New Franklin, however, continue another mile on US 40 to a roadside park on the right. Here are two historical markers. One is a bronze plaque set in a granite stone commemorating the "Forts of 1812." This refers to the family forts that defended the Boone's Lick Country during the War of 1812. The other marker is one of the attractive black-and-gold official Missouri Historical Markers. One side of this sign gives a capsule history of Franklin, the other side of Boonville. Both refer to the SFT.

From this roadside park return one mile to the junction of US 40 and SR 5. Turn right on SR 5 and go north about a mile to New Franklin. The one main business street of the town, Broadway Avenue, crosses the highway, which has become Missouri Street. Turn right one block to the center of the commercial area. In the middle of Broadway Avenue is a large red boulder and plaque surmounted by a three-bulb antique street light. This is the "Beginning of the Trail" monument placed with much ceremony by the DAR in 1909.

For modern travelers intending to drive (or walk or ride horseback) all the way to Santa Fe here is one of the Trail's highpoints. From this spot to the "End of the Trail" marker on the Santa Fe plaza lie almost a thousand miles, all studded with history. At the New Franklin monument your adventure into the past officially commences.

The heading on the plaque reads "Franklin, Cradle of the Santa Fe Trail, 1821." At the top, Becknell's first mule train to Santa Fe appears in sculptured relief. (Other Becknell trains in bronze relief will be seen along the Trail at Pawnee Rock and the Wagon Mound.) The full inscription, which I leave to your discovery, will stir all Trail buffs who respond to the drama and romance of history. Behind the DAR marker note a separate stone designating the "End of Boone's Lick Road." That road connected St. Louis with the start of the SFT.

Return ½ block to the junction of Missouri and Broadway. Turn right (north) on Missouri. In the middle of the first block on the left at 108 N. Missouri is the two-story, Federal-style, Harris-Chilton house built in 1832. Continue another 1½ blocks to Market Street and turn right. In mid-block on the left, at 110 Market, is a two-story white house with a sign in front, next to a wagon wheel, reading, "Seminary,

1832." The only surviving building from Old Franklin, it was moved to this site after flooding destroyed the rest of the town. First known as the "Franklin Academy," its construction is believed to date from 1826. (Private residence.)

From the Franklin area the early Santa Fe-bound caravans headed west to the vicinity of Boone's Lick where they crossed the Missouri by ferry to the village of Arrow Rock. Today no ferry exists there, or bridge, so you will have to return on US 40 over the steel bridge to Boonville and pick up I-70.

BOONVILLE

Old and New Franklin lay in the lowlands on the north side of the Missouri River. Opposite them on the south side steep limestone cliffs rose almost from the water's edge. Atop these heights, Boonville (named for Daniel Boone) was laid out in 1817.

Boonville is occasionally mentioned as a starting point for some Santa Fe caravans in the earliest years of the traffic, but its role in the trade was never a major one. Like Franklin and like other towns founded later up the Missouri, Boonville had its "landing" where cargos could be off-loaded from St. Louis steamboats and placed in freight wagons. A steeply sloped cobblestone street led upward from the landing to brick and frame warehouses.

Several early Boonville buildings, while having no direct association with the SFT, must have been familiar to the New Mexican traders. Christ Episcopal Church (northeast corner of Vine and Fourth Streets) dates from 1846 and claims to be the oldest Episcopal church west of the Mississippi. The Lyric Theater (Thespian Hall) at the corner of Main and Vine was begun in 1855 and is said to be the oldest theater west of the Alleghenies. Kemper Military School (Center and Third Streets) was established in 1844. Famed Santa Fe trader Franz Huning of Albuquerque placed his nine-year-old son Arno in this school about 1878.

SIDE TRIP TO COLUMBIA AND ST. LOUIS

Before continuing on to Arrow Rock an excursion can be made 27 miles eastward to Columbia and another 125 miles to St. Louis, both on I-70.

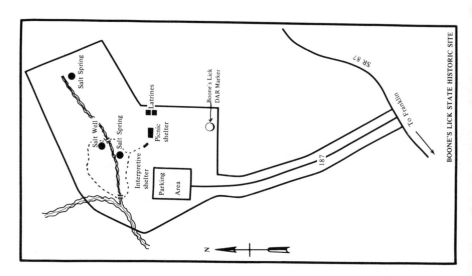

NEW FRANKLIN

N

"The Seminary"

Market

Church

Broadway

"Beginning of the Trail" DAR Marker

No. Missouri

Harris-Chilton House

SR 5

To Boonsville →

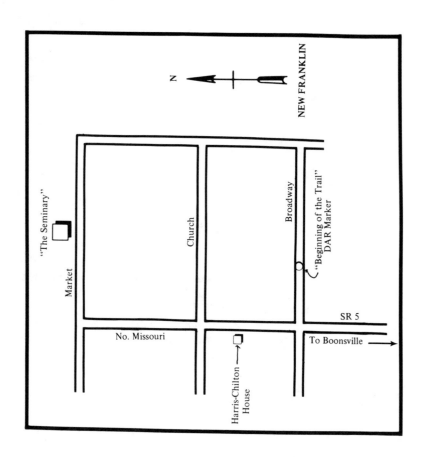

N

Salt Spring

Salt Well

Salt Spring

Salt Spring

Interpretive shelter

Latrines

Picnic shelter

Parking Area

Boone's Lick DAR Marker

187

SR 87

To Franklin →

BOONE'S LICK STATE HISTORIC SITE

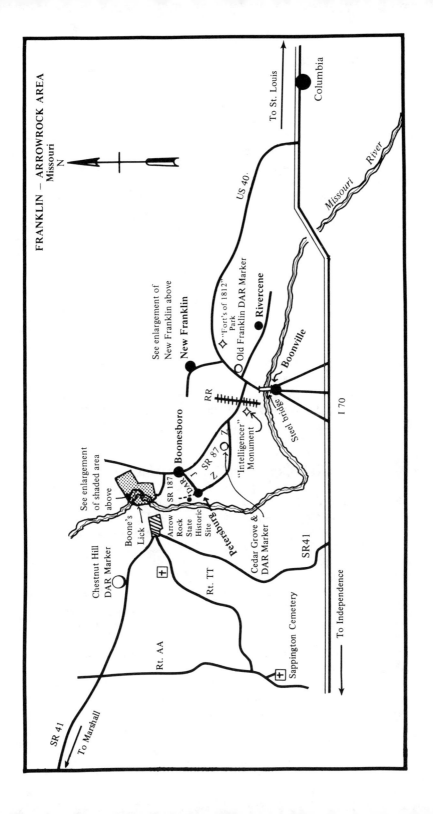

FRANKLIN – ARROWROCK AREA
Missouri

N

To St. Louis
Columbia
Missouri River
US 40
See enlargement of New Franklin above
New Franklin
"Fort's of 1812" Park
Old Franklin DAR Marker
Rivercene
Boonville
RR
Steel bridge
"Intelligencer" Monument
SR 87
Boonesboro
See enlargement of shaded area above
SR 187
DAR
Petersburg
Chestnut Hill DAR Marker
Boone's Lick
Arrow Rock State Historic Site
Cedar Grove & DAR Marker
I 70
SR41
Rt. TT
Rt. AA
SR 41
To Marshall
Sappington Cemetery
To Independence

Columbia

The State Historical Society of Missouri is located at 1020 Lowry Street on the campus of the University of Missouri. (Parking is available for visitors across the street.) Serious SFT researchers will find excellent facilities here, including:

(a) a library with rare Missouri and Western Americana materials;

(b) a newspaper library containing both original papers and microfilm of many early periodicals, among them the *Intelligencer*; and,

(c) the Western Historical Manuscripts Collection which holds an assortment of primary items relating to the SFT.

Each of these divisions has a separate room in the building, maintains good indices and provides photocopying services.

St. Louis

Located 15 miles below the confluence of the Mississippi and Missouri Rivers, St. Louis in the nineteenth century was the nerve center for western exploration and the fur trade. Its role in the history of the West is today symbolized by the Gateway Arch at the Jefferson National Expansion Memorial, which has exhibits relating to the SFT. (Easy access to the Arch and Museum from I-70.)

Four points of SFT interest in St. Louis are:

A. St. Charles Rock Road and Boone's Lick Road Marker

Located in Kiener Plaza, opposite the Old Courthouse in downtown St. Louis. This marker designates the beginning of the trunk line that connected St. Louis with the head of the SFT at Franklin.

B. Heroic statue of Missouri Senator Thomas Hart Benton

Located in Lafayette Park (bounded by Mississippi, Missouri, Park and Lafayette Avenues). Surrounding the park are once-beautiful homes, now being restored. It is a rough neighborhood, so visit only in midday. The splendid statue, cast in bronze in Munich and erected in 1868, is a gem. It was unveiled by Benton's daughter, Mrs. Jessie Benton Frémont, wife of the Pathfinder, John Charles Frémont. The statue faces west and at its feet are inscribed the words: "There lies the west; there lies India." It stands near the center of the park near another statue, of George Washington.

Benton, elected senator when Missouri achieved statehood in 1821, became the chief spokesman in Washington for the Santa Fe traders. He introduced the bill that led to the survey and marking of the Trail in 1825 and pressured the Secretary of War to provide military protection from the Indians for the wagon trains.

C. Bellefontaine Cemetery (pronounced "Bellefountain" locally)

Located between Florissant and Broadway, adjacent to I-70. Main entrance and office at 4947 W. Florissant. Cemetery gates open 7 days a week, but office has more limited hours.

The cemetery is huge, with a maze of lanes. Visitors need a map showing notable graves, available free from the office. Several SFT people are buried here, as are Manuel Lisa, a founder of the fur trade, and General William Clark of the Lewis and Clark Expedition.

Of primary interest to us is the Magoffin family plot. Brothers James W. (d. 1868) and Samuel (d. 1888) Magoffin were prominent traders well known in Santa Fe, El Paso and Chihuahua City. Samuel's young Kentucky-born wife Susan Shelby (d. 1855) kept the peerless diary of her SFT trip in 1846, as already noted in the introduction. The plot (in blocks 79-80, lot 1002, behind the elks statue) has markers for Samuel and Susan. There is no marker for James, although a diagram of the casket locations (photocopy available in the cemetery office) shows that he lies to the right of Susan.

A short distance away, under a 15-foot column, rests General Stephen W. Kearny, who led his army over the SFT in 1846. Before departing for California, he entertained Samuel and Susan in the old Spanish Palace of the Governors on the Santa Fe Plaza. Sterling Price, one of his subordinates, is buried under another tall column nearby. Price put down the revolt in Taos early in 1847 which had resulted in the death of Governor Charles Bent and others. You will also want to see the impressive monument marking the grave of Senator Thomas Hart Benton.

D. Missouri Historical Society, Jefferson Memorial Building

In Forest Park, on Lindell Boulevard. The museum on the first floor contains exhibits dealing with the Louisiana Purchase and exploration of the West.

The Society has its offices on the second floor. This organization is different from the State Historical Society of Missouri in Columbia. The collections include fine Santa Fe trade and fur trade materials. A daily fee is charged for use of the archive facilities.

ARROW ROCK

From Boonville go west on I-70 to the "Arrow Rock, SR 41" exit. Turn north on 41, 12 miles to Arrow Rock.

SR 41 crosses Main Street on the west side of Arrow Rock. Pause at this junction. When your tour is done return to this point and continue on 41 toward Marshall.

To the left, on the southwest corner of the junction, is the Arrow Rock DAR marker. The road that enters here on the left (from the west) is Rt. TT leading to the Sappington Cemetery. On the northeast corner of the junction is the Turley Service Station. Turleys from this area traveled the SFT and were prominent in New Mexico. Simeon Turley operated a distillery at Arroyo Hondo north of Taos, and he and his men were killed in the same January 1847 uprising in which Charles Bent perished.

Turn right at the junction and drive five blocks along Main Street to the center of Arrow Rock, which is a State Historic Site. Just beyond the town area is a bluff that drops off to the Missouri River. The ferry from Boone's Lick, immediately across the river, tied up at the landing at the foot of the bluff. Santa Fe traders, beginning with Becknell, crossed here coming from Franklin.

Although the site was long a camping place for caravans, the actual town was not laid out until 1829, by which time the jump-off for the SFT had moved westward to Independence. Still, people heading for New Mexico continued to pass through, and Arrow Rock (initially named New Philadelphia) remained associated with the Trail for the next couple of decades.

In the center of Arrow Rock, on the south side of Main Street, the Old Tavern is a focal point of interest. Nearby are a number of early homes of historical and architectural importance, but only SFT-related sites are mentioned here. (Note: The buildings are closed in winter.)

A. Old Tavern

A two-story white structure built about 1834 by Joseph Huston, the Arrow Rock Tavern is the town's most familiar landmark. A bronze plaque is on the front wall. Noted SFT travelers are known to have stopped here. Portraits and relics of early residents on display. Fine meals served. Historical brochure available.

Stone curb gutters of the kind cut and laid by slaves are in front of the tavern. Popular legend claims that upon returning from his second trip to Santa Fe Becknell cut open leather bags and Mexican silver coins rolled into these gutters. Historical evidence suggests that this actually happened in Old Franklin which had similar stone gutters.

B. Visitor Center

On Main Street, directly across from the tavern. Information and a map of the area are available here, as are historical publications.

C. "Arrow Rock" Official Missouri Historical Marker

Just past the tavern on the left. The sign contains a brief history of the town and reference to the SFT.

D. Santa Fe Spring, also called Big Spring and Arrow Rock Spring

Continue two blocks past the tavern on Main and turn right toward the picnic area. Then take the second right toward the Scout area. The spring is enclosed in stone and cement and covered by an open, four-post shelter. Here wagons for Santa Fe assembled after leaving the river landing, one-quarter mile away. A new sign identifies the site and refers to Becknell.

E. Arrow Rock Masonic Lodge

On north side of Main, 1½ blocks west of the tavern. The first floor houses a Craft Center. Founded in 1842, this lodge is known to have sent a number of its members over the SFT.

F. Sites House and Gunshop

Both buildings are behind the Masonic Lodge. These restored structures belonged to John Sites, Jr., who learned gunsmithing in his father's Boonville shop (est. 1835). He moved to Arrow Rock in 1841 and opened his own business. Thereafter, Sites Jr. catered to the needs of local citizens and supplied guns to persons heading west on the SFT and Oregon Trail.

G. Sappington Memorial Building and Museum

Located near the east end of High Street, next to the Lyceum. On Sappington's relation to the SFT, see the next section.

H. Sappington Cemetery

Return west on Main to its junction with SR 41. From there go southwest on Route TT. At .7 mile pass the Arrow Rock Cemetery on the right. Buried here is Joseph Huston (1784-1865), founder of the Old Tavern. Continue on another 4.3 miles, until the road ends in a T. There turn left, and a short distance beyond (on the left) is a sign and the gate for the Sappington Cemetery State Historic Site. A lane leads to the actual cemetery, which is surrounded by a low stone wall topped by an iron fence.

Close to the front on the left as you enter the cemetery is the grave of Meredith Miles Marmaduke (1791-1864), famed Santa Fe trader and later governor of Missouri. Two square columns over the grave were formerly connected by a marble arch. (Recently, the arch was on the ground.)

Marmaduke in 1824 was a member of the first large-scale caravan to Santa Fe, consisting of 81 men and 25 wagons. His famous journal of the trip was published in the *Missouri Historical Review* of October 1911. He married a daughter of Dr. John Sappington.

Dr. Sappington (1776-1856) and his wife Jane (1783-1852) are buried toward the right rear corner of the cemetery under large trees. The inscriptions on top of their above-ground tombs have almost weathered away.

The doctor indirectly played a major role in the development of the SFT. In 1832 he began distributing his famous "Sappington's Anti-Fever Pills" to western travelers. Intended for the prevention and control of malaria, they contained one grain of quinine compounded with gum myrrh and licorice. The pills were produced by the Doctor's twenty-five slaves and were distributed by traveling salesmen on horseback, one of whom was William Becknell.

Malaria, called *ague*, was then the most serious disease in western Missouri and eastern Kansas and was the scourge of the SFT. It was especially prevalent at Council Grove and along the Arkansas River where mosquitos abounded. (Not until 1895 was it learned that mosquitoes were malaria carriers.) Sappington revealed the formula for his pills in his treatise entitled *The Theory and Treatment of Fevers* (1844), the first medical book published west of the Mississippi. Susan Magoffin and many others on the SFT carried packages of Sappington's pills, and every traveler was familiar with his name.

The doctor's large two-story log house, located one-half mile southwest of the cemetery, burned in 1871. An 1834 portrait of Sappington and another of his wife Jane, painted by famed Arrow Rock artist George Caleb Bingham, hang in the Old Tavern. There too can be seen the doctor's medicine case and pill roller.

CHESTNUT HILL

From the cemetery return 5 miles to the junction with SR 41. Turn left (that is, northwest) on 41 toward Marshall. At 1.25 miles from the junction is the Chestnut Hill DAR marker on a bank above the east (right) side of the highway. Behind the marker 200 feet is "Chestnut Hill," the two-story white home of Santa Fe trader Phillip Thompson, built in 1844. (Now a private residence.) One of the area's first settlers, he purchased 1,400 acres of land just west of Arrow Rock as early as 1826. Owing to repeated trips to Santa Fe, Thompson was reported to speak Spanish better than English.

NEFF TAVERN

At 4.9 miles from the junction at Arrow Rock, SR 41 crosses a small bridge. At .5 mile past the bridge turn on a gravel road that angles in from the left and go .5 mile to the Neff Place DAR marker in the yard of a farmhouse on the left. Isaac Neff built a log tavern here on the SFT in 1837. According to Jean Tyree Hamilton: "The SFT went between the tavern and the barn which later became a stage station, then went west a quarter of a mile, bending around the Neff family cemetery and on northwestward down the grade. The tavern was torn down in 1890."

The brick residence behind the DAR marker is said to be on the original site of the tavern. To the left rear of this house and visible from the road is a two-story stone smokehouse, the only structure remaining of Neff's original complex. It is on the National Register of Historic Sites. Continue on up the road ¼ mile to the little Neff Cemetery, on the right marked by a small sign. It contains the graves of Isaac Neff, his wife and children. Faint traces of the SFT are said to exist beyond the cemetery, but the area is covered with heavy grass and brush.

MARSHALL TO LEXINGTON

From Arrow Rock the SFT headed west via modern Marshall and Lexington to Fort Osage. Before 1821 this route was called the Osage Trace. (Stocking's book shows the Trace on Maps 1 and 2.) Stay on SR 41 as far as Marshall. There, a DAR marker is located on the southwest corner of Courthouse Square.

At Marshall pick up US 65 west. On the west side of town, begin checking mileage at the junction of US 65 and SR 240. At 5.5 miles beyond this junction is the Kiser Spring DAR marker on the left (south) side of the highway. It sits on a bank in front of a house, within sight of a bridge ahead over Salt Fork Creek. Four miles farther, in the town of Malta Bend, is another DAR marker just past the only traffic light on the left (south) side of the highway. At 4.5 miles beyond is the Grand Pass DAR marker. It is in a landscaped area, framed by wagon wheels, on the northwest corner of US 65 at its junction with SR T.

At another 4 miles enter the town of Waverly. Turn right to the "Business District" and go 2 blocks to Kelling Street. A DAR marker is in the middle of the block on the lawn of a house directly across from the post office. At Waverly US 65 turns north, so leave it here and pick up US 24 to Lexington. At 10 miles beyond, in Dover, note a DAR marker in a small park on the left (south) side of the highway in the center of town. Lexington is another 10.5 miles.

LEXINGTON

This town is seldom mentioned in connection with the SFT but in fact was linked with the trail's history in several ways. Lexington, for example, was the center of the giant mercantile firm of the Aull Brothers—John, James and Robert. Branch stores in nearby Richmond, Liberty and Independence made this the largest business enterprise on the Missouri frontier and the first "chain store" in the state. In the 1830s the Aulls were leading outfitters for persons departing on the SFT. James followed the American army to Santa Fe and Chihuahua in 1846. The following year he was killed in a robbery at the store he had opened in Chihuahua City.

Lexington was also headquarters for the renowned freighting firm of Russell, Majors and Waddell which hauled both civilian and military freight over the SFT in the 1850s. It was also this company that operated the Pony Express (between April 1860 and October 1861) over the central route to California. Alexander Majors, the only one of the partners with extensive trail experience, made his first journey to Santa Fe in 1848.

Formally established in 1822, Lexington (like Boonville) sits atop a bluff on the south bank of the Missouri River. Its old steamboat landing at the base of the bluff was once a major shipping point. Many fine antebellum houses lend the town more of a southern than a western air.

In 1837, it was written: "Lexington is one of the towns from which outfits are made in merchandise, mules, oxen, and wagons for the Santa Fe or New Mexican trade. The fur-traders who pass to the mountains by land make this town a place of rendezvous, and frequently going out and coming in with their wagons and packed mules, at the same period of going and coming that is chosen by the Mexican traders. Lexington is therefore occasionally a thoroughfare of traders of great enterprise, and caravans of infinite value."

These sites are of interest to the SFT:

A. Lafayette County Courthouse

On Main Street between 10th and 11th. Built between 1847 and 1849, this structure was familiar to Trail travelers of the 1850s. Four columns hold up a clock-tower. In the east column is a cannon ball fired during the Civil War Battle of Lexington (September 1861). A sign in front of the courthouse calls attention to the cannon ball. On the east side of the courthouse is an official Missouri Historical Marker, "Lexington," with text. At the northwest corner of the grounds (facing Main) is a bronze Pony Express plaque with busts of Russell, Majors and Waddell.

B. Russell, Majors and Waddell Memorial

From the courthouse go east on Main to 16th Street. Turn north (left) and follow 16th several blocks until the street reaches a T near the entrance of College Park. Turn left (west) here and drive past the hospital which adjoins the park. You are still on 16th, now a winding street. The route curves to the right and goes along the west side of the hospital. Just past the hospital (and behind it) on the right is the Memorial, a black sheet metal sign with an ox-drawn wagon and an inscription honoring the three partners.

(Those interested in the Civil War should continue on 16th a block or so past the Memorial as 16th bends to the left. On the right is a marker and the entrance to the Lexington Battlefield, an 80-acre park on the bluff overlooking the Missouri. Here Confederate General Sterling Price defeated Union forces, taking 3,000 prisoners and many war supplies.)

Return to the courthouse on Main Street.

C. Sites on Main Street

Two minor points of interest lie on Main west of the courthouse. At the northeast corner of Main and 10th is the site (not the building) of the office of Russell, Majors and Waddell. Two doors west at 926 Main, between 9th and 10th (on the north or right side of the street) is a white sign and bronze plaque marking a two-story building that was Price's headquarters during the Battle of Lexington. Price, it will be recalled, led reinforcements over the SFT late in 1846 and later put down the revolt in Taos.

D. Pioneer Mother Monument

Continue one block on Main to Broadway, which angles to the right toward the river. You will be headed toward Richmond on SR 13. At the edge of the bluff above the river Broadway curves and starts downhill to the left. At this point, on the right, is a small park containing the first of four Pioneer Mother Monuments located along the SFT. Unveiled in 1928, the statue is of cast stone and stands 18 feet high. The four faces of the base contain historical inscriptions, those on the east and west faces being especially relevant to the SFT. Next to the monument is a smaller granite DAR marker. Both are clearly visible from the roadway. The DAR marker here was originally located at Tabo Creek east of Lexington (according to Long), but in recent years was moved to this site.

To get to the Lexington DAR marker, follow the highway from here down to the Missouri River bridge, as described in the next section. But, instead of crossing the bridge toward Richmond, continue west along the river .4 mile on SR 224 to a major intersection. The marker is on the left in a park surrounded by a chain link fence.

E. Lexington Historical Museum

Located at 112 South 13th Street, just south of Main. This fine small museum contains several items of SFT interest and an exceptional Russell, Majors and Waddell exhibit. Open afternoons, June to November.

SIDE TRIP TO RICHMOND

From the Pioneer Mother an excursion can be conveniently made to Richmond nine miles to the northwest. Follow the highway down to the bottom of the hill and cross the Missouri on SR 13. In Richmond find the courthouse square in the center of town. On the west side of the courthouse is a magnificent ten-foot bronze statue of Colonel Alexander Doniphan, head of the Missouri Mounted Volunteers, who accompanied Kearny on the SFT to the conquest of New Mexico in 1846. A plaque on the south base of the statue depicts a sword-waving Doniphan leading his troops at the Battle of Sacramento (north of Chihuahua City) on February 28, 1847. Doniphan died in Richmond on August 8, 1887, but is buried in nearby Liberty.

Return to Lexington and continue west on US 24 toward Buckner and Fort Osage.

FORT OSAGE

For a brief period in the 1820s, Fort Osage was the westernmost outpost in Missouri and a rendezvous for SFT caravans. Established in 1808 by William Clark (of Lewis and Clark fame), the palisade walls and log blockhouses sheltered both a military garrison and an Indian trading post run by the government (the latter called a "factory"). Sitting on the summit of a 70-foot bluff overlooking the Missouri River, the fort for a time figured prominently in the fur trade. It was abandoned by the government in 1827 with the founding of Fort Leavenworth farther up the Missouri.

It was from Fort Osage that a party of U.S. government

Fort Osage, Missouri.

commissioners set out in 1825 to survey the SFT, strangely making Taos and not Santa Fe their final destination. They began recording compass directions and chained distances to New Mexico at a point (the zero milestone) just south of the fort. (The spot was recently identified by Polly Fowler of Independence, although it is not marked.) George C. Sibley, the factor or government trader at Fort Osage, was the most visible of the commissioners so the enterprise is sometimes referred to as the "Sibley Survey."

In the community of Buckner US 24 intersects at the only traffic light with County Road 20-E. (It may not be marked.) On the southeast corner of this junction is the largest DAR marker on the SFT. Composed of three stone panels it sits in front of a chain link fence.

From US 24 at this point proceed north on County Road 20-E, 3 miles to Fort Osage. There are numerous turns in the road but follow the small signs. Nearing the fort, note the Sibley Cemetery on the right, where the paved road turns left in front of the new Visitors' Center and Museum. At the far back corner of the cemetery (that is, on the east side along the Missouri River) is one of the regular DAR markers. Beside it, a grassed-over dirt ramp leads down to the river through the trees. This was used by SFT wagons ascending from the landing on the flood plain.

The only grave here of major interest is that of famed fur trapper Zenas Leonard. After returning from the Rockies and California, he settled at the site of Fort Osage and became an Indian trader and steamboat operator. His *Narrative of the Adventures of Zenas Leonard* (1839) is a well-known account of western adventuring. The modern gray granite headstone, flat and level with the ground, is near the center of the cemetery and behind and to the left of the tall Harrelson monument.

The cemetery served the community of Sibley, founded in 1836 by Archibald Gamble after the dismantling of neighboring Fort Osage. He and George C. Sibley had married sisters, a relationship that no doubt helped him obtain the position of secretary to the commissioners on the 1825 SFT survey. Overland trader Alphonso Wetmore in 1837 wrote of the new town of Sibley: "It has already been made a point of landing for Santa Fe goods, and it will probably share largely in the increasing advantages of that trade. The landing and harbor of Sibley are excellent, made so by the eddy-water at the base of the bluff."

After touring the cemetery, stop at the neighboring Visitors' Center and see exhibits relating to the history of the fort and the local Indians. Then continue on the paved road 100 feet to the entrance of Fort Osage. An explanatory historical marker stands at the beginning of the sidewalk that leads to the fort gate.

The log fort, reconstructed on its original site in recent years, is today one of the highpoints of interest at the eastern end of the trail. Blockhouses, soldiers' quarters and the factory (trading post) can be toured. Shelves in the factory are stocked with trade goods, and that part of the building in which George C. Sibley and his wife lived briefly contains period furnishings. A porch at the rear provides a spectacular overlook of the Missouri River.

In 1962 Fort Osage became a Registered National Historic Landmark. It is operated as a facility of the Jackson County Parks System. A River Days celebration is held here each May.

SIDE TRIP TO LIBERTY

From Fort Osage return to Buckner and go west again on US 24 toward Independence. Within a mile or so pass the Independence City Limits sign, which is far out in the country. About 6½ miles past this sign on the right (north) side of US 24 is the new Salem Baptist Church. Just beyond it in a small park (also on the right) is the Salem DAR marker.

Continue west to the junction with SR 291. Turn right (north) on that highway and drive 8 miles to the town of Liberty. The one point of

SFT interest is the grave of Colonel Alexander Doniphan who led the Missouri Volunteers over the trail in 1846, the first year of the Mexican War. For a brief moment he played a major role in the history of New Mexico.

The Doniphan gravesite is in Fairview Cemetery at the south end of Gallatin Street close to the downtown area. Inquire locally for directions. Once in the cemetery the grave is easily found since it is marked by the tallest monument, a spire about 20 feet high near the center of the grounds. In his day Doniphan was one of the most renowned men in Missouri. Now he is scarcely remembered.

INDEPENDENCE

From its founding in 1827 until 1856 Independence served as a main outfitting point for the Santa Fe trade. Here goods bought in St. Louis, Philadelphia, New York and even Europe were transferred from Missouri steamboats to freight wagons bound for Santa Fe. Blacksmiths, wagon and harness makers, sellers of livestock and local merchants did a lively business in supplying the overland parties. By the early 1840s these included emigrants on the newly opened Oregon Trail.

Before the trail head shifted westward to Westport and Kansas City in the mid-1850s Independence was a noisy, bustling place frequented by such notables as Kit Carson, Josiah Gregg, Francis Parkman, Samuel and Susan Magoffin and the long-distance horseback rider Francis X. Aubry. The town is sometimes called the "Queen City of the Trails." Unfortunately, practically all the historic structures associated with overland travel have been callously demolished, some of them in recent years, by destructive urban renewal programs. A yearly Santa-Cali-Gon Days celebration honors the trail era.

All sites and markers noted here (with one exception) have some association with the SFT. Information about other places of interest can be obtained from the Chamber of Commerce, 213 South Main, or from the City of Independence Department of Tourism, P. O. Box 1827, Independence, Missouri 64050. Visitors interested in following the SFT route through town street by street should use Franzwa's Oregon Trail guide.

A. Harry S. Truman Library and Museum

Entering Independence from the east stay on US 24 which passes a few blocks north of the downtown area. At the junction with Delaware Street, the Library and Museum is seen on the right. An official

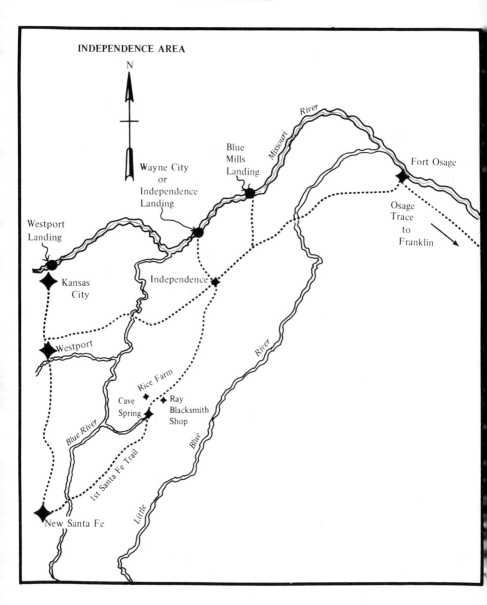

INDEPENDENCE AREA

N

Missouri River

Blue
Mills
Landing

Fort Osage

Wayne City
or
Independence
Landing

Osage
Trace
to
Franklin

Westport
Landing

Independence

Kansas
City

Westport

River

Rice Farm

Cave
Spring

Ray
Blacksmith
Shop

Blue River

Blue

1st Santa Fe Trail

Little

New Santa Fe

Missouri Historical Marker, "Independence," is at the entrance to the grounds and its text contains reference to the SFT and Josiah Gregg.

Although you may wish to tour the entire facility, the one point of interest for trail buffs is the massive and splendid mural by artist Thomas H. Benton entitled "Independence and the Opening of the West." It is located in the main lobby along with a sales desk which has items of historical interest.

The mural depicts scenes typical of the Santa Fe and Oregon Trails. At the far right blacksmiths are readying wagons for the westward journey. In the upper right can be seen a caravan heading for Chimney Rock, a famous landmark on the Oregon Trail. The left side of the mural is devoted to the SFT. There is a Pawnee warrior with his scalplock and behind him a Cheyenne chief bartering red fox furs with a trader. At the upper left appears Bents Fort, best known stop on the Mountain Branch of the SFT. Beyond it rise the Spanish Peaks, beacons for all travelers headed toward Santa Fe and Taos.

Two separate panels at the bottom show Independence in the late 1840s. The one at the left portrays a steamboat at the Missouri River landing. From it, covered freight wagons are taking on goods for the Santa Fe trade. The right-hand panel features a caravan forming up on Independence Square with the old 1840 courthouse in the background.

Here we can mention that there were two landings on the Missouri River north of town. The oldest, founded before 1832, was the Blue Mills Landing located six miles northeast of the square. (It was initially called Owens Landing after Santa Fe trader Samuel C. Owens.) In time Blue Mills was overshadowed by Wayne City Landing, commonly called Independence Landing, several miles upstream. This one was about 3½ miles north of the courthouse square.

To reach the Wayne City marker go north on River Boulevard (which is one block west of the Truman Library). At the "Sugar Creek Portland Cement" sign River veers left and starts downhill to the cement plant and the original site of the landing. (Note: As this book was going to press the cement company was petitioning to have the road closed to the public.) About one block after the turn on the left is a pull-out and Missouri River overlook. At the edge of the overlook is a beautiful new historical marker, dedicated in August 1983. Return south on River to Truman Road. Go east on Truman to Osage, then south on Osage to the vicinity of the courthouse.

B. Independence Courthouse Square

Early writers often described the bustle and color surrounding the Courthouse as wagons formed up for the departure to Santa Fe. None of the buildings on the square dates from the heyday of the Trail. The last, the Nebraska House (built 1849), located at the northeast corner of present Liberty and Maple, was torn down in 1980 to make way for a parking lot. Even more popular than the Nebraska House as a hostelry was the Merchants Hotel operated by Colonel Smallwood ("Uncle Wood") Noland. Situated on what is now the northwest corner of Main and Maple and also facing the square, the two-story brick building there at present is believed to incorporate some portions of the original structure. The hotel soon became known as the Noland House and was mentioned by Susan Magoffin, who passed a night under its roof before starting for Santa Fe in 1846.

On the southwest corner of the square (at Liberty and Lexington) the three-story Chrisman-Sawyer Bank Building is on the site of the Aull & Owens store. (Their role in the Santa Fe trade has been noted under Lexington above.)

The SFT divided at this corner, offering a choice of branches to wagonmasters. One route lay west along Lexington to the town of Westport. The second branch left the square on Liberty headed south through the present suburbs of Independence and then angled southwest through modern Raytown and passed the Cave Spring campground. The branches came together again at the village of New Santa Fe on the Missouri-Kansas border. (See map.)

C. The Courthouse

In the center of the square at 112 West Lexington. Inspired by Independence Hall in Philadelphia, this structure is now called the Truman Courthouse since Judge Harry S. Truman had an office there in the 1920s and 1930s. It incorporates the foundations and sections of several earlier Jackson County courthouses dating from trail days. See the restored courtroom on the first floor which dates back to 1852 and was used later by Truman. (Note: Offices of the Jackson County Historical Society Archives are also on the first floor.)

On the west side of the courthouse is a large equestrian statue of Andrew Jackson for whom the county is named. Flanking the statue are two monuments. One is the DAR marker for the SFT; the other marks the beginning of the Oregon Trail.

D. First Log Courthouse

At 107 West Kansas, one block south of the square. This small structure was built in 1827 to serve as a temporary courthouse until something more permanent could be constructed. It is the oldest courthouse remaining west of the Mississippi.

E. Site of Robert Weston's Blacksmith Shop

Southwest corner of Liberty and Kansas, just west of the First Log Courthouse. This shop catered to the needs of Santa Fe traders in the

1840s. The structure was demolished in the 1940s and the site is now a parking lot. A historical bronze plaque mounted on a red granite monument is on the corner. Robert's father, Samuel, also a noted blacksmith, is honored by a historical marker at his gravesite, noted in Woodlawn Cemetery below.

F. Kritser House

115 East Walnut. This small residence with a gable roof was built in 1847 by Martin L. Kritser. It is said that he went over the SFT in 1846 and with the profits from his trading venture built this house. A municipal historical marker with text is on the lawn.

G. Smallwood Noland House

1024 South Forest. Home of Independence's most famous innkeeper during trail days, this two-story white residence was erected about 1850. A rear section, however, may date from as early as 1831. There is no marker at the residence.

H. Bingham-Waggoner House

313 West Pacific. The SFT passed by this residence located just a few blocks south of the square. An early owner of the property was Jacob Hall, a prominent freighter in the Santa Fe and Chihuahua trade and operator of stage lines to New Mexico. His letters and business ledgers are preserved in the Historical Society Archives at the courthouse. A later property owner, John Lewis, built the two-story brick house. He was a saddle-maker, also associated with the Santa Fe trade. After changing hands twice more the estate was purchased by celebrated Missouri artist George Caleb Bingham who lived there with his wife for six years. In 1879 Peter and William Waggoner bought the house, which was destined to remain in the hands of their descendants for the next ninety-nine years. Today it is owned by the City of Independence and is being made available to the public.

Immediately north of this residence are red brick buildings associated with the Waggoner-Gates Milling Company (at 526 South Osage), which began operations on the site in 1875. The mill itself was destroyed by an explosion and fire in the 1960s. (Lately there has been talk of using these structures for a "Beginning of the Trails" interpretive center after the manner of the "End of the Oregon Trail Interpretive Center" in Oregon City.)

In the area north of the remaining mill office (between Osage and Spring Streets) is located the "Emigrant" Spring whose waters in trail days were said to flow in the volume of "about the size of a man's arm." Here wagons once gathered before departing for Santa Fe. Now the site is littered with construction debris, but it is hoped that it will soon be cleaned up and marked.

I. McCoy House

410 West Farmer. William McCoy arrived in Independence in 1838 and became the town's first mayor in 1849. He was heavily involved in the New Mexico trade, government freighting, and (with Jacob Hall) stagecoaching. The rear wing of this two-story brick residence is thought to have been constructed about 1840 for Samuel C. Owens, famed merchant and outfitter for the Santa Fe trade. The main section of the house dates from about 1856. A historical marker with text is near the street.

J. Woodlawn Cemetery

710 South Noland Road. Begun around 1837 (on an Indian burial ground according to tradition), this cemetery contains the graves of several persons associated with the SFT as well as Independence pioneers. Unfortunately, the attendant at the small Sexton's house in the traffic circle just inside the main gate cannot help you in finding graves of interest because no records are kept of persons buried here before 1900. However, the description of location and the map supplied below will guide you.

(a) Grave of John Taylor Hughes. (Drive on the right side of the Sexton's house and take the first lane leading east, toward the back of the cemetery. Hughes' waist-high stone is on the left next to the lane. Two large cedars are just to the north of it.) Private Hughes accompanied Colonel Alexander Doniphan's First Missouri Mounted Volunteers over the SFT to the conquest of New Mexico in 1846. He participated in the Navajo expedition to western New Mexico and later was in the Battle of Sacramento north of Chihuahua City. He became the official historian for these events upon returning home when he wrote and published (1847) the detailed book *Doniphan's Expedition*. The volume remains a standard source on the SFT and the Mexican War in the Southwest.

(b) Grave of Samuel Weston. (From Hughes' stone continue straight ahead, that is, east, to the rear of the cemetery where the lane curves to the right or south. The 6-foot high Weston marker of red granite is on the right in front of a large tree.) Samuel, father of Robert who was noted above, had a blacksmith shop on Lexington between Osage and Spring Streets. He was also a carpenter and did interior work on two of Independence's early brick courthouses. His headstone is of recent origin and more in the nature of a historical marker with reference to the SFT.

(c) Grave of Mother Mary Matilda Mills. (Across the lane from the

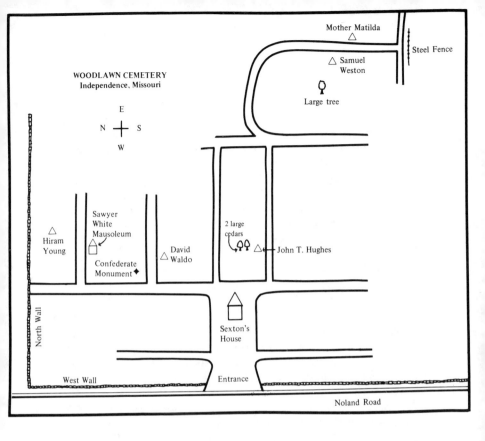

WOODLAWN CEMETERY
Independence, Missouri

Mother Matilda △

△ Samuel Weston

Steel Fence

Large tree

E
N ⊢ S
W

Sawyer White Mausoleum

2 large cedars

△ John T. Hughes

Hiram Young △

△ David Waldo

Confederate Monument ✦

North Wall

Sexton's House

West Wall

Entrance

Noland Road

Weston grave and a few feet south, her flat stone, level with the ground, is next to the edge of the pavement. It is in the Stayton family plot.) In July 1852 New Mexico's Bishop Jean B. Lamy was returning to Santa Fe with a party that included a group of Sisters of Loretto. From St. Louis they sailed up the Missouri on the steamer *Kansas*. Four days out cholera struck. Mother Matilda, superior of the nuns, died and others became gravely ill. Through fear of the disease the captain put Lamy's entire company off the boat six miles east of Independence, where they found refuge from the rainy weather in an abandoned warehouse. Mother Matilda lay in a hastily constructed coffin on the river bank. Lamy finally secured a hearse, but because some of his people still suffered the dread cholera local authorities refused them entrance to the town. A family named Stayton who learned of the problem offered to let Mother Matilda's coffin be carried to their burial plot in the present Woodlawn Cemetery. There, at night and in secret, Bishop Lamy and Father Donnelly, the local priest, performed the funeral services. (Note that in his biography, *Lamy of Santa Fe*, Paul Horgan tells of Mother Matilda's death but fails to mention where or how she was buried. That information is supplied here through the courtesy of Polly Fowler.)

(d) Grave of David Waldo. (From the rear of the Sexton's house take the lane leading north and turn right, or east, at the first intersecting lane. The large Confederate monument is immediately on the left and just past it, on the right side of the lane, is the Waldo monument.) David Waldo was one of the leading Santa Fe merchants, entering the trade as early as 1831. He made numerous trips over the SFT and played a conspicuous role in the conquest of New Mexico in 1846. His younger brother, Lawrence L. Waldo, also a trader, was killed near Mora, New Mexico, early in 1847 during the same disturbances that led to the death of Governor Charles Bent. In the early 1850s David Waldo was engaged in hauling military freight to New Mexico over the SFT and with Jacob Hall operated the stageline to New Mexico. A brief sketch of his life is included in Ralph E. Twitchell's *The Military Occupation of New Mexico*.

(e) Grave of Hiram Young. (On the next lane north of the Waldo monument is the small Sawyer mausoleum, white with a pitched roof. Across the lane from it, to the northeast, is the chest-high gray granite marker for Hiram Young.) In the decade before the Civil War ex-slave Young gained a reputation as a superb wagon maker. He also carved ox bows by the hundred for use on the SFT and Oregon Trail. A document of April 15, 1857 (supplied by Polly Fowler), refers to: "25 large new Santa Fe wagons with 2½ inch tread, with provision boxes and bows, now on the lot of said Young. . .and also 150 ox yokes." During the war he and his family fled briefly to Fort Leavenworth and when he returned to Independence he found that his shops (between present Main and Liberty Streets on the south side of 24 Highway) had been destroyed by Union occupation forces. Hiram Young is featured in the current trail exhibit at the Kansas City Museum of History and Science. He is also pictured, working at his forge, in the lower right corner of the Benton mural at the Truman Library.

K. Jim Bridger's Grave in Mount Washington Cemetery

Drive west on Truman Road to the entrance of the cemetery. Upon entering go straight ahead about 2 blocks. After crossing a little bridge, Bridger's tall monument is seen immediately on the right, standing alone in a small triangular lot. James Bridger (1804-81) had nothing to do with the SFT, but as a trapper with Kit Carson in the central and northern Rockies and an associate of Jedediah Smith (both closely identified with the SFT) Bridger was a leading figure in the history of the West.

L. Missouri Town 1885

Go east from Independence on 40 Highway to Woods Chapel Road. Turn right, or south, and proceed to Liggett Road which intersects from the east, or left. This is the entrance to Lake Jacomo Park. Continue east on Liggett across the low dam and go a mile or so beyond to the east side of the lake where a paved road joins from the right. At that point begin following the small signs around the lake to Missouri Town. This fine living museum is managed by the Jackson County Parks and Recreation Department. It consists of residences and businesses built between 1820 and 1860, which have been moved to the site from various locations in western Missouri. Although the place has no direct connection with the SFT, it is so well put together that it helps visitors catch the spirit of trail days. A pair of oxen is corraled on the main street in summer.

M. Santa Fe Trail Park

Entrance off Santa Fe Road, which was formerly McCoy Street, one block north of 31st Street. Caravans from Independence's Courthouse Square passed through the area of the park, headed in a southwesterly direction and occasionally camped here. Faint traces of ruts are visible on grassy slopes. Find the baseball diamond in the southwest corner of the park. Down in the creek to the right (north) of the diamond is a dirt ramp marked by a low stone retaining wall. This is believed to be a remnant of the SFT. In mid to late summer it may be lost in a tangle of trees and brush. Beyond the creek crossing, trail ruts can be found in the yards of modern homes—behind 3131 Santa Fe Terrace, for example.

Upon completing a tour of trail sites in Independence, the Santa Fe Trail Park is a good point of departure for Raytown. From the park entrance continue south on Santa Fe Road to 33rd Street and turn right 2 blocks to Crysler Avenue, a main thoroughfare. There turn left (south) and go to 47th Street. There turn right (west) 2 blocks to the intersection of Blue Ridge Boulevard. Turn left (south) on Blue Ridge and you will be directly on the SFT route leading into Raytown.

RAYTOWN AND CAVE SPRING

The people of Raytown are very conscious of their location on the SFT. Entering the city limits on Blue Ridge Boulevard note the Santa Fe Trail Professional Building on the left (east) side of the street. Every few blocks can be seen rustic green and white SFT signs placed along the trail route by the local Boy Scout troop. Blue Ridge Boulevard angles diagonally through the center of Raytown. As the original SFT it was following the high ground or ridge between the Little Blue and the Big

Blue Rivers, which made the easiest travel for wagons.

At 59th Street turn right (west) and drive 3 blocks to the intersection of Raytown Road. The new City Hall will be seen on the right. It is on the site once occupied by the home of George Washington Rhoades. He was the Jackson County Surveyor (1840-44), a commissioner of roads and "an advocate of the Santa Fe Trail." According to *Raytown Remembers*, a book published in 1975 by the Raytown Historical Society, George W. Rhoades in May 1839 "petitioned the County Court to establish a public highway to Santa Fe." The SFT was already well travelled, but owners of adjacent farmlands often put gates across the road to discourage wagons from crossing their properties. Rhoades advocated serviceable all-weather roads for heavy trail vehicles. He may have been engaged in trade to the Southwest because his estate inventory included "five Trading Wagons." A cast aluminum plaque containing reference to the SFT was placed at his homesite in 1975. It is set in a concrete monument next to the flagpole in front of City Hall.

From this point go south on Raytown Road to the intersection of 63rd Street. Just beyond the southeast corner, facing Raytown Road, is a historical marker with text commemorating the site of William Ray's Blacksmith Shop. Ray settled at this spot with his family in the late 1840s, built his shop and provided wagon repairs for travelers on the SFT. He charged 88 cents to shoe a horse. By 1854 the community that grew up around the smithy was known as Raytown, although by that time the smith himself had already migrated westward on the Oregon Trail.

From this intersection drive west on 63rd Street 1½ blocks to the Raytown Museum on the left (at 9705 E. 63rd). Some of its exhibits relate to the era of the SFT. Continue west on 63rd Street .3 mile to Blue Ridge Boulevard which veers off to the left and after .6 mile intersects with Blue Ridge Extension. This is still the original SFT route. Turn left (south) on Extension and immediately 66th Street intersects from the left. There on the southeast corner in a large lot and hidden by trees is the original farmhouse of Archibald Rice. (Its address is 8801 East 66th Street.)

The white frame structure, built in the late 1830s, is little changed except for the later addition of dormer windows in the steep pitched roof. The SFT passed just north of the house and once beyond it turned left (south) along present Blue Ridge Extension. A DAR marker is on the corner facing Extension.

New Orleans journalist Matt Field, who made a trip over the SFT in 1840, wrote: "About half a day's travel [from Independence] brings the Santa Fe bound traders past the flourishing plantation of Farmer Rice, where leisure travelers often linger to enjoy his sweet bacon, fresh eggs, new milk and other nutritious and unsophisticated luxuries that appease appetite without encumbering digestion."

On the west side of the Rice house, facing Blue Ridge Extension, is a small log structure with a stone chimney known as Aunt Sophie's cabin. The restored cabin, said to have been built in 1837, was one of several Rice provided as quarters for his slaves. All have disappeared except this one, which housed the slave remembered as "Aunt Sophie." Before her death in 1896 at age 77 she often spoke of the Santa Fe caravans that had passed by in the early days. She is said to be buried in Independence's Woodlawn Cemetery in the Rice family plot, but I have been unable to locate her grave. Along the street by the cabin is one of the Boy Scout SFT markers.

Continue south on Blue Ridge Extension about 4 blocks to the intersection of Gregory. Turn right (west) on Gregory and almost at once on the left (south) is the entrance to the William M. Klein Park. (This park is too new to appear on most maps.)

Located on the western edge of modern Raytown, the Klein Park's chief point of interest is the Cave Spring. It was a natural camping site furnished with a fine stream of water issuing from the mouth of a small limestone cave. SFT travelers in the early 1820s would have found it a good overnight stop. After Independence was established in 1827 wagon trains leaving Courthouse Square could conveniently "noon" at Cave Spring before pushing on toward the Kansas border. Few references to the site occur in the trail literature but old-timers in the vicinity have reported SFT ruts just west of the spring and beyond in Swope Park.

Klein Park is the recent creation of a group of dedicated Raytown citizens who formed the Cave Spring Association to protect and interpret the site. The first portion of a visitors' center, the Art Clark Nature Center, was dedicated in 1982. (Be sure to note the story of young Art Clark in the Center's interpretation.) A map is provided so that visitors can follow a trail through woodlands to the cave. Future plans call for the addition of historical exhibits.

This is one of the most promising and exciting projects now underway along the SFT. Trail buffs can receive more information and apply for membership in the Cave Spring Association by writing the Executive Director, Sylvia Mooney, 7120 Harecliff Drive, Kansas City, Missouri 64133.

Return to the intersection of Blue Ridge Extension and Gregory, turn right and start south on Blue Ridge along the east side of Klein Park. About 2 blocks from Gregory is a DAR marker on the right. It is still in Klein Park but separated from the grounds by a thick wall of trees.

CAVE SPRING TO NEW SANTA FE

From Klein Park continue south on Blue Ridge Extension (which inexplicably becomes Blue Ridge Boulevard again) about 5 miles to the intersection of Red Bridge Road. Here turn right (west) and proceed on Red Bridge (using a city map to follow its jogs) about 3½ miles to the crossing of the Big Blue River. Here is an actual "red bridge." The SFT forded the river at this point.

Several blocks beyond the bridge, 110th Street joins Red Bridge Road from the right (north). On the left is the entrance to Minor Park and a wooden sign, "Santa Fe Trail Historic Site." Drive into the parking lot and beyond the back right corner is a SFT map under glass with extensive historical text. From here, walk south along the wire fence about 100 yards to a large red granite DAR marker. It sits in the deep swale of grassed-over SFT ruts that cut through a ridge above the Big Blue River. After the wagons had forded they moved up the slope below the present marker and their wheels sliced a path in the brow at the top. These are some of the most interesting trail remains in the Kansas City area.

From the park entrance go west to the intersection of Holmes Road and turn left (south) along the west side of Minor Park. Continue south on Holmes about a mile to the intersection of the street called Santa Fe Trail. There turn right and go west (crossing Wornall Road) until you come to the Santa Fe Bible Church on the right (north) side of the street.

Enter the Church parking lot on the west. Adjoining it in the rear is an old cemetery, all that remains of the hamlet of New Santa Fe. At the front of the lot near the street is an official Missouri Historical Marker, "New Santa Fe," with text and references to the SFT. A half block west on the northeast corner of Santa Fe Trail Street and State Line Road is a DAR marker.

This little community was at the junction of the two branches of the SFT that had parted back at the square in Independence. The older branch, which you have been following, descended directly from Independence (22 miles) in a southwesterly direction via Raytown and Cave Spring. It was finally abandoned in 1856. The second branch went west from Independence Square to the community of Westport near the state line, then led almost due south (just inside the Missouri border) to New Santa Fe. The historical sites and markers along that route are described below.

The early history of New Santa Fe is fuzzy. A tavern was on the site by the mid 1840s, selling whiskey to persons who crossed the State Line from the "dry" Indian reservation on the Kansas side. The townsite was platted in 1851. Two years later the place boasted two general stores, an inn, shoe shop, drugstore, blacksmith shop and post office. New Santa Fe, never much to begin with, withered away after the glory days of the trail had passed.

KANSAS CITY AND OLD WESTPORT

Some 11 miles west of Independence, John Calvin McCoy built a two-story log cabin in 1833 to serve as a trading post on a branch road to Santa Fe. His effort marked the beginning of the new community of Westport. McCoy began luring trail outfitters away from the stores in Independence with considerable success. He picked up his mercantile stock from steamboats tying up at Westport Landing, 4 miles to the north. The landing, on the Missouri about 1½ miles below its junction with the Kansas (or Kaw) River, had a fine ledge of rock jutting out into the water. Goods were first deposited in warehouses, then freighted up a bluff and on to stores in Westport.

The small settlement that grew up around the landing afterward took the name Kansas City. As the century advanced it expanded and eventually engulfed Westport by 1897. In the beginning, however, it was Westport, newly booming as a jump-off point for the far West, that gave promise of becoming the region's chief population center.

By the mid-1840s Independence's monopoly over the Santa Fe trade had been broken and by 1853 Westport virtually controlled the overland traffic. In the decade before the Civil War it fairly hummed with activity as Santa Fe traders, mountain men, Indians and Oregon-bound emigrants mingled in the streets.

Westport remained the main eastern terminus of the SFT longer than any of the places that preceded it—Franklin, Arrow Rock, Fort Osage or even Independence. However, the outbreak of the Civil War in 1861 brought border disturbances and caused most of the Santa Fe traders to move their business upriver to Fort Leavenworth, which was more secure. After the war, Westport briefly recovered some of its lost trade but by 1866 the railroad had pushed into Kansas and the head of

Westport Landing.

the SFT moved with it.

A surprising number of sites and markers exist in the Westport-Kansas City area. Those unfamiliar with the region will need to rely upon an up-to-date city map. Franzwa's guides will also prove useful in reaching many of the places noted below.

Points of SFT interest fall into three clusters from north to south: (1) Kansas City, (2) Old Westport, and (3) the trail south to New Santa Fe. Both Westport and New Santa Fe today lie within the greater metropolitan area of Kansas City.

Kansas City

A. Site of the Westport Landing on the Missouri River

In the vicinity of First and Grand. During the 1840s as many as five or six steamboats might be tied up at this landing at one time. There is not much to be seen now but it is a historic location. For the history of this area see Franzwa, OTR, pp. 119-21. From the foot of Grand

Avenue a river boat, the "Westport," offers excursions during the summer. On several Sundays a 25-mile trip down river to Fort Osage can be taken. For a brochure write: Kansas City River Boat, Inc., One Grand Avenue, Kansas City, Missouri 64106.

B. Main Kansas City Library

Downtown at Main and Grand. Some good research materials on the SFT are available here in the Missouri Valley Room. Murals around the ceiling depict the early history of the city, including scenes associated with the trail. Just outside the room hangs a copy of the Spalding Map of 1855, which shows the area in the heyday of the SFT.

C. City Hall

Downtown between Eleventh and Twelfth and Oak and Locust. Major episodes in the city's history are depicted in a frieze of sixteen panels directly above the sixth story.

D. Penn Valley Park

Directly south of downtown at Pershing Road and Main Street; accessible from I-35. The east side of the park was located astride the road from Westport Landing to Westport. There are three trail monuments of interest here:

(1) A special DAR marker

On Memorial Drive on the north side of St. Mary's Hospital and south of the 300-foot shaft of the Liberty World War I Memorial. A bronze plaque showing a covered wagon and oxen in relief is attached to a stone monument. Four more of these special DAR bronze plaques will be found at points along the eastern end of the trail as far as Lost Springs.

(2) Pioneer Mother Memorial

In the park west of the DAR marker and St. Mary's Hospital. The Memorial is a larger-than-life group of bronze figures surrounding a pioneer mother on horseback. This sculpture is unrelated to the series of stone pioneer mothers on the SFT, the first example of which has already been noted at Lexington. With the Kansas City skyline rising behind it, this work is a beauty. Don't miss it.

(3) The Scout

On the west side of the park beyond Penn Valley Drive. An equestrian statue of a Sioux warrior gazes toward the skyline of Kansas City. The Sioux from the north occasionally made attacks on the SFT in central Kansas.

E. Thomas Hart Benton Memorial

In a traffic circle at the intersection of Gladstone and Benton Boulevard. Senator Benton's role in developing western trails was mentioned in connection with his statue at St. Louis. Here a seven-foot

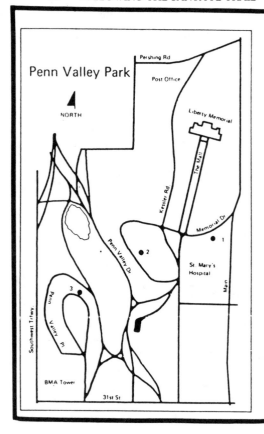

PENN VALLEY PARK IN KANSAS CITY

1. Santa Fe Trail Marker
2. Pioneer Mother Memorial
3. The Scout

granite monument holds two bronze plaques, one of which bears Benton's likeness.

F. The Kansas City Museum of History and Science

At 3218 Gladstone Boulevard, two blocks from the Benton Memorial. Splendid exhibits of the mountain men, Indians, Oregon Trail and SFT are some of the best to be seen anywhere. The SFT is well represented.

G. The Independence to Westport Road

To follow this route street by street through Kansas City refer to Franzwa's OTR. There are four markers between the crossing of the Big Blue River and Westport on this branch of the SFT:

(1) Marker at 27th Street (not 27th Terrace) and Topping on the southeast corner of the intersection. This brass plaque refers to the site as being on the "connecting link" between Independence and Westport. In the park behind the marker a wide path leads downhill at a

diagonal through the trees about 2 blocks to the Big Blue Crossing. This was the route of the SFT. The actual trail ruts, visible a few years ago, are now too faint to see. Franzwa, OTR, pp. 98-99, calls it a strenuous walk down to the crossing. To avoid that, drive east on 27th alongside the park for 2 blocks until the street ends at a T and a large pile of white limestone blocks. Turn right and go 1 block to where the street ends in a traffic circle. Park and follow a path on the east side of the circle down to the Big Blue. If you don't want to walk, at least catch a glimpse of the river through the trees at the start of the path. This was a very difficult crossing for wagons because of the steep banks.

(2) Marker at Askew School. Return to 27th and Topping and drive north on Topping 1 block to Askew School on the left (west) side of the street. This is the route of the SFT as it followed a ridge north briefly before turning southwest toward Westport. A fine bronze marker on a granite monument is in front of the main entrance of the school.

(3) Marker at Linwood and Euclid Streets. On the north side of Linwood in the center of a vacant lot is a red granite monument. Unfortunately, the bronze SFT plaque that it once held has been stolen. This spot on the trail was about half way between the Big Blue Crossing and Westport.

(4) Gillham Marker. Located in the center parkway just south of the intersection of 38th and Gillham, this red granite monument has a beautiful metal plaque showing in relief a wagon train under attack by Indians. Franzwa, OTR, p. 101, says this marker is on the exact location of the trail just before it reaches Westport.

Westport

A. Trail Markers

A cluster of trail markers is in the vicinity of Broadway and 40th just north of the Broadway and Westport Road intersection and a block northeast of the center of Old Westport:

(1) Plaque bearing the relief of a Pioneer Mother and her children affixed to a six-foot granite boulder in a small triangular park at Broadway and 40th.

(2) "Westport, Gateway to the West," a wooden trail marker about chest high with reference to the SFT across the narrow street northwest of the Pioneer Mother plaque.

(3) Old Westport Historical Interpretive Sign suspended from a large wooden ox yoke in a narrow parkway on Broadway just southeast of the Pioneer Mother.

B. Harris Home

4000 Baltimore. Built in 1855 by Colonel John Harris who was a participant in the Santa Fe trade, the house was moved to the present site in 1922 from its original location a half-block away at Westport and Main, a spot now marked by a plaque. The beautiful two-story brick house is currently the headquarters of the Westport Historical Society which has restored several rooms for public view. (Address inquiries to the Society at Box 10076, Westport Station, Kansas City, Missouri 64111).

C. Site of the Harris House Hotel

Northeast corner of Westport and Penn in the center of Old Westport. Colonel Harris bought the log building at this location in 1846, when it was known as the McGee Tavern and Hotel or more popularly the "Catfish House," catfish being a specialty of the chef. Owner Allen McGee was selling out to enter the Santa Fe trade. When the building burned, Harris rebuilt a three-story brick structure in 1852. It was razed in 1922. A plaque now marks the spot. The SFT passed by both the Harris home and his hotel.

D. The Ewing-Boone Building

Northwest corner of Westport and Penn. Westport's leading historian William Goff has established that this structure was built in 1850-51, not in 1837 as a plaque on the east wall facing Penn indicates. Owners were George and William Ewing, prominent traders with the Shawnees whose lands lay just across the Kansas line. Albert G. Boone, a grandson of Daniel Boone, bought the building in 1854, the year the Shawnee lands were extinguished and the Indian trade died.

E. Jim Bridger's Store

Next to the Ewing-Boone Building on Westport Road. Sometimes described as the most historic building remaining in Old Westport, the structure was built in 1850 by Cyprien Chouteau, member of a prominent fur-trading family of St. Louis. Before coming to Westport in that year, he had operated a trading post at Council Grove on the SFT. Chouteau sold the two-story store and warehouse in 1866 to aging Jim Bridger, known in his younger days as "The King of the Mountain Men." Bridger ran a grocery business there for several years. A bronze historical plaque is attached to the outside front wall. The building is presently occupied by a restaurant, "Stanford & Sons."

F. Covered Freight Wagon

Three blocks west of Bridger's Store on Westport Road (which is also 43rd Street) at Southwest Trafficway. This large wagon on the west side of the intersection under the Old Westport sign is a replica commemorating trail days.

A freight wagon of the kind that traveled the Santa Fe Trail.

The Westport To New Santa Fe Road

From the Old Westport square the SFT ran almost due south 10 miles to the junction hamlet of New Santa Fe. From the square the trail crossed Brush Creek, climbed Brush Creek Hill and, following today's Wornall Road, continued on to the "great camping ground." At this well-watered and grassy site caravans organized for their departure on the SFT. That area now lies between Wornall Road and the State Line and is bounded on the north by 67th Street and on the south by 71st Street. Not far below the camping ground, the Olathe cut-off of the SFT branched toward the southwest, rejoining the main trail near present Gardner, Kansas. (See Franzwa, MOT, p. 27.)

The following sites all lie below Old Westport and can be visited in sequence, moving south toward New Santa Fe:

A. Shawnee Mission State Park

Mission Road at 53rd Street. Between 1825 and 1854 the Shawnee Indian Reservation extended 25 miles south from the Kansas (or Kaw) River through these Indian lands. The Shawnee Mission, whose beginnings date from 1829, was maintained as a manual training school for Shawnee children. SFT travelers and emigrants bound for Oregon often stopped here. Three of the original brick buildings on twelve landscaped acres have been preserved and a historical marker with text is in front of each. On the northeast corner of Mission and 53rd is one of the white oval SFT markers of the American Pioneer Trails Association, nailed to a tree.

To reach the mission from the covered freight wagon (mentioned above) drive south about 6 blocks on Belleview to the intersection of Ward Parkway, which is also US 56 (the SFT highway across Kansas) as well as US 50 and 169. Turn right (west) on Ward, but a few blocks later when it turns south, continue west on US 56. A few blocks after crossing the State Line, watch for the mission sign pointing to the park, which will be about 1 block off 56.

B. "The Wagon Master"

On the southern drive of Ward Parkway just west of its intersection with Wornall Road. This bronze, ten-foot-tall equestrian statue of a SFT wagon master is a dandy and should not be missed. Note the authentic detail of the "Santa Fe style" saddle and the long rifle across the pommel. Cast in Italy, the statue was dedicated in 1973.

The statue is a bit difficult to find because of the confusing nature of the streets in the immediate vicinity. Also, Kansas City residents seem unaware of it, and I found no one who could provide me with directions to it.

Return from Shawnee Mission on US 56, recross the State Line and continue to the intersection of Broadway in the midst of the Country Club Plaza shopping area. Turn south on Broadway and cross Brush Creek, which is here a cement-lined, wide ditch. As Broadway crosses the creek it becomes Wornall Road. (This is not clear on most city maps.)

Note that the streets paralleling Brush Creek on its north and south sides are both called Ward Parkway. Just beyond the bridge, the high-rise Alameda Plaza Hotel stands on the southwest corner. (If you become lost this hotel is the landmark to look for.) Turn right (west) on the southern Ward Parkway. About ½ block beyond, shortly before you reach the intersection of Sunset, is the Wagon Master on the left. It sits on the hotel grounds facing north across Brush Creek toward the

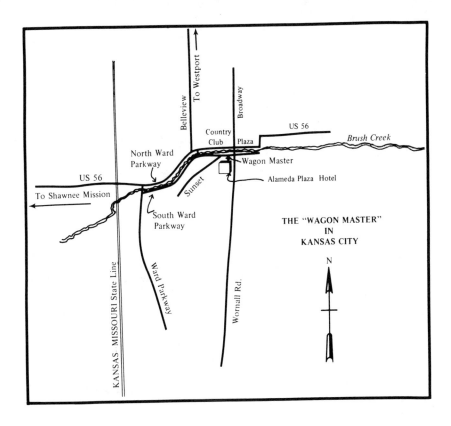

Country Club Plaza.

C. William Bent House

At 1032 West 55th Street, about ½ mile west of Wornall Road. In the yard is a black historical sign with text in gold letters. The two-story white house in front belonged to Seth Ward, who served as post sutler at Fort Laramie on the Oregon Trail. Ward also traveled for a brief period on the SFT, at least part of the time in the employ of famed merchant Ceran St. Vrain. He was a friend of Kit Carson as well. Later he became the patriarch of Westport. Ward Parkway is named for him. (Private residence.)

Note: The only sketch of the life of Seth Ward appears in LeRoy R. Hafen's *The Mountain Men and the Fur Trade of the Far West*, III, pp. 357-84.

To the rear of the beautiful Ward residence is a second house that was owned for a time by William Bent, one of the founders of famed Bent's Fort on the Mountain Branch of the SFT. Bent commuted between this house, which was the center of a farm, and his fort via the SFT. His daughter was married here in 1860. Most of the wording on the historical sign refers to the Civil War Battle of Westport which took place in the immediate area in October 1864.

D. John Wornall House

On the northeast corner of Wornall Road and 61st Terrace. A handsome ante-bellum residence built in 1858 by one of the area's most prominent citizens, it was the center of a 500-acre farm. The SFT passed in front on its way to the great camping ground just beyond. The home was briefly used as a hospital during the Battle of Westport. Restored, the house is opened to the public by the Jackson County Historical Society.

E. Alexander Majors House

At 8201 State Line Road amid the trees on a large lot on the northeast corner of 83rd and State Line Road. As noted in Lexington (above), Majors with his partners Russell and Waddell operated the largest overland freighting firm in the early West. This two-story frame house, built in 1856, was on lands the company used as a "home corral." Just across present State Line were ox barns, mule sheds, blacksmith and wagon shops. Below the house was a caravan camp where the heavy wagons were loaded with goods brought by light wagon from Westport Landing. Majors died in 1900 and is buried in Union Cemetery (Warwick Trafficway and 28th and Terrace). His house has been recently restored and furnished. Behind it are a smokehouse and a large barn (with exhibits), reconstructed on the original foundation. The site is open to the public and administered by the Alexander Majors Historical Trust.

F. Fitzhugh Mill Site

From the Majors House continue south on State Line Road to 103rd Street. There, turn left (east) and go 1 block. Approaching the bridge over Indian Creek, turn right into the parking lot of a shopping center. On the east side of the lot, steps lead down to Indian Creek and a bronze historical marker with text. With the marker is one of the original mill stones.

The Fitzhugh mill, built here in 1832, became a favorite rendezvous for some Oregon Trail emigrants and Santa Fe traders, no doubt because of the abundance of water and pasturage. Anthony B. Watts acquired the mill in 1850. It was dismantled in 1942. In 1985 plans were announced to reconstruct the mill.

From this site, continue south on State Line Road to the intersection of Santa Fe Trail Street and the New Santa Fe DAR marker noted previously.

Fort Dodge.

KANSAS

ENTERING KANSAS

A little over half of the total length of the SFT fell within the present boundaries of Kansas. US 56 (and beginning at Kinsley, Kansas, US 56/ 50) generally follows the original route of the trail. Scattered along it are nearly one hundred DAR markers and other monuments.

Kansas DAR marker number one can be found at Overland Park, a suburb municipality of Kansas City. The marker is located on the northeast corner of 80th Street and Santa Fe Drive (Kansas Highway 58). A granite monument bears a bronze plaque reading "Santa Fe Trail, 1822-1872." The latter year represents the date the SFT was extinguished in eastern Kansas.

Overland Park and the town of Lenexa which adjoins it on the southwest were on the Olathe cut-off that led from the aforementioned great camping ground down to the main trail coming from New Santa Fe.

LENEXA

From the Overland Park DAR marker go southwest on Santa Fe Drive (which is also US 58). At 87th Street, US 58 turns west. Follow it just under 1.5 miles to the intersection with I-35 (which here is also US 56) coming down from Kansas City. After passing to the west side of I-35 on the crossover turn left at the first street going south, which once more is Santa Fe Drive. (Note: For those skipping the Overland Park DAR marker and descending directly from Kansas City via I-35/US 56, take the Lenexa exit to arrive at this same point.)

Go south on Santa Fe Drive about 1 mile to Lenexa. Kansas DAR marker number two will be found on the left in Railroad Park, next to the tracks, just before reaching the junction with Noland Road.

OLATHE

Continue southwest on what has now become Santa Fe Road. Entering the next town, Olathe, the name changes to Old Kansas City Road. The entire route, since leaving Overland Park, has followed the original SFT fairly closely.

Immediately beyond the intersection of Old Kansas City Road and Ridgeway, on the right, can be seen one of the white oval SFT markers of the American Pioneer Trails Association. This is actually one of several replicas recently placed along the SFT in Olathe by Michael Duncan, director of the Mahaffie House.

At 1 block past the Ridgeway intersection on the right (1100 Kansas City Road) is the Mahaffie House and Farmstead, a registered National Historic Site. The fine two-story residence was built in 1865 as a farmhouse, but it soon came to serve as the first noon stage stop beyond Westport. Caravans also rested here overnight. It is the only remaining stage station on the SFT that is open to the public. The place is being restored as a living farm and additional interpretive exhibits are planned, including several relating to the trail.

Continue southwest on Old Kansas City Road about 1 mile to the intersection with Santa Fe Avenue. Turn right (west) four blocks to the Johnson County Courthouse on the left. On the southeast corner of

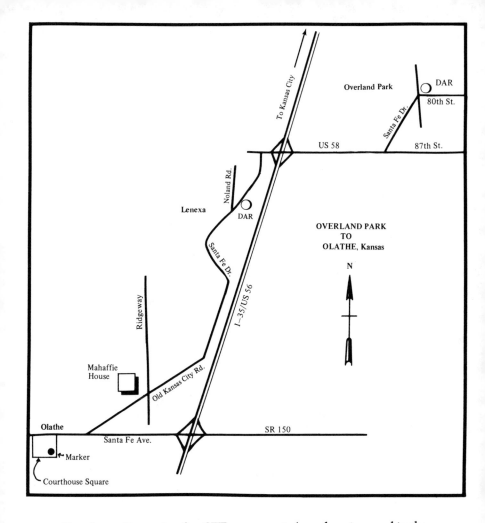

Courthouse Square is a fine SFT monument. An oxbow is carved in the stone at the top. Below is a bronze plaque with an ox-drawn covered wagon in relief, like the one noted earlier in Penn Valley Park.

In the Kansas Room of the Olathe Public Library, a good collection of SFT materials and maps is available for researchers and trail hounds. The reference librarian is very helpful. Its location is one block east of the courthouse, at Park and Chestnut Streets.

SOUTH OF OLATHE

Two markers of interest can be visited on back roads below Olathe. Proceed to the interchange at the junction of I-35 and US 169 south of town. There pick up 151st Street (also called on some maps Morse

Olathe Road) and drive east 7 miles to the Blue Valley Baptist Church on the right (just west of the intersection with Antioch Road). A new Santa Fe and Oregon trails marker, with text, was placed here in 1984, in an open area west of the church. The SFT, coming from New Santa Fe and heading for the Lone Elm Campground, crossed present 151st at this location.

Return to the above interchange and go south on US 169. At the intersection of 167th (at this writing, a gravel road) turn right (west) 1 mile to Lone Elm Road. On the southeast corner of 167th and Lone Elm is the DAR marker for the oft-mentioned Lone Elm Campground. First known alternately as "Round Grove" and "Elm Grove," this site came to be called "Lone Elm" by 1844 when all the surrounding timber had been cut by travelers for firewood and only a single tree remained. By the end of the decade the Lone Elm itself had fallen to the ax. The campground took in 40 acres or more behind the marker. For a description and map of the site consult Franzwa's OTR, pp. 131-33; and his MOT, p. 41. Many caravans from Westport made this place their first stop on the trail.

Pick up US 56, the SFT route, on the south side of Olathe. If a side trip to Fort Leavenworth has not been made before now, this will be the last opportunity. Driving west on US 56 continue to the junction with SR 7 and turn north about 33 miles to the fort.

FORT LEAVENWORTH

From anywhere in the Kansas City area a convenient side trip can be made up the Missouri River to Fort Leavenworth. Established in 1827 by Colonel Henry Leavenworth, the fort saw branches of the Santa Fe and Oregon Trails cross its grounds. An arm of the SFT extended southwestward from here to a link-up with the main trail west of New Santa Fe. General Stephen Watts Kearny's Army of the West as well as the celebrated Mormon Battalion used this route when they marched over the SFT in 1846 to conquer New Mexico.

Border disturbances associated with the outbreak of the Civil War disrupted the Westport market and many Santa Fe traders began to use the protected "Government Lane" from Fort Leavenworth south to the main trail. In the 1850s and 1860s emigrants heading for New Mexico or California increasingly debarked at the fort from Missouri River steamboats and organized caravans for a crossing of the SFT. There are two clusters of SFT-related sites, one in the town of Leavenworth and another on the grounds of the fort immediately to the north.

The Town

Entering the south side of Leavenworth watch for the junction of SR7/US 73 with SR 5 which enters from the right (east) along the south side of the large VA hospital grounds. Turn right at this intersection onto SR 5 (which is also Muncie Road) and go two blocks to the entrance of the Leavenworth National Cemetery on the left. (Note: This cemetery is distinct from the Fort Leavenworth National Cemetery, on the fort grounds and described below.)

Here is buried William Sloan who, as a boy, accompanied his mother Eliza and sister Marian on several SFT crossings in the 1850s. True trail buffs, addicted to Marian Sloan Russell's memoirs, published under the title *Land of Enchantment*, will want to visit the grave of her brother who figured prominently in the narrative. He served as a corporal in the Civil War, which entitled him to be buried here, and he died at the neighboring VA hospital in 1917. Will's marker is in Section 30, Row 14, Grave 7, near the flagpole. (Directions to his sister Marian's grave west of Raton Pass near Stonewall, Colorado, will be given later in this Guide.)

Back at the cemetery entrance turn left (east) on SR 5 which quickly curves to the right. Beyond the curve on the left (east) is the gate to Mt. Muncie Cemetery. (It is .4 mile between the gates of the two cemeteries.) Enter and take the first lane to the right. The Fred Harvey family stone is on the left about 50 yards up this lane. It is the largest one in the immediate vicinity. The Harvey name is on the back of the stone and thus not visible from the road.

Beginning in the 1870s, Frederick Henry Harvey (1835-1901) began developing a chain of famous restaurants and hotels along the Santa Fe Railroad, the successor of the SFT. His splendid company encouraged tourists to travel the "new Santa Fe Trail" by rail. Harvey's name remains legendary in the Southwest and much has been written about his career.

Return to SR 7/US 73, turn right, and continue north into Leavenworth. Approaching the center of downtown, turn left (west) on Olive Street and go 4 blocks to the Fred Harvey House on the northeast corner of Olive and 7th. The beautiful two-story mansion, once the residence of Harvey, now houses the offices of the local Board of Education. The exterior of the structure is well preserved, except for an awful modern door at the entrance. A metal historical sign on the front lawn has a text concerning Harvey.

Again, return to SR 7/US 73 (that is, 4th Street) and turn left (north) toward downtown. On the northwest corner of 4th and

Delaware Streets is a two-story brick building now occupied by the Guarantee Land Title Company. Originally the freighting firm of Russell, Majors and Waddell, whose role has been mentioned above under Lexington, maintained general offices here in the late 1850s and 1860s. Two plaques are attached to the side of the building facing 4th Street. One commemorates the freight company; the other, its famous Pony Express line.

The first street north of Delaware is Shawnee. On it, between 5th and 6th Streets, is the Chamber of Commerce which offers fine maps and brochures on local points of historical interest.

Continue north on 4th (SR 7/US 73) until that street ends at a T at Metropolitan Avenue. Turn left (west) and proceed to the entrance of Fort Leavenworth on the right.

The Fort

A. Main Entrance
Entering the fort, visitors are on Grant Avenue. On the right is the post information building. Stop and obtain maps and a self-guiding tour booklet of the fort. Here too, behind the building, is the official Kansas Historical Marker for Fort Leavenworth with reference to the SFT.

B. Post Museum
Go north on Grant past the lakes to Reynolds Avenue and turn right 1 block to the museum. Here are displayed objects of pioneer and army life, "emphasizing the drama of Westward expansion." One of the largest collections of pioneer vehicles in the world can be seen, including a freight wagon and army vehicles of the type that traveled the SFT.

C. Old Stone Wall
Continue north on Grant to the intersection of Kearny Avenue. Here in a traffic circle is a statue of President U. S. Grant. Behind it and across the street is a section of the Old Stone Wall. Two plaques are mounted on it, one placed by the DAR.

D. The Rookery
One block northwest of Grant's statue at 12 Sumner. Constructed in 1832, this is the oldest building in Kansas. It was in use as the post headquarters during the heyday of the SFT.

E. Mormon Battalion Marker
At the northeast corner of Kearny and Sumner Place, to the left rear of Grant's statue. It is the first of five such markers placed in Kansas and Oklahoma by the LDS Church to commemorate the march of the

Mormon Battalion over the SFT in 1846.

F. National Cemetery

Go west on Pope from Grant Avenue to Biddle Boulevard and the cemetery entrance. Bodies of civilians and soldiers killed on the SFT were brought here for burial. A tall column over General Leavenworth's grave is near the flagpole. Another interesting monument is that for Colonel Edward Hatch, once commander of the Department of New Mexico who pursued Apaches led by Chief Victorio. Graves of Tom Custer (brother of General Custer) and other soldiers killed at the Little Big Horn are also here. Ask at the cemetery visitors' center for the location of individual graves.

G. Santa Fe Trail Ruts and Monuments

Beginning at Grant's statue follow Riverside Avenue's loop down to the Missouri River. A deep cut running from what was once a boat landing on the river to the top of the hill represents the track left by ox-drawn covered wagons. In the 1830s the river swept along the base of the hill and the landing was where one now sees a warehouse. Stone columns with brass plaques designating the Oregon and Santa Fe Trails are located at the top and bottom of the cut.

Upon completing a tour of the Leavenworth area return to Olathe via US 73 and SR 7 and pick up US 56 leading to Gardner.

GARDNER

On US 56 at 1 mile west of the junction with SR 7 is the Olathe city limits. Here on the right are two houses, the first a two-story red brick and the second a long white bungalow. Just past the bungalow on the right side of the highway is an open field leading down to a creek. This is the site of a major SFT campground, and before that an Indian campground. The trail wound along the foot of the slope that rises to the present highway. Across the creek and the bridge, trail ruts briefly parallel US 56, just inside a farm fence.

About 2 miles west of the junction of US 56 and SR 7, US 56 curves to the left. Here, 151st Street, really just a section line road, continues straight ahead. In the small triangle formed where the two roads split is a DAR marker.

A. SFT Monument

At the main intersection in the center of Gardner turn right (north) off US 56 onto Elm, which has no street sign. Drive 1 block to the monument in the schoolyard located on the northeast corner of

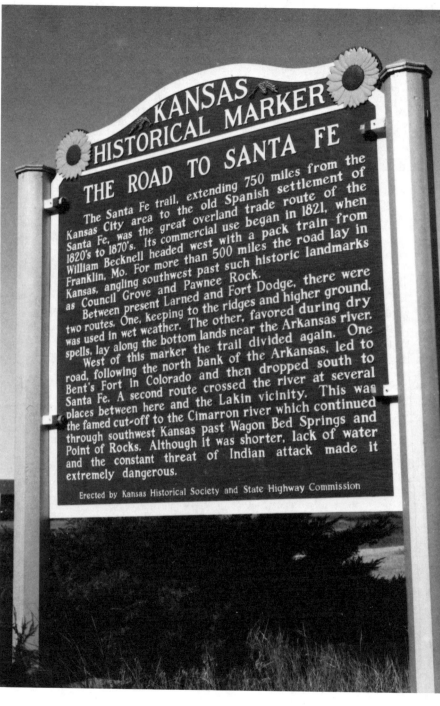

KANSAS HISTORICAL MARKER

THE ROAD TO SANTA FE

The Santa Fe trail, extending 750 miles from the Kansas City area to the old Spanish settlement of Santa Fe, was the great overland trade route of the 1820's to 1870's. Its commercial use began in 1821, when William Becknell headed west with a pack train from Franklin, Mo. For more than 500 miles the road lay in Kansas, angling southwest past such historic landmarks as Council Grove and Pawnee Rock.

Between present Larned and Fort Dodge, there were two routes. One, keeping to the ridges and higher ground, was used in wet weather. The other, favored during dry spells, lay along the bottom lands near the Arkansas river.

West of this marker the trail divided again. One road, following the north bank of the Arkansas, led to Bent's Fort in Colorado and then dropped south to Santa Fe. A second route crossed the river at several places between here and the Lakin vicinity. This was the famed cut-off to the Cimarron river which continued through southwest Kansas past Wagon Bed Springs and Point of Rocks. Although it was shorter, lack of water and the constant threat of Indian attack made it extremely dangerous.

Erected by Kansas Historical Society and State Highway Commission

One of the fine Kansas Historical Markers, east of Dodge City.

Elm and Shawnee. This handsome SFT marker with a bronze plaque is like the one in Olathe. Continue another block north on Elm to a fine Oregon Trail DAR marker on the right in the schoolyard.

B. Junction of the Santa Fe and Oregon Trails

Two miles west of Gardner on US 56 at a small roadside park on the right (north) side of the highway. Near this point the two historic trails parted, the SFT going left and the Oregon Trail branching off to the right. An official Kansas Historical Marker in the park briefly tells the story. (See Franzwa, OTR, pp. 133-37.)

LANESFIELD DAR MARKER

The setting of this DAR marker is especially nice and hence worth seeking out. Approaching the eastern limits of Edgerton on US 56 and before crossing a small bridge turn right (north) on a gravel section line road which has a sign reading "To Sunflower." Go .9 miles to the first intersection and turn right (east) on 191st Street, really a gravel section line road. At .6 mile turn left (north) on Dillie Road and drive .5 mile to the grounds of the old Lanesfield School on the right. The school building is now a museum. The DAR marker is in the southwest corner of the grounds next to the road.

Behind and to the left of the DAR marker is a large oak tree. Nailed to it is a red, white and blue sign designating the SFT as part of the National Old Trails Road. It was placed long ago by the Auto Club of Southern California. The Club must have placed other such markers along the trail, but if so this is the only one remaining.

The SFT passed diagonally north of the Lanesfield School grounds from northeast to southwest, going from the trail junction near Gardner to the Narrows at present Baldwin City.

BALDWIN CITY

Just east of Baldwin City begins the Narrows, a ridge or divide separating the waters of Wakarusa Creek on the north from those of the Marias de Cygnes (pronounced locally Mara du Seen) on the south. The SFT caravans kept to this ridge because it was the easiest way to travel, at least in dry weather. When it rained wagons sunk to their axles in the deep mud. The Narrows, merely a broad hump of high ground, is scarcely noticeable today as a geographical feature.

A. Douglas County Prairie Park

On the south side of US 56 about 3 miles east of Baldwin City. This small roadside park was near the beginning of the Narrows. A half-circle drive enters from the highway at the east end of the park and exits at the west end. Near the entrance on the left is a Pioneer Meeting House of native logs. A replica, it was placed and dedicated in 1971.

At the exit are three markers. One, an official Kansas Historical Marker, describes the Battle of Black Jack, ¼ mile south of the park. This small battle on June 2, 1856, was the first open conflict between free and slave forces, an early prelude to the Civil War.

The second, a DAR marker for the SFT, sits just west of the exit. Amelia Betts and Katharine Kelley, a pair of dedicated women in nearby Baldwin City, painted the worn, incised inscription on this marker (and the other six DAR markers in Douglas County) so that it is easily readable by visitors. The third is a handsome new metal marker, "Black Jack Park," with reference to the SFT.

B. Trail Depressions

Enter the gravel road that leads south from the highway along the west boundary of the roadside park. Behind the row of trees along the back of the park is a 40-acre field containing fine traces of the SFT, seen as wide swales and ridges in the sod. They are directly behind the large wooden sign reading "Depressions Made by Traffic, Santa Fe Trail," which faces the gravel road.

The ease of viewing the depressions will depend upon the time of year. In April the dead grass is burned off and they are clearly visible in the blackened field. Later in the summer when vegetation is thickest they are difficult to see. But on the ridge to the right-rear of the sign they show as indentations against the sky. During June wild strawberries can sometimes be found growing in the depressions. Wagon travelers mentioned their pleasure in collecting the fruit in this area.

At the back of the field a small access road veers off to the left and leads to an overlook and to the vicinity of two stone monuments of the Sibley SFT survey of 1825. The eastern-most stone has an inscription. Continue on the gravel road past the field about ⅛ mile to find the entrance to the Battle of Black Jack Park, site of the conflict mentioned above, on the right.

C. Official Kansas Historical Marker, "Baldwin"

On US 56 at a turnout on the north (right) side of the highway about 2 miles west of the roadside park as one approaches the limits of Baldwin City. It contains reference to the SFT and local history.

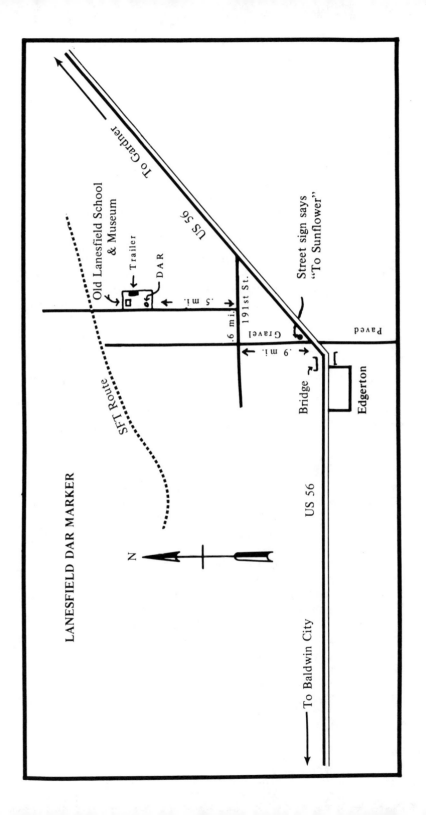

LANESFIELD DAR MARKER

D. Old Castle

On 5th Street, 5 blocks south of US 56. Built in 1858 during trail days, this three-story native stone structure was the first building of the first college in Kansas Territory. Now a museum, it is open afternoons. A green and white SFT Historic Point sign is on the front lawn.

E. Palmyra Town Site

On the northern edge of modern Baldwin City. Palmyra, founded in 1854 near the beginning of the Narrows, was known as a "repair stop" during the latter days of the SFT. Here blacksmiths and wagon makers maintained shops for the benefit of travelers. After entering Baldwin City on US 56, turn north (right) on Eisenhower Street (a sign here points to the high school) and go 1 block to the first intersection. A "Palmyra" sign on the northeast corner indicates the center of the old town. The SFT passed through the grounds of the high school on the left.

At this intersection turn right (east) and go 1 block. Then turn left (north). In the middle of the block on the right is a modern blue house. That was the site of Palmyra's Santa Fe Hotel, which burned a few years ago. Continue past it to the sign on the right that marks the Santa Fe Well. It was a watering place for the Santa Fe caravans. The restored well now has a pitched roof over it.

Continue past the well to the first little lane that turns to the left (really a driveway) and follow it back to Eisenhower and the school grounds. There turn north (right) and go up Eisenhower. About ½ block beyond the point where the pavement changes to gravel is a marker on the east (right) side of the road. It is a wooden sign locating the site of the original Palmyra Blacksmith Shop. Climb the grassy ridge behind the sign and look back toward the southeast (in the direction of the roadside park and ruts visited earlier) and the eye will follow the route of the Narrows.

Go back to the high school, about a block, and note the markers on the grounds between Eisenhower and the teachers' parking lot. One is a DAR marker, recently moved here from the blacksmith shop site. The second is a new Palmyra historical sign installed through the efforts of Amelia Betts and Katharine Kelley. The sign refers to the SFT.

From here at Palmyra the SFT headed off in a northwesterly direction to the present Trail Park. To get there, return down Eisenhower to US 56 and turn west (right). Go west on 56 a short distance to the intersection of 6th Street (which is also marked State Road 1055). Turn north on 6th and go ¾ mile to Trail Park.

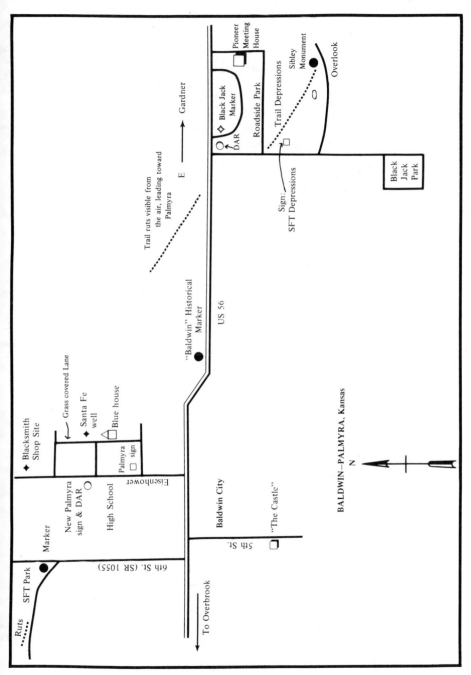

BALDWIN–PALMYRA, Kansas

F. Trail Park and DAR Monument

A small park on the west (left) side of SR 1055. Originally the DAR monument here had a fine bronze plaque like the ones in Olathe and Gardner, but it was stolen in 1968. A marble replica of the plaque was placed on the monument in 1969 by the local Santa Fe Trail Historical Society. Recently two new SFT historical signs have been added to the park. The gravel road that here intersects with SR 1055 and runs along the southwest side of the park is the actual route of the SFT. In dry weather follow this road west about 1 mile to the point where it curves to the left. On the right, just before the curve, is a farm. In the open areas around it are traces of SFT ruts. Return to US 56.

BALDWIN CITY TO OVERBROOK

A. Brooklyn

At 3 miles west of Baldwin City (from the junction of 6th Street and US 56) turn right (north) on a gravel road. (A white farmhouse is on the northwest corner.) Go 2.5 miles to two markers on the right designating the site of Brooklyn, "early trading center on the SFT." Return to US 56.

B. "Sibley Hill"

North (right) side of US 56 about 12 miles west of Baldwin City. Drive west from Baldwin City on US 56 about 11 miles to the Globe crossroads (the old Globe Rock Store is on the southwest corner of the intersection). SR 1029 crosses US 56 here. A DAR marker is 1 mile north on the west side of SR 1029. Just past Globe on US 56 a rounded hill with a tall red and white relay tower can be easily seen. It lies a short distance to the right of the highway. The Sibley survey line of 1825 ran over the summit, but the SFT itself swung around the south flank, that is, between the hill and present US 56. (See Stocking, *Road to Santa Fe*, p. 74.)

C. Flag Spring DAR Marker

About 3½ miles west of Globe, or a mile east of the county line on the south (left) side of US 56. A two-story white farmhouse with white barn can be seen across the highway and a bit to the west of this marker and can help locate it. Here the SFT crossed the present highway from north to south heading toward modern Overbrook. The actual Flag Spring, a noted landmark in early trail days, was about a mile to the north, its precise location uncertain.

A DAR marker near Baldwin City, Kansas.

OVERBROOK

Approaching Overbrook on US 56 look to the south (left) and the town cemetery, through which the SFT passed, can be seen in the distance. To get to it take the first street to the left, which is Cedar. Go south on Cedar several blocks and just before it turns east note a white house on the left. After the turn an open field is on the left behind that house. In the center of the field is a spring marked by a stack of railroad ties and a small tree. This was a watering place of the SFT.

A short distance beyond, the lane enters the cemetery gate. Drive straight ahead. The graves on the immediate left lie in the faint ruts of the SFT which here is headed toward the spring just passed. At the back of the cemetery where the gravel road turns left is a 1½ foot gray wooden post in the ground. It marks the center of the trail ruts.

From the cemetery return to US 56 and continue several blocks west to the intersection of Overbrook's one main commercial street. Turn left (south) to the DAR marker in front of the town post office.

Continue west on US 56 and about 1 mile from Overbrook watch to the right for a tall tower on legs. Just beyond it cross a highway bridge. From the bridge and from the road just past it look to the right (north) of the highway. "Santa Fe Trail Spring" can be seen in a large depression, its location marked by a windmill and cattle tank. Immediately to the west of the windmill is a red barn with a white roof. This is reported to have been a major watering stop for trail travelers, although no details about its history are available. There is no historical marker here.

SANTA FE TRAIL HIGH SCHOOL

The school is located 6 to 7 miles west of Overbrook on the south side of US 56. Approaching the entrance there used to be a sign on the right side of the highway reading: "Santa Fe Trail Crossed Here," but recently it disappeared.

The school name is on a large sign attached to a native rock monument at the main entrance. Above it is a metal covered wagon. In front of the monument and sign is a separate granite marker placed by the Sons of the American Revolution. As far as I know, it is the only SFT marker originating with the Sons, in contrast to the numerous ones placed by the Daughters. The school grounds lie atop the ruts of the trail.

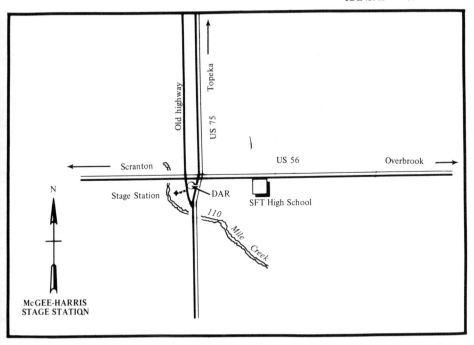

McGEE-HARRIS
STAGE STATION

Continue west from the high school on US 56 to an intersection
with a sign pointing left (south) to the Osage County Lake. (A cement
silo is on the southeast corner.) Drive south .2 mile to SFT ruts seen in
the unplowed field on the left (east). They show as indentations on the
skyline. Here the trail, coming from the school grounds, is heading
toward the crossing at 110 Mile Creek.

McGEE-HARRIS STAGE STATION AT 110 MILE CREEK

In the early 1820s the stream here was known as Oak Creek.
When Sibley made his trail survey in 1825 it was determined that the
crossing was 110 miles from Fort Osage and Sibley's Landing on the
Missouri River (the start of the survey). Soon the stream was being
called 110 Mile Creek, retaining that name to the present day.

About 1854 Fry McGee, who had been over the Oregon Trail and
back, settled with his family on the east bank at the SFT crossing. He
farmed, built a toll bridge and provided overnight accommodations for
wagon travelers and stage passengers. The toll was 25 cents per wagon.
In the late 1850s the coach for Santa Fe stopped twice a month.

A Mr. Harris married McGee's eldest daughter, who had the unlikely name of America Puss. He built a residence and store adjacent to his in-laws and after McGee's death in 1861 operated the stage station until the SFT closed here in 1866. (See Stocking, *Road to Santa Fe*, pp. 75-77.) A major building of stone and frame remains, apparently a residence and station. Ruins of other structures nearby may include the blacksmith shop that was part of the original complex. Traces of the trail are visible at the creek crossing about 100 yards west.

To reach the stage station go a short distance beyond SFT High School where US 56 crosses US 75. Continue ½ mile south on US 75 to a DAR marker on the west (right) side of the highway. It is surrounded by a steel pipe fence. Behind it an old paved highway comes in from the north and joins US 75. Behind the marker and across this old highway is a dim dirt road that leads .2 mile toward the stage station and 110 Mile Creek. The site is on private land. Do not attempt the road in bad weather.

A glimpse of the darkly weathered, slope-roofed stage station can be had from the highway. Drive south on US 75 from the DAR marker about 1 mile to the highway bridge over 110 Mile Creek. Turn around and return to the marker. About midway back look to the left and a sharp eye can catch sight of the upper part of the stage station rising from the thick foliage.

SIDE TRIP TO TOPEKA

At this intersection of US 56 and US 75 a side trip can be made to the State Capitol of Topeka 15 miles north on US 75. The Kansas State Historical Society has its headquarters downtown at 120 West Tenth Street. Here SFT buffs will find excellent research materials in the archives as well as rare books and early newspapers. In 1984 the excellent historical exhibits (including the SFT) that were on display in this location were moved to new quarters at the Pottawatomie Baptist Mission in west Topeka adjacent to I-70, at 6425 South West Sixth. Featured is the oldest surviving AT&SF steam engine, used in the 1880s over Raton Pass. Return to junction of US 75 and 56.

BURLINGAME

At 2½ miles beyond the McGee-Harris Stage Station, US 56 leads to the town of Scranton. The SFT passed through its southern limits.

Formerly there was a sign on the outskirts that greeted visitors with the words: "Welcome to Scranton on the Santa Fe Trail," but it disappeared about 1980. In the center of town, turn left at the first street past the post office and go one block to Jones Park on the right, which has a DAR marker moved here in the 1970s.

At 5 miles beyond Scranton, US 56 reaches the edge of Burlingame. Just after the highway passes under a railroad trestle, cross a bridge over Switzler Creek. Here was a major trail crossing. The creek was named for John Switzler who built a log toll bridge at this point in 1847.

After crossing the highway bridge, Santa Fe Avenue leads 2 blocks to the center of town. Burlingame claims to be the only town in Kansas whose main street was once a part of the SFT. Notice the businesses along it named for the trail. The community was founded in 1857 as Council City and later renamed for Anson Burlingame, a famous minister to China and an anti-slavery advocate. It is said blacksmiths here shod thousands of oxen and mules destined for New Mexico. Tracks of the AT&SF arrived in 1869. Burlingame titles itself the place where "Trail Meets Rail."

In the center of Burlingame US 56 reaches a main intersection and turns to the left (south). Instead of turning, continue straight ahead 1 block on Santa Fe Avenue (which is also SR 31) to a schoolyard on the left. In the northeast corner of the yard is a special DAR marker honoring Fannie Geiger Thompson, the woman who initiated the marking of the SFT in 1906.

Note: This is the DAR marker which Margaret Long (SFT, p. 62) locates on the west side of the Switzler Creek bridge. Since she wrote in 1954 it has been moved to its new site in the schoolyard.

From Fannie Thompson's marker continue west on SR 31 about 3 miles to the bridge over Dragoon Creek. According to Stocking (Road to Santa Fe, p. 79), the creek was named by a Lieutenant Fields who brought a company of dragoons (that is, mounted infantry) over the SFT in 1852. Cross the bridge and go 1.5 miles to a DAR marker next to a wire fence on the north (right) side of the road. It commemorates the nearby Dragoon Creek Crossing. The trail here was actually another branch road leading down from Fort Leavenworth to join the main SFT not far to the south.

From the DAR marker look across the road to the southeast and in a field about 100 yards from the pavement see the ruins of the Havanna Stage Station. The small community of Havanna was founded by German and French settlers in 1858, according to information supplied me by Amelia Betts of Baldwin City. In addition to the stage station, there was a store and hotel, both of which have disappeared.

To reach the site return east .2 mile to a primitive road that leads to an old cattle loading chute next to the highway. Park here. Next to the chute is a fence and beyond that a field. Toward the back of the field are the fine limestone walls of the station which reach up to roof level. In summer months much of the building is obscured by brush and trees. Behind it is a more recent weathered gray barn and to the left rear is a red barn with a tin roof. Both are easily seen from the road and will serve as landmarks helping to find the station.

Return to the DAR marker and continue west on SR 31 another .2 mile to a wide highway maintenance pull-out that extends along the north (right) side of the road. Recently there have been piles of gravel and dirt and a black portable water tank on legs in this long pull-out, but these features can change. At the back of the pull-out (and past the water tank if it is still there), in the field just across the wire fence, is the grave of Private Samuel Hunt of Kentucky who died on the SFT in 1835. It is surrounded by a pipe railing. The information on the modern gravestone was supplied by the War Department when a new marker was installed a century after Hunt's death.

Return to Burlingame and rejoin US 56 going to Council Grove.

Note: For the 40 miles from Burlingame to Council Grove a Boy Scout hiking trail has been established along the original SFT, which lies north of US 56. The starting point and a base campground are located on the east side of Burlingame at the crossing of the trail and the Santa Fe Railroad. For information and a map write: Chamber of Commerce, Burlingame, Kansas 66413.

TO COUNCIL GROVE

At 10 miles west of the Town of Allen, US 56 crosses the Morris County line. At 1 mile beyond the line is a crossroads and sign that points south to Dunlap. Turn right (north) on the section line road and go .2 mile to a DAR marker on the right. It is at the end of a line of evergreen trees, in the front yard of a house and next to a propane tank. The marker sits in the ruts of the SFT, which here cross the section line road. Return to US 56 and continue to Council Grove.

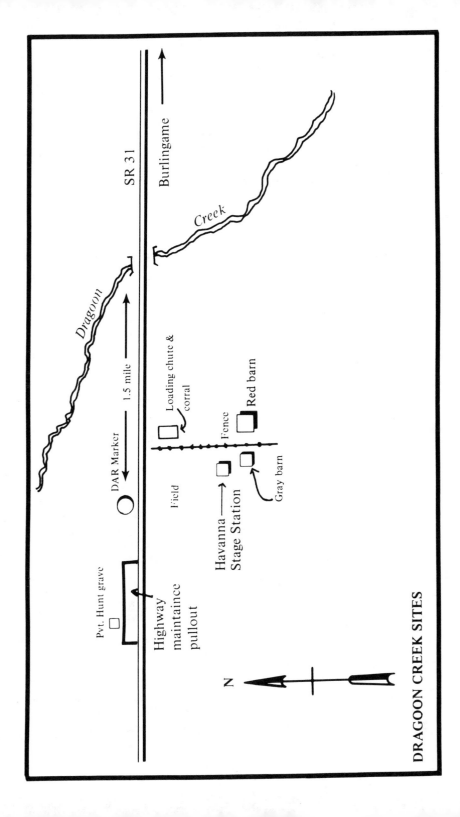

DRAGOON CREEK SITES

COUNCIL GROVE

Approaching Council Grove, travelers enter the region of the Flint Hills and the prairie grasslands. Here is one of the largest remaining tracts of tallgrass prairie (mainly bluestem) in the Midwest. In trail days leaves of the bluestem grew three feet tall and the seed stems reached six feet. Susan Magoffin in 1846 likened the grass to "a waving sea of green."

Council Grove on the Neosho River is one of the most historic places on the SFT. It was a natural way-stop on the route to New Mexico, well-watered with plenty of pasture and timber. Past this point no hardwoods grew on the plains so spare axles were cut along the Neosho and stored under the wagons for later use. Here too caravans organized their military defenses for they were now on the edge of hostile Indian country. Modern visitors should read Josiah Gregg's description of Council Grove in the heyday of the Santa Fe trade.

The site was named by Commissioner George Sibley in 1825 when he made a treaty with the Osage Indians guaranteeing safe passage for wagon trains and providing a right-of-way to Santa Fe. During the Mexican War the army built a wagon repair depot and a few years later, when stagecoach service began on the SFT, the firm of Waldo, Hall & Company operated a station, shops and corrals. Traffic on the SFT ended about 1866 with the building of the Kansas Pacific Railroad 50 miles to the north.

A. Official Kansas Historical Marker, "Council Grove"

On the old highway at the east edge of town. The sign gives a capsule history of the town, including extensive reference to the SFT. A DAR marker is next to it. Both are often overlooked since they are easily missed by first-time visitors. Approaching Council Grove from the east turn right on the paved road that runs along the west side of the Ritz Drive-in Theater. Go .2 mile and take the first left at an intersecting paved road. At another .3 mile, just past the Hill Top Cafe, on the right, is a roadside turn-out and the two markers. This site is probably "the bluff" mentioned by some wagon travelers from which one can see over the Neosho Valley. From here continue ahead about .5 mile and the road rejoins US 56. Turn right (west) on US 56 toward the center of Council Grove. US 56 becomes Main Street.

B. Council Oak Stump

On the right just beyond the junction of Main and 3rd Streets. A jagged stump is all that remains of the famous council oak that blew down in 1958. The tree was purported to be the one under which Sibley signed his treaty with the Osage. The "stump shrine" is now covered by a roof and surrounded by an iron fence. An interpretive historical sign, a special DAR marker, and the Registered National Historic Landmark plaque for Council Grove are also at the site.

C. Post Office Oak

On Main Street 1½ blocks past the Council Oak Stump on the right (north). SFT travelers are said to have left letters in a crevice at the bottom of the tree which were picked up and carried back to the States by returning caravans. Marked by a sign.

D. Madonna of the Trail

In Madonna Park on the right of US 56/Main Street just beyond Post Office Oak and facing the Neosho Bridge. This statue of the Pioneer Mother, placed by the DAR in 1928, is a duplicate of the one already noted in Lexington, Missouri. The park is on part of the old SFT campground at the Neosho Crossing.

E. Neosho Bridge

Over the river on US 56/Main Street, at the original trail crossing. Stands of giant hardwoods, used by early travelers for spare axles and wagon tongues, can still be found on the river both north and south of town. A nice SFT plaque was blown to bits in 1984 when the old bridge was replaced by a new one.

F. Hays House Restaurant

One-half block west of the Neosho Bridge at 112 Main Street. Seth Hays, a great grandson of Daniel Boone and a cousin of Kit Carson, in 1847 became the first white settler at Council Grove. He established a trading post for the neighboring Kaw Indians, then in 1857 built this tavern and hostelry to serve wayfarers on the SFT. A popular story has it that he hired a bagpiper to play from the outside balcony of his place to draw customers.

The building has been remodeled but some of the interior fabric is original, including stone walls and a large walnut beam that can be seen in the basement and a hand-hewn beam mantlepiece in the dining area. On the wall near the outside entrance is one of the oval SFT signs of the American Pioneer Trails Association. An ox yoke is also here. The Hays House is a fine restaurant, open seven days a week, and a boon to modern travelers on the trail. It claims to be the oldest eating establishment west of the Mississippi.

Just past the Hays House, on the southwest corner of Main and Neosho Streets, is the Farmers and Drovers Bank which occupies the site of Waldo, Hall & Co.'s log depot and warehouse for its mail wagons to Santa Fe.

Note: Across the street from the Hays House is the Chamber of Commerce which has a variety of historical maps and brochures of the area.

There are two other points of interest associated with the Hays House. One is Seth Hays' residence, located 2 blocks south of Main on Wood Street, just across the railroad tracks on the right. This neat brick house, built about 1866, is now the museum of the Morris County Historical Society, open by appointment only. There is a bronze plaque on the corner of the building.

The second point of interest is Seth Hays' grave in Greenwood Cemetery (established 1862). The cemetery is on US 56/Main, 5½ blocks past the Last Chance Store (described below). After entering the main gate go straight up the lane to a small house. Seth Hays (1811-73) is buried under a tall white column to the right. Next to it is the broken tombstone of Sarah Taylor (Aunt Sally), ex-slave of Hays. After her liberation she remained with his family.

G. Becknell Monument

On the southwest corner of Main and Mission Streets on the library lawn. This monument and plaque commemorate the 100th anniversary (in 1921) of William Becknell's first packtrain to Santa Fe. The monument is not mentioned in local historical guides. Behind it, a large cornerstone set in the library building has an inscription on the SFT Indian treaty of 1825.

H. Old Kaw Mission

Go west on Main, 1½ blocks from the Hays House to Mission. Turn right on Mission and drive 5 blocks to Huffaker Street. The Kaw Mission is on the right. This beautiful two-story native stone structure was built in the winter of 1850-51. It first served as a school for children of the Kaw (or Kansas) Indians upon whose reservation Council Grove was founded. After 1854 it became the school for local white children. As the most imposing building in Council Grove, the Mission often accommodated prominent travelers in the later days of the SFT. Now a state museum, it has some trail relics on display.

On the grounds is a stone house built by the government for Kaw families. It was moved from its original site 3½ miles southeast of Council Grove on Big John Creek. Other houses and a commissary building for the Kaw are still there. Directions can be obtained at the Chamber of Commerce. It is said that the Kaw stabled their horses in the stone houses, preferring to live in their native lodges. Also on the mission grounds is one of the new Mormon Battalion markers.

I. Old Bell

One and a half blocks north on Belfrey from US 56/Main Street. Installed here in 1863, the bell warned of floods, fires and Indian raids and also summoned children to school.

J. Hermit's Cave

Two blocks north of Main on Belfry, just past the Old Bell. In this small cave lived for a brief period in the early 1860s a religious mystic, Giovanni Maria Augustini, who was closely associated with the SFT. Born in Italy in 1801, the son of a nobleman, he lived in caves in South America and Canada before landing in Council Grove. In 1863 the hermit approached the wagon train of wealthy merchant Don Eugenio Romero of Las Vegas and asked to be allowed to accompany it to New Mexico. He walked beside the caravan the entire 550 miles over the SFT. (His fate in New Mexico will be described under the entry for Las Vegas below.)

Note: Much of the information found in tourist brochures about the hermit is in error.

K. Last Chance Store

Northwest corner of Main and Chautauqua Streets. A small stone building erected in 1857, the store later served as a post office and government trading post. Closed now, it took its name because for a time it was said to be the last place where supplies could be obtained between Council Grove and Santa Fe. An interpretive historical sign is on the grounds.

L. Custer Elm

Five blocks south on Neosho Street from Main at the bridge over Elm Creek. Under this hundred-foot tree, said to be one of the largest elms in the United States, George Armstrong Custer camped in 1867 while pursuing hostile Indians. At several points in Kansas, Custer's personal history crossed that of the SFT. Only the trunk of the elm remains.

M. Father Padilla Monument

Go south on Neosho Street from the Custer Elm. That street is also SR 57/177. After 3 blocks the highway starts up a hill. Half-way to the top of that hill turn right on a small gravel road and go .7 mile. At the third turn in the road is a gate on the right and beyond the fence is the tall pyramid monument on a hill. A member of the Coronado expedition of 1540-42, Father Juan de Padilla remained in Kansas to minister to the Indians. He was soon martyred. This is the first of at least five monuments and markers scattered along the SFT that commemorate his passing. The exact site of his death and burial is not known, although this monument claims to be it.

Return to US 56 and go west. On the western limits of Council Grove (as on the eastern), the town has placed handsome signs claiming to be the "Birth Place of the Santa Fe Trail." At about 3½ miles from the city limits is an intersection with a gravel county road. Pump jacks are near the southeast and northwest corners and a windmill is near the northeast corner. Turn left (south) off US 56 and go ½ mile to a sign, "SFT Crossed Here." Ruts on both sides of the road are represented by a wide trough. Return to US 56.

DIAMOND SPRING

This famous spring, a day's wagon journey west of Council Grove, was mentioned in the accounts of many trail travelers, including Gregg, Magoffin and Russell. Commissioner Sibley in 1825 likened the rushing water to the "Diamond of the Desert," a celebrated spring in Arabia. It was he who called it Diamond Spring. Waldo, Hall & Company built a stage station at the site in 1849. The base of a stone corral was visible until a few years ago when it was covered over with dirt.

Most travelers today will wish to by-pass the spring. Since it is on private ranch land, permission must be obtained to visit, and the access road may be impassable in bad weather. The daring, however, should drive 14 miles west of Council Grove on US 56. At the intersection of SR 149 go south 2.3 miles on a gravel road to the entrance of the Diamond Spring Ranch. It is on the right and unmarked, but there are short sections of white board fence on either side of the cattleguard. From this entrance drive across open ranch land, 1 mile, to a large two-story white house where permission should be obtained. (Beware of dogs.) To the right of the house is a barn and a road that turns left in front of it. Just after the turn, on the left, is the Diamond Spring, and a DAR marker a few feet above it on a knoll under a tree.

Note: The Diamond Spring Post Office and community, 4 miles south and shown on some road maps, is NOT the SFT site and has nothing to do with it.

Return to US 56 and continue west. Past Delavan just over 2 miles is a paved crossroads that leads south to Burdick. Turn left toward Burdick and go 3.2 miles to a bridge over Six Mile Creek. At .1 mile past the bridge on the left (east) is a DAR marker. Park next to it and walk through deserted farm buildings on a lane leading 150 yards to the SFT crossing of Six Mile Creek. The next stream to the east is Three Mile Creek, and east of that, One and A Half Mile Creek. The names, given by wagonmasters, were based on distances from Diamond Spring. Charley Owens established his Six Mile Ranch here in 1866. But two years later a war party of Cheyennes burned it to the ground while he and his wife were absent. Return to US 56.

FORT RILEY

Continue west on US 56 to the junction with US 77. From this point a side trip can be made 25 miles north on US 77 to Fort Riley and Junction City. One of the functions of the fort, founded in 1853 at the junction of the Republican and Smokey Hill Rivers, was to provide military protection for the SFT to the south. It was named for General Bennet Riley, a Mexican War hero and leader of the first military escort along the SFT in 1829.

Fort Riley remains an active post. An official Kansas Historical Marker, with reference to the SFT, is in a roadside turn-out on the grounds. Of chief interest at the fort is the official U.S. Army Horse Cavalry Museum, which includes some SFT exhibits. Associated with the museum is the "Custer House," dating from 1854, once occupied by Lieutenant Colonel and Mrs. George Armstrong Custer, who were stationed here in 1866.

That same year, the Union Pacific Railroad reached neighboring Junction City, which then became the railhead and starting point of the SFT for a brief period. Woolworth and Barton Overland Transportation Line built a large warehouse next to the railroad depot and in January 1867, dispatched its first wagon train to Santa Fe, the shipment being destined for the Spiegelberg Brothers of that city. As the Union Pacific advanced westward across Kansas the starting point of the SFT moved with it.

HERINGTON

Return to the highway junction of US 56 and US 77 on the main SFT route. Here US 56 turns south with US 77. Before taking it, however, go west on the highway into Herington. When a main thoroughfare (Broadway) crosses the road turn right (north) on it. After 2 blocks cross the railroad tracks, then cross a bridge and turn left (west) into the City Park. At the back of the circle drive is a tall sandstone monument commemorating the death of Father Padilla.

Note: The first Padilla monument was seen in Council Grove.

Once more, return to the junction of US 56 and US 77. Go south 1½ miles to a roadside turn-out on the right. Here is an official Kansas Historical Marker with text on the Coronado Expedition, which is believed to have followed part of the route of the later SFT.

LOST SPRING

About 5 miles south of the Coronado marker on US 56/US 77, a small sign on the right (west) marks the spot where the SFT, coming from Diamond Spring and heading for Lost Spring, crosses the highway. In the weeds on the left (east) side of the highway is a DAR marker. A tall silo with a red and white top is just beyond this site on the right.

Continue south on the highway and cross the railroad tracks. Just beyond them, a sign points to a paved county road leading 1 mile to the modern community of Lost Springs. Turn right (west) on this road. Entering the small community turn right on either the first or second gravel street that intersects from the north. Drive 1 block to the municipal park. On the west side of the park is a DAR marker with a bronze plaque like the ones noted at Olathe and Gardner.

Return 1 block to the paved county road and turn right (west). Continue to the post office and Zinn Cafe on the right, which form most of the town's "business district." At the street that enters along the west side of the cafe, turn right (north) and drive several blocks toward the railroad tracks. Just before the tracks, a sign indicates where the SFT crossed the street. Return to the paved county road and again turn right (west).

Go one block to the next intersection, make a right turn, and drive north one block. Here on the northwest corner is a waist-high limestone monument that reads "SFT, July 4, 1908." Behind it is a two-story green house. This is one of three "homemade monuments" installed in the area on that date by local resident Dan McNicol. Return to the paved county road, turn right and go west 2.3 miles to the original Lost Spring on the SFT. Although less renowned in trail days than Diamond Spring, it is now far better preserved, more accessible and one of the most scenic spots on the eastern leg of the SFT. A large DAR granite marker is on the south (left) side of the road surrounded by a pipe railing. Across the road on the north is a historical interpretive sign and behind it pools of water are seen during most seasons of the year.

40 ft.

30 ft.

Station House

20 ft.

30 ft.

Stockade

**PLAN OF THE
LOST SPRING STAGE STATION**

Lost Spring, Kansas, a major trail landmark west of Council Grove.

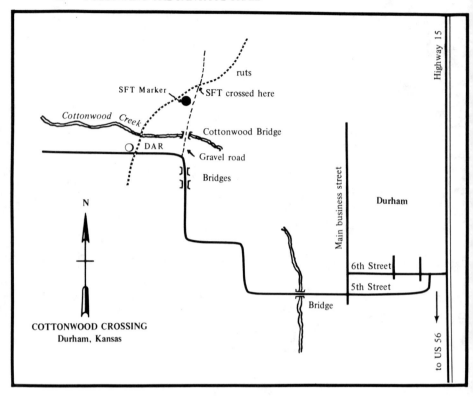

COTTONWOOD CROSSING
Durham, Kansas

Early geologists declared that the water originated in the Rockies and followed a fault line to this location. Wagon travelers claimed it tasted like mountain water. In the late 1840s the army planted water cress and strawberries around the spring hoping soldiers on patrol would eat them and thus prevent scurvy. The last berries disappeared twenty-five years ago but the cress still grows.

In 1859 George Smith built a stage station, hotel and tavern. The station with its sod roof was on a knoll southeast of the present county road. Late the same year a soldier, Jack H. Costello, returning from New Mexico on the SFT, won the station from Smith in a card game. The place became a haven for gamblers and outlaws. Eleven men died in shoot-outs and were buried near the station.

The SFT crossed the county road at the DAR marker and angled southwest down to a creek crossing. From the interpretive sign walk about 50 yards south of the road to see trail ruts, in the form of a cut or swale, leading down to the creek. The cut is in a diagonal line with the DAR marker.

COTTONWOOD CROSSING

From the Lost Spring site continue west on the paved county road 2.6 miles to a paved crossroad. (Note: A dirt road continues straight ahead.) Turn left (south) .7 mile to a DAR marker on the right, behind a barb wire fence. The SFT crosses here and the marker sits in faint ruts extending diagonally toward the trees behind it.

Continue south another .3 mile to an intersection. Turn west (right) on a gravel road toward Tampa, 5 miles. After a railroad crossing continue to the next intersection on the edge of Tampa where the pavement begins. The SFT crossed the road just before the intersection and faint ruts can be seen in the cemetery on the right. Just beyond on the southwest corner is a large DAR marker with extensive inscription.

Continue straight ahead (west) 4 miles to join SR 15 and there turn left (south) toward Durham. At 1.5 to 2 miles after entering upon SR 15, the SFT, coming from Lost Spring and heading for Cottonwood Creek, crosses the highway. (This site is about 3 miles north of Durham.) A small sign marks the point. Long grooves of SFT ruts can be seen in the grassy field on the west (right) side of the highway.

Continue on to the small community of Durham. Turn right (west) off the highway into the center of town. Take the one paved county road leading west. It begins as 5th Street at the southern end of "downtown." As 5th leaves town it crosses a bridge. Beyond, it turns to the right (north), then left (west) and then right (north) again. Finally, after crossing two bridges in quick succession the county road makes another sharp-angle turn to the left (west). At this turn of the paved road a gravel road continues straight ahead (north) across Cottonwood Creek.

For the moment, though, make the lefthand turn on the pavement and a few hundred yards beyond is a DAR marker on the right (north) side of the road. In the summer it may be obscured by weeds. In front of it is a faded green sign on a post stating: "Santa Fe Trail Crossed Here." Behind the marker is a small tilled field and at its far edge is a line of trees bordering Cottonwood Creek. The famous crossing was there. Several parties of travelers were hit by blizzards at this spot. Susan Magoffin mentions it at length in her diary.

Go back to the last turn of the paved road and, turning left, take the gravel road north. Upon crossing the bridge over Cottonwood Creek look left to see the approximate area of the old wagon crossing.

Not far beyond the bridge, on the left under a tree, is a waist-high marker for the SFT with two bronze plaques. It was placed by Kansas school children. In summer the marker is surrounded by poison ivy. Behind it and to the right on a hill is a farmhouse. The farmer has plowed up numerous trail relics in his fields down along the creek.

A short distance beyond the marker is a sign on the right stating: "Santa Fe Trail Crossed Here." Behind it on a slope to the right of the road can be seen ruts of the SFT coming from Lost Spring and leading down to the Cottonwood Crossing.

Return to Durham and pick up SR 15 leading south 10 miles to rejoin US 56, which then goes west.

HILLSBORO TO McPHERSON

At the junction of SR 15 and US 56 a side trip is recommended 3 miles east on 56 to Hillsboro, one of the tidiest and most energetic small towns in Kansas. Entering the eastern limits watch for the Adobe House Museum on the right (south) side of the highway. A granite marker commemorating the SFT and the Chisholm Trail is in the yard. The museum contains a small trail exhibit. The "Adobe House" was built in 1876 by Mennonite immigrants from Russia who settled this area. The furnished rooms contain splendid examples of their folk culture.

Continue one block past the museum on US 56 and turn left (north) on Main Street. At 102 Main, on the corner, is the Chamber of Commerce offering maps and brochures on area points of historic interest. One block beyond on the east side of Main is a fine two-story building completed in 1887. Now called "Olde Towne," it contains interesting shops. Across the street is a bookshop containing a good selection of titles on Mennonite history. Hillsboro holds a Folk Festival in late May and an Arts and Crafts Fair in September. The Chamber of Commerce can supply the dates. Return west on US 56 toward McPherson.

At ½ mile beyond the Marion-McPherson County line, which is well marked, the SFT crosses the highway. At 1 mile from the county line turn right (north) on a gravel road. (This intersection on US 56 is about 2 miles east of Canton.) Go north on the gravel road ½ mile to a railroad track. Just before (south of) that track turn east (right) on dirt car tracks (in fair weather only) and go about ¼ mile to the Jones Cemetery on a rise surrounded by trees and hedges. Here are a DAR marker and next to it the gravestone of eighteen-year-old Ed Miller, a mail courier (not a Pony Express rider) killed on the SFT in 1864 by Cheyennes. They are in the center of the cemetery near a large dead tree. Return to US 56 and continue west.

Watch for the Canton junction, that is, for the sign pointing north to Canton. At 5 miles west of that junction, US 56 intersects with paved County Road 307. Turn left (south) and go 2 miles to a tall white brick monument on the left (east). A bronze plaque marks the Running Turkey Creek Campground on the SFT. This was also the site of Fuller's Ranch, 1855, the first settlement in McPherson County. Return to US 56.

McPHERSON

Approaching the eastern limits of McPherson, leave US 56 and drive 7 miles north on I-35 to a roadside park located in the wide median of the highway. There are two separate units of the park, one for northbound traffic and the other for southbound. Turn left into the first unit, drive to the rear and take a small road that leads to the second (or southbound) unit. Here is located one of the newly installed Mormon Battalion markers. Also note the trails map, "Historical Kansas," on the building adjacent to the marker.

Return to McPherson and pick up US 56. On the west side of town it intersects with SR 153. Turn south (left) onto SR 153 and go about 5 miles to the little community of Elyria. At ½ mile beyond that place, on the right (west) side of the highway, is a roadside turn-out. Here is the DAR marker for Dry Turkey Creek. (Its earlier name, Sora Kansas Creek, is on the marker.) Inscriptions are on the front and back.

An official Kansas Historical Marker is also here. Its text describes the treaty made on Dry Turkey Creek in 1825 between the U. S. Commissioners and the Kaw tribe, granting access to travelers on the SFT. A line of trees marks the creek about a mile to the west. Look across the field behind the markers.

LITTLE ARKANSAS CROSSING

The crossing of the Little Arkansas was a spot well-known to early teamsters and merchants. The stream was comparatively small, but it had a muddy bottom and steep banks. There were actually two crossings about ½ mile apart. The SFT split several miles to the east, drivers taking the fork leading to whichever crossing their scouts reported as being in the best condition.

A short distance beyond the Little Arkansas the two branches came together to form one trail again. The north crossing, or what I call the "upper crossing," was the older and more important. In trail days there was no thick lining of timber as now, but there was one large "marker cottonwood" that could be seen far out on the plains. It guided wagons to the upper crossing. That cottonwood still stands on the east side of the ford. At about the height of a man, the huge trunk forks into two smaller trunks.

About 1865 a notable landmark, the Stone Corral, was built on the west bank near the lower crossing. It was 200 by 400 feet and had 30-inch-thick walls 8 feet high. The structure not only held livestock but doubled as a fort. A stage station was nearby and a toll bridge was also erected in the middle 1860s. In the 1880s, after abandonment of the SFT, local residents hauled away the quarried stone from the corral and no trace remains today.

Stocking (*Road to Santa Fe*, pp. 105-10) describes his visit to the Little Arkansas Crossing but his sketchy directions will never get you there. From McPherson go west on US 56 to Windom (which is actually off to the right ½ mile). A mile beyond the Windom turnoff, paved County Road 443, which is on the county line, crosses US 56. Turn left (south) and drive exactly 5 miles to an intersection. (Note: County roads here are laid out on a grid with intersections 1 mile apart. Thus you will pass 4 crossroads before reaching the 5-mile intersection.) At this point, on the southeast corner, can be seen a DAR marker and sign pointing west to the Stone Corral.

At this intersection turn west (right) as the sign directs. Go ½ mile to a small dirt road that turns to the left just before the bridge over the Little Arkansas. A hand-lettered sign on a pipe frame (put up by the property owner) is titled "Stone Corral" and gives a brief history. The corral was not here but across the county road and west of the river. Behind the sign are some depressions reputed to be the remains of trenches dug by troops of Colonel George Custer when he was here guarding the ford briefly in the 1860s.

Continue down the small dirt road a short distance to a sign on the right: "Cottonwood Grove Cemetery." Depressions behind the sign are remains of graves of soldiers who were killed by Indians while stationed at the crossing. Later their bodies were removed to Fort Leavenworth

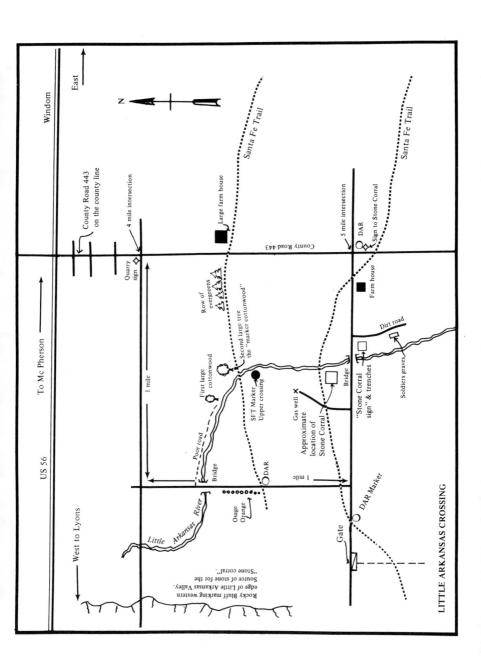

LITTLE ARKANSAS CROSSING

Cemetery.

Note: A small picnic ground at the graves is private. For permission to use it see the farmer whose house can be seen to the east across the fields.

Return to the county road and continue west across the bridge over the Little Arkansas. Just beyond, on the right, is a new access road leading to a gas well out in the field. Turn onto this road. To the right toward the river note a low mound with some small trees on the north end, in the middle of the field. The Stone Corral is thought to have been in the field immediately north of the mound. Continue to the end of the road and park at the gas well. Beyond (north), about ¼ mile, under the fringe of trees is a granite SFT marker at the upper crossing and the site of the toll bridge. The "marker cottonwood" is across (that is, on the east side) of the river.

From the access road return to the county road and go west to the next intersection. Continue straight ahead ½ mile to a DAR marker on the left (south) side of the road. Past this marker turn left through the first gate leading into pasture land. At .1 mile from the gate the SFT crosses the road. The deepest ruts are to the left (east). A small iron cross is in one of the ruts. Return to the last intersection and go north to another DAR marker on the right (east) side of the road. It is a replacement for an older marker that had a bronze plaque, which was stolen. The plaque later turned up at a farm sale and is now preserved in the museum at Lyons. The present DAR marker (placed in 1979) is the most recent I have found on the trail.

Here on the west side of the road is a line of Osage Orange trees. One of the early conditions for homesteading was that the farmer plant such tree rows to serve as a windbreak and provide firewood. Except in middle and late summer when the crops are up and the foliage heavy along the Little Arkansas, it is possible to look east across the fields behind the DAR marker and see the white granite SFT marker at the crossing. Return to US 56.

LYONS

Entering Lyons proceed to the intersection of US 56 and SR 96/ 14 near the downtown area. At that junction turn left (south) toward Sterling. At 1.4 miles watch for an oversize marker erected by the Sterling Chapter of the DAR. It is on the right (west) side of the highway and stands between two large evergreen bushes. Return to the last intersection, in the center of Lyons, and turn west 1 block on US

56 to Courthouse Square.

The new Coronado-Quivira Museum is located at 221 East Avenue South, 1 block south of the courthouse. This excellent facility contains exhibits relating, among other things, to the Coronado Expedition and the SFT.

FATHER PADILLA CROSS AND COW CREEK CROSSING

Four miles west of Lyons on the south side of US 56 is a small roadside park. Its most conspicuous feature is a 30-foot marble cross honoring Coronado's well-traveled friar, Father Padilla. In the same park is an official Kansas Historical Marker with a text describing Coronado's search for Quivira. Next to it is a Rice County Historical Society sign for the Cow Creek Station on the SFT. In the plowed field behind the cross was once a huge Quivira Indian village.

On the east edge of the park is a gravel road running south to Buffalo Bill's Well and Cow Creek. Follow this county road 1 mile to the well-marked site. Next to the well (which is covered by a shelter) is an interpretive sign and a DAR marker. Just beyond, the bridge over Cow Creek is very near the original crossing of the SFT.

Cow Creek marked the boundary between the tallgrass country on the east and the shortgrass prairie stretching westward, the latter being the prize range of the buffalo. The site was also on the margin of hostile Indian country, so that beginning in the 1850s soldiers were often stationed at the crossing to protect passing caravans. Their flagpole is said to have been placed on a low hill just north of the well. Many massacres and bloody fights with Indians are recorded for Cow Creek.

Buffalo Bill Mathewson operated a trading post and ranch at the crossing beginning in the 1850s. (His grave is in Highland Cemetery, Wichita.) For a time a youth named William Cody worked for him. Later, when Cody served as a hunter for the Kansas Pacific Railroad, supplying meat for the construction crews, he too took the nickname "Buffalo Bill."

PLUM BUTTES

Midway between Cow Creek and Fort Zarah was the Plum Buttes noon stop. Several low buttes, so-called, were really sand hills surrounded by plum thickets. Wagons paused here for lunch but there was no water or firewood. Today the Buttes are still in evidence, although difficult to recognize.

About 8 miles west of the Father Padilla Cross and the roadside park on US 56, a blacktop road crosses the highway. Approaching the intersection, a sign points south (left) to the town of Raymond. At the intersection itself is a small white sign pointing north to Salem Methodist Church. Here, turn north (right) on the blacktop. At about ¼ mile cross a railroad track. After another ½ mile watch for a small sign on the right reading: "Santa Fe Trail Crossed Here." Beautiful ruts in the form of a deep swale are visible on the east (right) side of the road. West of the road, where the ruts are fainter, is a DAR marker by the fence. The ruts on the east are carefully preserved by the owner, Ralph Hathaway.

Continue straight ahead (north) to the next intersection. Turn left (west) and go 1.5 miles to a high point in the road. There on the right and left are the remnants of the Plum Buttes, unmarked but recognizable as low sand hills. Originally they stood over 100 feet before erosion reduced them. The Buttes could be seen by teamsters from the Cow Creek crossing, ten miles in the distance. In those days there was no timber to obstruct the view as is the case now. Look for the wild plum bushes that still grow along the road and at the base of the Buttes. Drive on to the next intersection and turn left (south), continuing 1 mile, past a grain elevator, to rejoin US 56. Turn right (west).

FORT ZARAH AND WALNUT CREEK CROSSING

The next town after Plum Buttes is Ellinwood. Two blocks past its one traffic light is a DAR marker on the right.

Continuing west on US 56, cross a highway bridge over Walnut Creek about 2 miles east of the town of Great Bend. Just past the bridge on the right (north) side of the highway is a spacious roadside park commemorating Fort Zarah and the Walnut Creek Crossing. Near the entrance is an official Kansas Historical Marker, "Fort Zarah," with reference to the SFT.

For a brief period (1864-69) the fort guarded one of the most dangerous sections of the SFT. In those years Barnum, Veil & Vickery operated a stageline and held the government mail contract between Kansas City and Santa Fe. They built a fortified stage station and corral at the Walnut Crossing. Fort Zarah troopers provided escorts for the coaches. No trace of the sandstone fort or station remains today. However, I have been told that Fort Zarah was in the field across the creek from the present park.

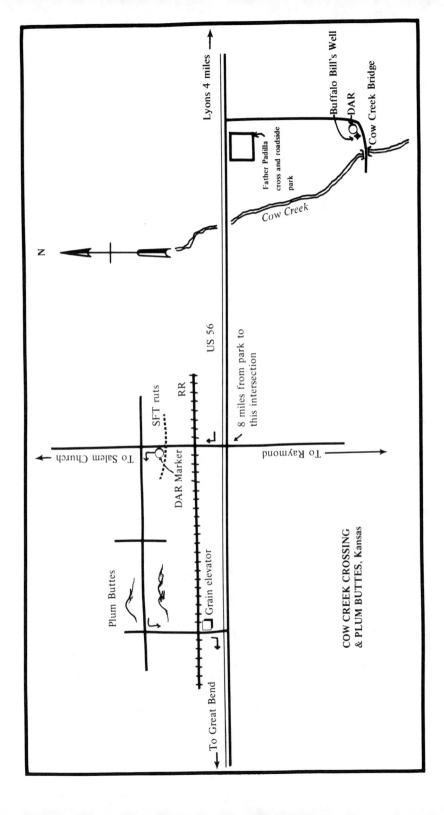

COW CREEK CROSSING
& PLUM BUTTES, Kansas

GREAT BEND

The SFT joined the Arkansas River at its great bend, sometimes called the north bend, and followed its broad valley toward the southwest and Pawnee Rock. The present town of Great Bend was not founded until 1871, after the SFT had closed in this area. The trail ran through the grounds upon which the Courthouse now stands downtown. Entering Great Bend from the east on US 56, a DAR marker can be found on the left side of the road, next to some evergreens adjacent to the Sands Motel.

Continue into the center of Great Bend. At Kansas Street turn left (south) 4 blocks to the railroad station. A DAR marker is located about 50 yards east of the station, at the corner of a large white metal building and adjacent to the tracks. Return to US 56.

Note: On the west side of Great Bend US 56 makes an unexpected turn to the left at the drive-in theater. The turn is easy to miss.

PAWNEE ROCK

The most famous natural landmark along the SFT in Kansas, Pawnee Rock was an Indian ambush site and a major campground for the caravans. Colonel Henry Inman claimed that every square yard of sod below the Rock contained the grave of a SFT traveler. Practically everyone who wrote about the trail took pains to describe Pawnee Rock, which is merely a small hill with a rock face. Anywhere but on the flat plains of Kansas it would pass unnoticed.

Modern visitors who are carrying a copy of Susan Magoffin's diary should read her description of the place under the entry for July 4, 1846. She carved her name here, as did many other passers-by, but those priceless inscriptions were lost in later years when Pawnee Rock was heavily quarried for building materials. Now it is a state park and protected.

Entering the small community of Pawnee Rock on US 56, turn right (north) at the sign in the center of town which points to the historic site. Go about ½ mile to the park entrance. On the right side of the gate, almost hidden by a lilac bush, is a DAR marker.

The road passes through the gate and leads to the base of Pawnee Rock. Imbedded in its face are two bronze plaques. One shows William Becknell's first packtrain of 1821 in relief. (An identical plaque will be encountered later at Wagon Mound, New Mexico. They were designed

Monument atop Pawnee Rock, Kansas.

and cast by an anonymous citizen of Larned and placed in 1971.) The second plaque commemorates the SFT. Most inscriptions seen on the Rock are from post-SFT days, but about 25 yards to the left of and below the plaques are a couple of original signatures with early dates.

The road makes a circle on to the top of the Rock. Here is a stone shelter and a tall white marble SFT monument with inscriptions on four sides. This is the only marker I know of on the trail that mentions the women as well as the men who ventured forth on the SFT. Look south across the town to the line of trees marking the Arkansas River. The SFT ran about 100 yards south of the Rock.

Return to US 56 and turn right toward Larned. Leaving the western outskirts of the community of Pawnee Rock stop at an official Kansas Historical Marker in a roadside park on the left. The text gives a brief history of the Rock and recounts a bogus story about a youthful Kit Carson making his first trail trip and shooting his own mule on night guard duty here.

ASH CREEK CROSSING

About 1 mile past the aforementioned roadside park look to the right (west) of the highway about a quarter-mile to a long trending bluff or ridge. The feature is most conspicuous at this point although it actually extends all the way from Pawnee Rock to Ash Creek, paralleling the trail. I call it Kirwan's Ridge, after Private John S. Kirwan, 4th US Cavalry. He was with a small patrol from Fort Riley operating on this section of the SFT in 1859. Escorting a party of east-bound Pikes Peakers (returning Colorado gold seekers) with their families, the patrol encountered hostile Indians who the day before had attacked the Santa Fe mail coach killing the driver and conductor. Says Kirwan in his journal: "Pretty soon we came in sight of the Indians scattered along the bluff as far as we could see, moving up and down the sides of the slope. They did everything possible to draw us on, and away from the wagons, but Lt. Otis gave positive orders that we were not to fire...and under no circumstances to leave the wagons. The women were brave and even the children were plucky." The strategy was successful and the train escaped without a fight. (Kirwan's complete journal is in the *Kansas Historical Quarterly*, Winter 1955, pp. 569-87.) A farm structure or two can be seen on the low bluff today. Try and imagine the same scene, with menacing Indians, as Kirwan and his companions saw it in 1859.

Just over 3 miles past the above roadside park, an unmarked gravel

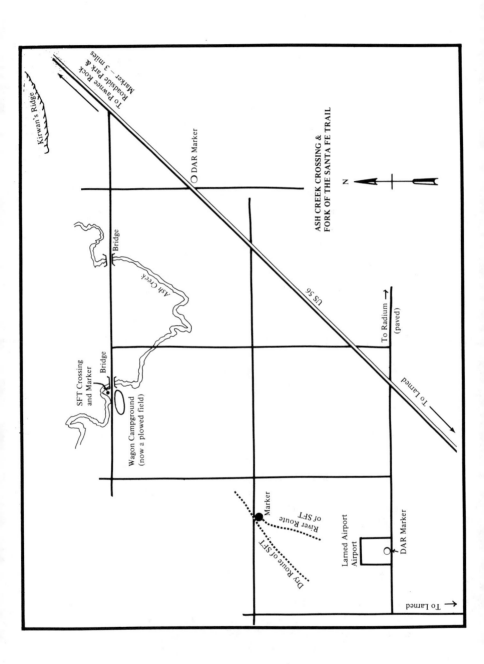

ASH CREEK CROSSING &
FORK OF THE SANTA FE TRAIL

road crosses US 56. Turn west (right) and go 2 miles to the Ash Creek Crossing. (It is about 50 yards past the second bridge.) Stop on the road. Just to the right (north) of the road is the tree- and brush-filled bed of Ash Creek, usually dry. This site, identified by Earl Monger of Larned, has been recently marked with a nice sign.

Across the creek due north is a white farmhouse and a silo with a silver dome. Wagons coming from Pawnee Rock crossed here (if you know where to look you can see the line of trees marking Ash Creek from the top of the Rock) and camped in the plowed field just to the south of the road.

This unspectacular crossing is significant because it was here that young Susan Magoffin's carriage turned over, throwing her to the ground unconscious. The injuries she suffered led to a miscarriage later at Bent's Fort. Read the account of the incident in her journal.

Return to US 56 and turn right (southwest) toward Larned. At the next intersection, at .7 mile, is a DAR marker on the left between the highway and the railroad tracks.

At just under two miles past the DAR marker, US 56 intersects with a paved road from the left at mile marker 185. A large tree is on the right and a highway sign just beyond the junction reads: "West, 56, 156." Here, turn west (right) on a gravel road and drive 1.3 miles to the Larned-Pawnee County Airport, which is on the right (north) side of the road. A DAR marker is at the Airport near the hangar facing the road. The SFT passed across the present runways, coming down from Ash Creek Crossing and heading toward the Pawnee Fork River.

From the airport turn back toward US 56. But at the first intersection with a county road turn left (north) and drive 1 mile to a crossroads. Here go left (west) about ¼ mile to a sign in the field on the left reading "Santa Fe Trail to Fort Mann." The airport can be seen in the distance behind the sign. At this point, as described below, the SFT forked, the two branches eventually meeting at Fort Mann (later, when the trail was rerouted, at Fort Dodge). Return to US 56 and continue toward Larned.

THE LARNED COMPLEX

In the vicinity of the town of Larned are a variety of SFT points of interest, probably enough to warrant designating the area a "complex." The only complex formally established thus far is the "Clayton Complex" comprising a cluster of trail sites in eastern New Mexico. At

Larned a fairly substantial river, the Pawnee Fork, flows from the west and joins the Arkansas on the southern edge of town. When the Pawnee Fork was running high it made crossing treacherous for wagons and men on muleback. There were several branches and sub-branches of the SFT in the environs of Larned. (For a detailed description see Stocking, *Road to Santa Fe*, pp. 125-30; and Long, *SFT*, pp. 94-95.) The trail split north of the present airport. One branch, the River Trail, stayed close to the Arkansas as it dipped to the southwest. The other branch, called the Dry Route or sometimes the Hill Trail, left the river and took a more direct path to the west. This latter trail was some 10 miles shorter than the River Trail, but usually it could not be used after July 1 because the ephemeral ponds in swales and buffalo wallows dried up. The two branches came together again at Fort Dodge on the Arkansas.

Entering the northeastern outskirts of Larned, note several green and white "SFT Historic Point" signs posted along the highway. Follow US 56 to its junction with Broadway at the first traffic light. At this intersection US 56 turns south on Broadway toward downtown Larned. Here SR 156 continues west (that is, straight ahead). Your main route will remain US 56, but before taking it follow SR 156 west to several major and minor SFT points of interest.

A. Larned Cemetery

At 2 miles beyond the abovementioned intersection a paved road crosses SR 156. Turn left (south) ½ mile to the cemetery entrance on the right. One branch of the SFT passed through the southern edge of the cemetery, which is on elevated ground, then headed down toward the crossing of the Pawnee Fork about 1 mile to the southwest.

Continue past the entrance on the paved road toward the cemetery's southeast corner. Approaching that corner, some very, very faint buckles or ripples can be seen on the grassed-over ground that passes under the chain link fence to the right. An aerial survey has established that they are the dim remains of the SFT. Had not Earl Monger of the SFT Center shown them to me, I would never have noticed them. Continue to the corner where the road ends at a T at 8th Street. Turn right (west) on 8th along the south side of the cemetery. Almost at once, there is an iron gate on the left leading into a pasture. Wide SFT ruts coming from the cemetery extend at a diagonal toward the southwest from just inside the gate. They are represented by faint depressions visible only when the thick pasture grass has been grazed down. From this point a good view of Jenkins Hill can be had in the

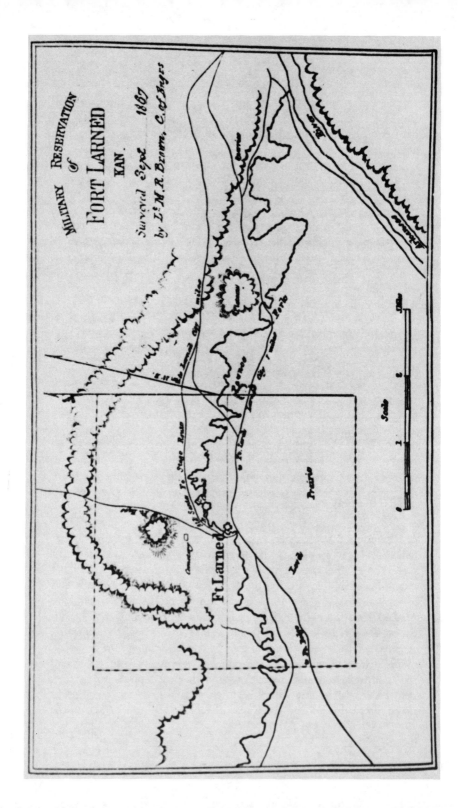

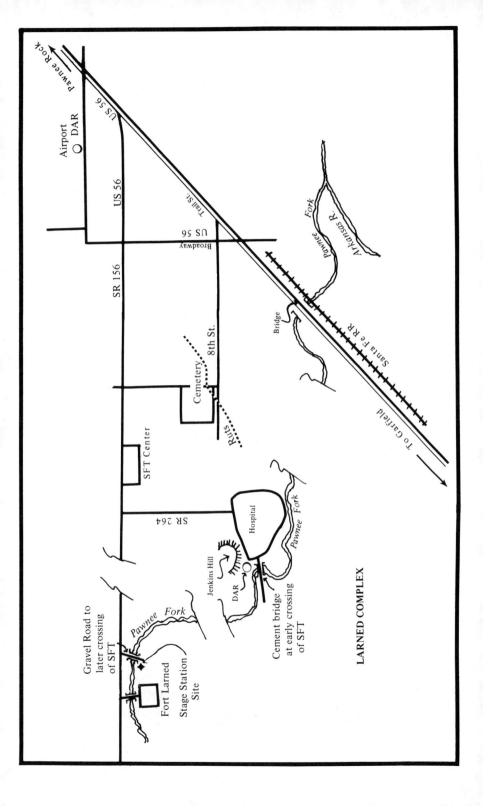

LARNED COMPLEX

distance at the Pawnee Fork Crossing. Return to 156 and turn left (west).

B. Santa Fe Trail Center

On the south side of SR 156 at 2½ miles west of Larned. Built and dedicated in 1974, the beautiful SFT Center interprets both the trail story and Kansas pioneer history with a series of fine museum exhibits. For researchers there is a small but growing library and archive. Various trail-related special events are held during the year. (See Appendix I.) A covered wagon stands outside the main door and one of the new Mormon Battalion markers is located near the northeast corner of the building. This is one of the highpoints of the modern trail.

Serious trail buffs will want to join the Fort Larned Historical Society which established and administers the Center and issues a newsletter called "Trail Ruts." Requests for information can be addressed to: Director, SFT Center, Route 3, Larned, Kansas 67550.

C. Pawnee Fork Crossing on the "Dry Route"

At ½ mile beyond the SFT Center turn left (south) off SR 156 onto SR 264 and drive 1 mile to the Larned State Hospital. Entering the hospital grounds Jenkins Hill, surmounted by a large water tower, can be seen on the right. Originally it was known as Lookout Hill and was used by SFT scouts (more commonly called "pilots") who scanned the surrounding country for hostile Indians. Many skirmishes took place at its base. In the latter 1850s the army considered placing a fort on the hill's summit but instead chose a location 3 miles up the Pawnee Fork. When Fort Larned was built, stone was quarried on Lookout Hill and hauled to the construction site.

SR 264 ends at a T. There, turn right and follow the road a short distance until it begins to curve left at the foot of Jenkins Hill. On the right at the curve is a DAR marker designating the Dry Route Crossing of the Pawnee Fork. The river is through the trees immediately behind and below the marker. Faint traces of the trail can be observed on the banks. This site was later known as Boyd's Crossing for a saloon established here by A. H. Boyd in 1867.

Just past the DAR marker is a red brick building, boarded up. On its south side a dirt lane leads right, off the paved road down to a cement bridge over the Pawnee Fork. It is best to walk down to the bridge. From its center look up to the water tower and the top of Jenkins Hill, which hangs over this historic crossing. The view gives a good idea why the look-outs were stationed there.

Return to SR 156 and turn left (west) toward Fort Larned. At 2.5 miles from the SFT Center is a road junction. Here, turn left (south), drive .8 mile, and stop. Across a field to the right, a line of woods marks the course of the Pawnee Fork. The tallest tree, rising above the others, sits in a weed-filled swale or cut that leads down to the river. There is no ramp on the opposite bank. It has been washed away. The swale represents an alternate branch of the Dry Route of the SFT. This river crossing came into use in the 1850s and probably supplanted the earlier one at Jenkins Hill on the Hospital grounds. A wooden bridge was built for convenience of stagecoaches, but it was burned by Kiowas in 1864 during a general uprising and never replaced. Once across, the trail ascended the river about .5 mile to a civilian mail station. Nothing is known about that station (it was recently excavated), but it may have been built by the firm of Hall and Porter which had the mail contract in the 1850s. About ⅛ mile beyond the station was Fort Larned. Earl Monger says it is not known whether the station or the fort was established first, but he suspects the station came first and the fort was later built nearby to protect it. Return to SR 156.

D. Fort Larned Historical Site

Located west on SR 156 about 6 miles from Larned. Established by the army in 1859, the fort was intended to protect caravans, stagecoaches and travelers on the eastern leg of the SFT. It also served as a base for offensive operations against the southern Plains Indians and later guarded construction crews on the AT&SF Railroad.

Today the nine surviving stone buildings around the parade ground have been restored and contain military and SFT exhibits. SFT books are sold at the information desk, and visitors should ask about the trail film shown in the theater room. At the desk also ask for the brochure entitled "Fort Larned History Trail." It provides directions for a walking tour of outlying points of interest, including the site of the stage station mentioned above. Special historical events are scheduled from time to time. Direct inquiries to: Superintendent, Fort Larned National Historic Site, Route 3, Box 69, Larned, Kansas 67550.

At the fort entrance alongside SR 156 is a roadside park containing a National Park Service interpretive sign, a DAR marker, and a SFT map. An official Kansas Historical Marker, "Fort Larned," has been removed recently. Turn left on the west edge of the park on a road that crosses the Pawnee Fork and enters the fort.

E. Trail Ruts

Go west from the Fort Larned entrance on SR 156, ½ mile to a paved county road that intersects from the left (south). Drive 4 miles on this road; then go right (west) 1 mile, then left (south) on a gravel farm road ½ mile to a well-marked parking area on the left. From the small, elevated observation booth out in the field the visitor can observe

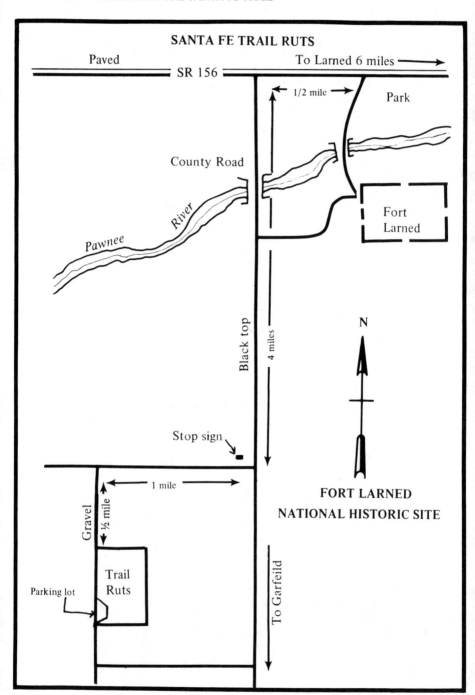

SANTA FE TRAIL RUTS

Paved   SR 156   To Larned 6 miles →

1/2 mile

Park

County Road

Pawnee River

Black top

4 miles

Fort Larned

N

Stop sign

1 mile

FORT LARNED NATIONAL HISTORIC SITE

Gravel

½ mile

Trail Ruts

Parking lot

To Garfeild

excellent SFT ruts that have been preserved in an undisturbed 40-acre pasture. An interpretive historical sign is in the booth. A sharp eye can also discern shallow oval depressions about six feet in diameter. These are old buffalo wallows where the big animals rolled in the dust seeking relief from biting flies. The ruts are now administered as a detached unit of Fort Larned.

Return to SR 156 and to its junction with US 56 on the north side of the town of Larned. At this intersection turn right (south) on US 56, which is also Broadway. On the left at Eighth Street and Broadway is the Jordaan Memorial Library containing excellent materials on local history and the SFT.

Continue south on Broadway until it joins Trail Street angling in from the left. Broadway continues straight ahead, but US 56 turns right onto Trail Street. One block beyond at the junction of Santa Fe and Trail Streets is a DAR marker on the right. Continuing several more blocks, Trail (or US 56) crosses the Pawnee Fork. To the left of the highway bridge is a railroad bridge which is the site of the crossing of the River Branch of the SFT. A short distance below the railroad bridge the Pawnee Fork joins the Arkansas River.

LARNED TO DODGE CITY

Continue southwest on US 56 to Garfield. A DAR marker is in the northeast corner of the town park, on the right side of the highway opposite the post office. From this marker continue on US 56 .9 mile to Coon Creek Crossing on the River Route of the SFT. Approaching the highway bridge over Coon Creek, a faint dirt road turns right into a field. A tree is at this junction. Stop under the tree after entering the road. The field to the right was the site of a wagon campground. To the left, marked by a new wooden sign, is the crossing. To reach it, a one-strand electric fence must be crossed. Just beyond, several indentations in the cut-bank are wagon ramps leading down to the crossing. Remains of a shallow pit filled with logs can also be seen here. Earl Monger believe the pit may be either the site of a dugout hut or the place where soldiers buried 102 ox yokes when their stock was stolen by Indians. The yokes were later recovered.

At 7.4 miles past the Coon Creek bridge on US 56 is a DAR marker on the right, between mile markers 162 and 163.

Continue on to Kinsley. There pick up US 50 going east and drive

3 miles to the Arkansas River bridge. Shortly before coming to that point the road crosses a smaller bridge again over Coon Creek. The creek is mentioned in many early trail journals. At ½ mile past the Arkansas River in a roadside turn-out on the right is an official Kansas Historical Marker, "The Battle of Coon Creek." Its extensive text refers to the SFT. Return to US 56 in Kinsley.

On the western limits of Kinsley is a large roadside park. A DAR marker stands beside a black railroad engine. The Sod House Museum is also in this park.

Continuing on US 56, at 4.7 miles from the roadside park is a pullout on the left side of the highway. It contains another DAR marker. At 3 miles beyond is the town of Oferle. On the west side of the town and to the right of the highway is a small park with a DAR marker.

FORT DODGE AND DODGE CITY

Continue southwest on US 56 to the intersection with US 283 which comes in from the north (right) 8 miles east of Dodge City. On the northeast corner of this junction is a large roadside park with an official Kansas Historical Marker, "The Road to Santa Fe." Its interpretive text on the SFT is one of the most detailed of any found in Kansas.

US 56 continues west to Dodge City, but at this intersection it is best to go due south on a paved county road 4 miles to US 154. The main tour route at that junction turns right (west) toward Fort Dodge. But for those with plenty of time, a sidetrip can be made by turning left (east) on 154. Drive about 8.5 miles down the valley of the Arkansas. The road here parallels the River Route of the SFT. As the highway curves toward a bridge over the river, a paved county road to Spearville intersects from the left (east). Follow it ½ mile to where the paved road makes a turn to the left and goes north. Instead of turning on the pavement continue straight ahead 1.5 miles on a gravel road to excellent SFT ruts. They begin in the vicinity of a windmill located in a grassy pasture on the left (north) and run about ½ mile parallel to the road toward a brick farm house. A short distance before the farm house, the trail crosses the county road into a wheat field on the right.

Return 2 miles to US 154. There turn left (south) toward the town

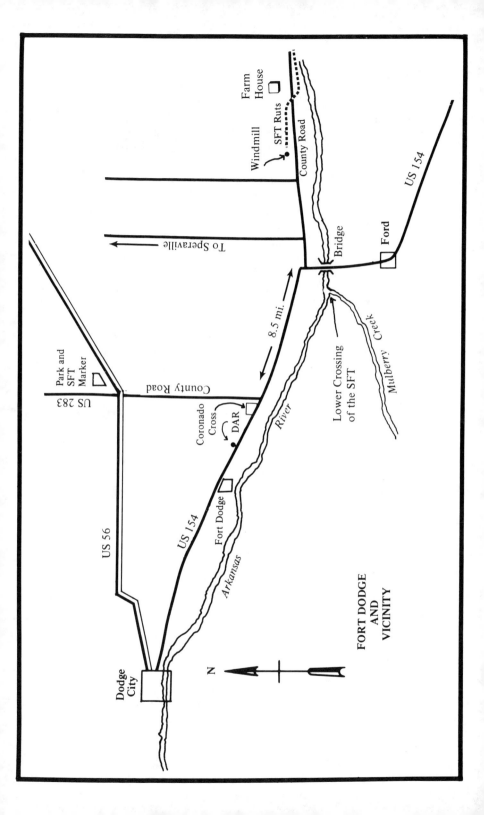

FORT DODGE
AND
VICINITY

of Ford. Very quickly the highway crosses the Arkansas River. Once off the bridge on the south side stop and look west across an open field. A line of trees about ½ mile away marks the course of Mulberry Creek as it approaches its union with the Arkansas. An early branch of the SFT heading southwest across the Cimarron Desert forded the Arkansas at the mouth of Mulberry Creek. This point was known as the Lower Crossing. (Stocking, *Road to Santa Fe*, pp. 133-34, describes the site in some detail.) It is about a half-hour hike across the wide field to the mouth of Mulberry Creek, which is easily located. But the area is thickly grown with trees and brush and I have been unable to find traces of the trail. Return about 9 miles to the intersection where you first joined US 154.

From that junction go west on 154 about ¼ mile to a small park on the right (north). Behind it on a hill is the large Coronado Cross. The 38-foot cross of pre-stressed concrete was erected in 1975 as a bicentennial project. It commemorates a religious service believed conducted in this vicinity on June 29, 1541, by Father Padilla after the Coronado Expedition successfully crossed the Arkansas River.

At .3 mile west of this park, on the right side of the highway, is a DAR marker under a tree. It is near the spot where the Dry Route and the River Branch of the SFT, which parted near Larned, came together again.

Continue on US 154 west .5 mile to the entrance of Fort Dodge (on the left), now maintained as a soldiers' home. In a roadside park to the west of the entrance .2 mile is an official Kansas Historical Marker, "Fort Dodge," with reference to the SFT. Founded in 1864, Dodge like Fort Larned provided soldier escorts for wagon trains and mail coaches during the dangerous 1860s.

Because the place has been adapted to modern use little remains among the often-remodeled structures to suggest the primitive life of frontier days. Two of the original adobe barracks dating from 1864 do survive but are now faced with native stone. Of greatest interest is the Custer House (turn right on Custer Street a couple of blocks inside the entrance), once the post headquarters and briefly the residence of George A. Custer and other noted military men of the time. It is now a white two-story structure with pitched red roof and a columned porch across the front. (Private residence; not open to the public.)

From the fort drive west on US 154 to Dodge City, 5 miles away. (Note: If you have followed the route just described you will miss an official Kansas Historical Marker, "Dodge City, the Cowboy Capital," which refers to the SFT. It is located on US 56 3 miles east of Dodge

City at an overlook of a giant cattle feedlot and stockyards. The turn-out for the sign is on the south side of the highway.)

Entering Dodge City from the fort on US 154 follow that highway to the center of town and its intersection with 2nd Avenue (which is also US 56). There go left (south) on US 56 1 block to a DAR marker just inside the entrance of Wright Park on the right.

Return north 2 blocks, cross the railroad tracks and turn right (east) on Wyatt Earp Boulevard. Drive 2 blocks to the Santa Fe Railroad Depot on the right. Santa Fe Park is on the east side of the depot, hidden from the street by an adjacent building.

In Santa Fe Park are two large sundials made of poles and white stones, whose shadows mark the time. The western dial records Mountain Time and the eastern Central Time. Between them is a stone tablet marking the north-south line of the 100th Meridian. Before the United States conquered the Southwest in 1846, territory of the Mexican Republic began west of this line, south of the Arkansas River. (Here the Arkansas is several blocks south of the depot.) That meant that from this point on as the wagon trains ascended the valley, the Americans could look south across the river to Mexican Territory.

The 100th Meridian also marked the beginning of what was once called the Great American Desert. East of the line there was generally enough rain to support agriculture. West of it there was not.

From the depot return west on Wyatt Earp Boulevard 4 blocks to Front Street and Boot Hill on the right (north) side of the street. Both are Disneyesque replicas commemorating Dodge City's heyday in the mid-1870s when it was a shipping point for cattle driven up from Texas. The Boot Hill Museum at the west end of Front Street has excellent exhibits relating to the SFT and Forts Dodge and Mann.

Behind Front Street (at Spruce and 4th) is the two-story building containing the Chamber of Commerce. It offers a variety of historical brochures and maps of the area. In front of the building is a crude concrete statue of a pair of yoked oxen bearing the inscription: "My Trails Have Become Your Highways."

Modern trail travelers may also find it useful to visit the Kansas Heritage Center at 1000 2nd Avenue. It too provides a variety of historical publications and services. One of the Center's published books is David K. Strate's *Sentinel of the Cimarron, The Frontier Experience of Fort Dodge, Kansas.*

Another point of interest in town is the modernistic metal statue of "The Plainswoman" erected in 1972 on the campus of Dodge City Community College. It honors early pioneer women. To reach the campus drive west on Wyatt Earp and turn north on 14th Avenue.

After a mile or so the campus and statue can be seen on the left (west) side of the street.

Returning south on 14th watch for a major intersection, with traffic lights, at Comanche. Turn east on Comanche and go about 5 blocks to Chilton Park. Turn left (north) on Manor Drive and proceed 2 blocks along the east side of the park. Watch for a six-foot-high white stone monument in the center of the park. The inscription on it honors Major Robert H. Chilton, commander of Fort Atkinson which was located on the SFT just west of Dodge City. In 1853 the Major presided over a large council with the Comanches, Kiowas, and Apaches designed to provide safe passage for travelers on the trail. A vivid description of the event is given by Sergeant Percival G. Lowe in his *Five Years A Dragoon* (Norman: University of Oklahoma Press, 1965), pp. 103-108. An ox yoke that was originally suspended near the top of the Chilton monument has long since disappeared.

Return to Wyatt Earp and turn right (west) heading out of Dodge City. You are now on US 50, which will be your SFT route as far as La Junta, Colorado. On the western outskirts of town is a Holiday Inn on the right. Across the highway from it on the south side of US 50 is a roadside turn-out with a DAR marker and an official Kansas Historical Marker, "Dodge City, the Cowboy Capital." Its text contains reference to Forts Mann and Atkinson and to the SFT.

WEST OF DODGE CITY

At ¾ mile past the Holiday Inn, US 50 By-pass joins your highway (US 50 Business) from the north. At 1.3 miles beyond that junction, on the north (right) side of US 50 is a tall white monument at the intersection of a dirt section line road. The road crosses a cement bridge over a ditch.

The monument is easily missed. It commemorates the Caches (a famous SFT campsite), Fort Mann (1847) and Fort Atkinson (1854), all located in the immediate vicinity and figuring prominently in the trail's history.

At 1 mile past this monument on the right is a large sign, "Suburban Santa Fe Trail," advertising a fancy subdivision. Just beyond are several low rounded hills that come down to the edge of the highway. Until recently one of the hills had a rocky cliff that faced south. Called "Point of Rocks" (the first of several such features by that name on the trail), it was a major landmark for travelers.

Two of the earliest trading expeditions, the Cooper party on its way to Santa Fe and the Fowler party returning, met here on June 12, 1822. Until 1846, persons standing on top of the Point of Rocks could look south across the Arkansas River to Mexican territory on the other side. The river then had no timber, but today its banks are marked by a line of trees seen to the left of the highway.

In 1981 the local highway department widened the road and destroyed the Point of Rocks. A remnant of the hill from which it projected is all that remains. It lies on the right at .9 mile past the "Suburban" sign mentioned above. A telephone pole is on top and a fence corner.

Continuing west on US 50, at 6 miles from Dodge City or 4.5 miles past Point of Rocks, can be seen a fine and well-marked set of SFT wagon ruts. They are located on the right (north) side of the highway, and at the approach a sign advises: "Historic Point of Interest." At the site is a turn-out and parking area with a large billboard-type sign decorated with a covered wagon and reading: "Santa Fe Trail Tracks."

A turnstile admits visitors through the fence. Near the turnstile is a DAR marker. From this point follow the path about 150 yards up a grassy ridge to a National Park Service Monument adjacent to the ruts. In trail days the Arkansas River looped toward the north, about where the highway is now, to the foot of the sandy bluffs. The SFT therefore swung out of the bottomlands and made about a 2-mile arc over the high ground to the north before returning once more to the valley farther west. The splendid set of ruts seen here, perhaps the longest and best preserved in Kansas, are part of that arc.

RIVER CROSSINGS

Continue west on US 50 to the town of Cimarron. There at the traffic light and main intersection turn left (south) on SR 23. Four blocks south, just before the bridge over the Arkansas, is the entrance (on the right) to the Cimarron Crossing Park. Just inside the entrance on the right hand is a large red granite marker with text and map showing the two branches of the SFT.

Behind the marker stands a white brick pavilion and beyond it a new official Kansas Historical Marker, "The Santa Fe Trail." Its extensive text includes reference to Becknell's inaugural trip. To the right of this marker is a covered wagon. The park is one of the most pleasant spots on the SFT today in western Kansas.

The Cimarron Crossing of the Arkansas River was a major

landmark for travelers. It was the midpoint of the journey, roughly halfway between Independence and Santa Fe. Here the SFT split into two great divisions—the Cimarron Cut-off or Desert Route; and the Mountain Branch, also called the Bent's Fort Cut-off. The Cimarron Cut-off forded the river here (or at other crossings 6 miles up the Arkansas as far as the modern town of Ingalls) and struck off in a southwesterly direction 50 miles across the waterless desert (or Jornada), which ended at the Cimarron River. To the water problem was added the threat of attack from Comanches and Kiowas. However, this was the shortest route to Santa Fe so it was preferred by most traders.

This area of the river was called the Middle Crossing and the fords here were those most used. The Lower Crossing (the least used) was downriver at present Ford, Kansas (14 miles east of Dodge City), while the Upper Crossing was near modern Lakin (roughly 60 miles upriver from the town of Cimarron). All the crossings eventually led travelers to the Cimarron River.

The Mountain Branch made no crossing of the river in Kansas but continued up the Arkansas to Bent's Fort in southeastern Colorado. There it forded the river and then headed for Raton Pass. Although it was about 100 miles longer, the Mountain Branch had fewer water problems and Indian worries. After the mid-1830s there was also the attraction of Bent's Fort which offered travelers a welcome stopover. The two branches finally converged at La Junta (Watrous), New Mexico, and continued the last 75 miles to Santa Fe as a single trail.

Continue west on US 50 up the Arkansas Valley to Ingalls. The old railroad depot 2 blocks south of the railroad tracks on the left has been converted into the "Santa Fe Trail Museum." Although there are nice displays of pioneer artifacts, none actually relate to the trail. Directly across the street to the west is a DAR marker on the corner in a small park.

GARDEN CITY

Approaching the eastern limits of Garden City, a roadside park is on the left (south) side of US 50. Here is a DAR marker and an official Kansas Historical Marker, "The Indian and the Buffalo," with an interesting text.

Enter Garden City on US 50 and proceed to the intersection of US 83 in the center of town. There turn left (south) on US 83, which is also Main Street, and drive 3 blocks to Maple. Turn left (east) on Maple and go 2½ blocks along the north boundary of Finnup Park to a DAR marker in the park on the right. Continue past the marker to Maple and Fourth and turn right (south) into the park.

The Finney County Historical Society Museum is on the right. In addition to exhibits, it contains a small research library with items of SFT interest. The facility is open afternoons only.

Return on Maple to US 83, turn left (south) and drive about 2 miles to the bridge over the Arkansas River. Its bed at this point is dry much of the year. Just beyond the bridge on the right is the information office for the Garden City Buffalo Refuge operated by the Kansas Fish and Game Commission. It contains the largest buffalo herd in the state. Late in the last century a local resident, C. J. "Buffalo" Jones, helped save these animals when they were on the verge of extinction.

Return to the center of Garden City and rejoin US 50. In the center of town note on the left side of the street the imposing four-story Windsor Hotel put up in 1887. Although built after the close of the SFT, it is worth a serious look. On the courthouse lawn behind the Windsor is a statue of Buffalo Jones.

The next town west of Garden City is Holcomb. A DAR marker is located on the southwest corner of US 50 and Wiley Street, 1 block before reaching the town's single main intersection.

TO LAKIN

Continue west on US 50 to the small community of Deerfield. Turn left (south) at the main intersection and drive 5 blocks to a park on the right. A DAR marker is on the southeast corner of the park.

Back at the main intersection go 3 miles west on US 50 to a highway bridge. Just past it on the right is a white "Wildlife Conservation" sign. Immediately beyond the sign is a dirt road leading to a grass-covered earth dam across a wide swale. Nice grass-filled ruts of the SFT come out of this swale from behind the dam and angle westward toward the highway. A corner fence post is in the middle of the ruts. By walking across the top of the dam, a wide band of ruts can be seen running up the grassy slope toward the east. This site has recently been donated to the local Kearny County Historical Society by Paul Bentrup of Deerfield. There are plans to place an interpretive marker here.

Drive on to Lakin and the intersection of US 50 and SR 25. Turn left (south) on SR 25 and go 2 blocks to the Kearny County Courthouse on the left. A DAR marker is on the lawn.

Continue south 2 blocks to Waterman and turn right (west) 2 blocks to Buffalo Street. The Kearny County Historical Museum, a complex of five buildings, is on the left. Turn left on Buffalo 1 block to the entrance, which faces the railroad tracks. This excellent museum has a number of trail-related exhibits, including one of the finest original Conestoga freight wagons to be seen anywhere. Superb railroad memorabilia is displayed in the restored AT&SF depot.

Lakin was in the vicinity of the Upper Crossing of the Cimarron Cut-off. Motorists wishing to follow that route should continue south on SR 25 to Ulysses and the Wagon Bed Springs site, picking up US 56 beyond at the town of Hugoton. This Guide, however, will continue west on US 50 following the Mountain Branch to Springer, New Mexico. At that point, we will return and describe the Cimarron Cut-off, beginning here at Lakin.

Bent's Fort

THE MOUNTAIN BRANCH

TO CHOUTEAU'S ISLAND

West of Lakin 1 mile on US 50 is a roadside park on the left (south) side of the highway. Here is an official Kansas Historical Marker, "Chouteau's Island." The island, a major landmark mentioned in all SFT histories, was in the Arkansas River about 5 miles southwest of the marker.

From the park go a bit over 2 miles west on US 50. Just past a highway bridge, a gravel road intersects from the left (south). It is marked by a green street sign that reads: "M 23." Turn south on this road and drive a little over 2.5 miles to an open gate in the wire fence on the right. (Just beyond this point M 23 crosses a canal and then ends in a T.) Turn into the gate on a dirt road and drive just over 1.5 miles to the base of the Indian Mound, which was originally known as Chouteau's Mound. One can drive to the top but it is better to park below and walk up. On the summit is a DAR marker. Sand-blasting winds have nearly obliterated the inscription.

The Mound is a low, flat-topped hill rising conspicuously above the floor of the Arkansas Valley. In trail days it was a prominent landmark denoting the location of Chouteau's Island immediately to the south. With changes in the river the island has long since disappeared. From the Mound's summit look south and slightly east to the tree-lined Arkansas. That was the approximate location of the island in a bend of the river. In the plowed field between the railroad tracks and the river was the Bluff Stage Station, of which no trace remains. Trees seen along the river are now mostly dead owing to a drastic fall in the water table in recent years.

Wagon caravans taking the Cimarron Cut-off crossed the Arkansas several miles east at modern Lakin and then followed the south bank of the river to Chouteau's Island. Here they left the Arkansas and started south through a wide band of sand hills via Bear Creek Pass. The "pass" was merely a shallow valley whose level floor offered an easy route of travel.

Once out of the pass and through the hills, the caravans were on flat prairie for the next 35 miles to the Cimarron River. Those trains using the Mountain Branch stayed on the north bank of the Arkansas and passed between Indian Mound and Chouteau's Island as they ascended the valley. Return to US 50.

West of Lakin and Chouteau's Island, modern drivers at high points on the highway can look south across the Arkansas Valley and see long, undisturbed vistas that were familiar to wagon travelers. In this vicinity one first gets the sense that the crowded East has been left behind and that the spacious West has been reached.

TO THE COLORADO BORDER

On US 50 at 16 miles west of Lakin is the small community of Kendall. At the Kendall sign turn left (south) and follow a gravel road to the town. A DAR marker is on the right, 1 block north of the railroad tracks. Kendall was originally named Aubry in honor of famed SFT freighter and long-distance rider Francis X. Aubry, but the Post Office Department later forced the change to Kendall because a town with a name similar to Aubry already existed in eastern Kansas.

About 8 miles west of Kendall on US 50 and 1 mile south of the highway are traces of the remains of Fort Aubry, a temporary post used to guard the SFT in 1865-66. However, the site is on private land and not accessible to the public. In this vicinity, a secondary branch of the SFT, known as the Aubry Cut-off, left the Arkansas and led southwest to Cold Spring on the Cimarron Route.

Continue west on US 50 to Syracuse. Approaching the one main intersection in the center of town, note the Hamilton County Museum on the right. It is housed in an old commercial building. In front is a DAR marker.

The next town, 15 miles beyond, is Coolidge, the last place in Kansas. Take note of the fine two-story stone building on the right which houses the post office. One block beyond, on the left (south) side of the highway is a DAR marker, the last in Kansas on the Mountain Branch.

At the state line on the right (north) side of US 50 on the northeast corner of an intersecting dirt road is the first Colorado DAR marker. The word "Kansas" is incised on the east side of the base and "Colorado" on the west side. The Colorado markers are of gray granite, in contrast to the red ones in Kansas.

HOLLY TO GRANADA

Holly is the first town encountered in Colorado on US 50. At the intersection of Main Street turn left (south) 3 blocks to the railroad tracks and depot. Cross the tracks. Straight ahead is an abandoned two-story red brick building. I am told that it was once used by the Arkansas Valley Land and Irrigating Company, set up by English engineers in 1896, and later by the famous Holly Sugar Company which harvested sugar beets.

Take the little road that runs along the right (west) side of this building. At the rear is a large white limestone barn in beautiful condition. According to local lore the barn was erected in the latter 1860s within the SFT era. The small square openings along the sides, it is claimed, are portholes used by early settlers in fending off Indian attacks. Note also the fine arched opening in the loft. From the barn look west up the driveway of a large two-story stone house. On the right side of the drive, a DAR marker sits in front of a lilac bush.

Return to the junction of Main and US 50 and continue west. At 4.3 miles from the junction at the Amity crossroad is a DAR marker. It is near the southeast corner, about 75 yards east of the junction and nearly hidden by weeds against the fence.

A short distance past the Amity DAR marker, US 50 crosses the Arkansas River to its south side, leaving the SFT on the north bank. About midway between the Arkansas bridge and the next town (Granada), a cut-off of the SFT called the Two Buttes Branch crosses the highway. (The location is unmarked.)

This route was laid out by the army in 1851 and was used by freighters going to Fort Union and Santa Fe. It saw heavy traffic in the period 1873 to 1875, when Granada as a new railhead was the actual beginning of the Santa Fe wagon road. This little known cut-off was named for two buttes located about 30 miles south of US 50. It passed near modern Folsom, New Mexico, and joined the Cimarron Cut-off near the Rock Crossing of the Canadian River. (A good description of the route is provided by Stocking, *Road to Santa Fe*, pp. 236-40.)

The town of Granada was platted in 1872 by the SFT freighting and mercantile firm of Chick, Brown and Company. Later Fred Harvey established one of his famous trackside restaurants here and developed a huge cattle company to supply beef to all his "Harvey Houses" and to dining cars on the AT&SF.

GRANADA TO LAMAR

To rejoin the original route of the SFT (left when US 50 crossed the Arkansas east of Granada) take US 385 that goes north from the center of Granada. At just over 2 miles the highway crosses the Arkansas River. At .4 mile beyond the bridge is a DAR marker on the right. Continue 1 mile north on 385 to a junction and turn left (west) on SR 196. At 5.5 miles from the junction is an intersection with a white house on the right. Turn left (south) off SR 196 and drive .2 mile toward the river to a DAR marker on the left (east) side of the road. Good SFT ruts existed in the field behind the marker until 1968, when they were silted over by a flood that covered the Arkansas Valley here. Return to 196 and turn left (west). At 6 miles is an intersection, with a DAR marker on the northwest corner. At another 5.3 miles intersect with US 50 in Lamar.

LAMAR

At the intersection of US 50 and SR 196 turn left (south) and drive across the Arkansas bridge and into the center of Lamar. On the east side at the corner of Main and Beach Streets is another Pioneer Mother statue, or "Madonna of the Trail." It is in front of the Chamber of Commerce, which offers a brochure on the history of the statue.

An inscription on the statue's base refers to the "Big Timbers," a 45-mile-long grove of cottonwoods extending up and down the valley of the Arkansas. The grove served as a popular campground for Plains Indians and was a familiar landmark to SFT traders and mountain men. It was the first significant stand of timber on the trail west of Council Grove.

Return north on US 50 (Main Street) and recross the Arkansas bridge. Just past the bridge watch for a pull-out on the right side of the highway. It contains a DAR marker. Just beyond the pull-out, US 50 curves to the left (west), but continue straight ahead to the large red brick building housing the Big Timbers Museum. To the left of the Museum's main door is a metal historical plaque with extensive text. (The facility is open afternoons only.)

At a bit over 4 miles from the river bridge and DAR pull-out, traveling west on US 50 watch for a huge stone barn that lies about ½ mile south of the highway and is clearly visible across tilled fields. It forms part of a private ranch headquarters. This structure was built in 1891 with limestone hauled from the ruined walls of Old Fort Lyon a few miles upriver. The keystone in the giant arched door on the west end is inscribed: "1st C[avalry] 1860." Part of the tin roof is missing and the building is rapidly deteriorating.

BENT'S NEW FORT

At 7.5 miles from the Arkansas River bridge at Lamar, US 50 crosses the Bent-Prowers county line. One mile beyond the line is a gravel crossroad, SR 35. Turn left (south) and go 1 mile, where the road ends in a T. At this point look straight across the field directly ahead to a stone monument barely seen on a hill. That is the site of Bent's New Fort.

To get to the fort, turn left (east) at the T, drive .2 mile to the first road intersecting on the right (south) and follow it .5 mile to a wire gate on the right. Park at the gate, cross the fence and hike .2 mile to the site. Aim for a telephone pole on top of the hill and it will bring you to the monument. Around it are the stone foundations of the fort. A few feet north is a fine DAR marker.

The original Bent's Fort, completed by the Bent brothers and Cerán St. Vrain in 1834, was located about 30 miles west up the

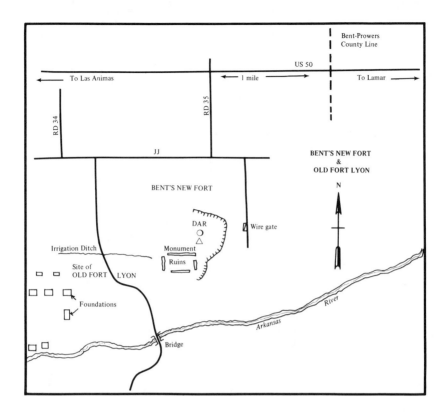

Arkansas. It was abandoned by the one surviving Bent, William, in 1849. The winter of 1852-53 he began building a new stone fort here in the Big Timbers on a bluff overlooking the Arkansas.

Like the earlier fort, the new one also served as a way station for SFT travelers, as well as a trading post and Indian agency. William Bent leased his fort and surrounding land to the army in 1860, which soon built a new post on the bottom land between the present monument and the iron bridge over the Arkansas just to the west. The army first called its establishment here Fort Wise, in honor of the governor of Virginia. In 1862 it was renamed Fort Lyon after Nathaniel Lyon, the first Union general killed in the Civil War. Following a flood in June 1867, this site was abandoned and Fort Lyon moved 20 miles upstream to its present site.

Return to the T and go straight ahead (west) to the first intersecting road from the left. Take it and start south toward the iron bridge over the Arkansas. At about ¼ mile, an irrigation ditch crosses the road. Stop just beyond it. In the distance to the left (east) can be seen the monument at Bent's New Fort. Fort Lyon was to the right (west). Across a plowed field about 200 yards, a slightly elevated pasture, resembling an island of grass, can be seen from the road. Extensive foundations of the fort remain in that area, including a row of eight buildings in line with the irrigation ditch, and between them and the ditch a string of low mounds representing the sites of sentinel boxes or stations. The SFT passed along the north edge of the fort, just above these stations. Stone bases of other buildings are in evidence to the south, extending down to the fringe of trees along the river bottom.

Return to US 50 and continue west about 4 miles. Watch for the McClave junction. At that intersection, SR 196 goes right and gravel county road 34 turns left (south). Hud's Campground is on the northwest corner. Turn south on 34 and at 1.9 miles, where the road curves right and starts down toward the bridge over the Arkansas, watch for a DAR marker on the left. It rests in an open field in the middle of excellent SFT ruts. Return to US 50.

TRAIL RUTS

At the community of Hasty turn left (south) off US 50 on paved road SR 260 leading to John Martin Reservoir, the largest in Colorado. The lake, completed in 1948 with the damming of the Arkansas, has destroyed sections of the SFT but one patch of ruts is nicely preserved.

At 1.8 miles south of Hasty SR 260 forks to the left and continues on to the dam and a campground. At the fork (with a wooden "Welcome to the Reservoir" sign in the middle of the Y) a dirt road goes straight ahead. (It is really the right fork of the Y.) Follow it and a short distance beyond a dirt road intersects. Turn right (west) and drive .1 mile to a small access road entering from the left (south). A wooden sign here calls attention to the SFT ruts. Follow the access road .2 mile to a fenced area with a turnstile at the entrance. Inside, a DAR marker sits upon faint SFT ruts.

Return to the Y and turn south ½ mile toward the dam on the paved road. Just before that road starts across the top of the dam, another road, leading to the picnic and camping area, intersects from the left. Take it. The road descends below the dam. Near the bottom it makes a curve to the left. As it does, note on the left a toadstool-shaped rock formation with a flat top. This feature was a prominent trail landmark known as Red Shin's Standing Ground. Stanley Vestal in his *The Old Santa Fe Trail*, pp. 234-35, tells how the rock got its curious name. In 1833 Cheyennes were camped on the river below. A warrior

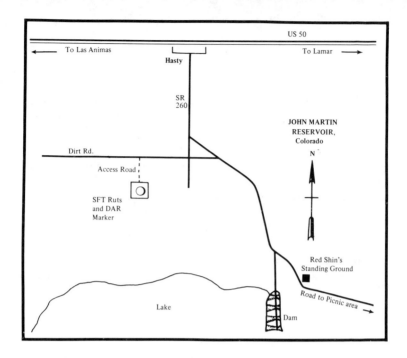

named Red Shin got in an argument with some of his tribesmen over a woman. The quarrel became violent and taking his weapons Red Shin fled to the top of the flat formation behind camp. His foes attacked him furiously but he successfully drove them off. Ever after the rock was known as Red Shin's Standing Ground.

This interesting site narrowly missed destruction when the John Martin Dam was built immediately to the west. In fact the location of Red Shin's rock had been lost until recently, when Paul Bentrup identified this formation as the one. From a pull-out, climb to the top and stand on the same spot where the Cheyenne warrior made his stand.

Return to US 50 at Hasty and continue west.

NEW FORT LYON

At the intersection of SR 183 with US 50 (6 miles east of Las Animas) is a sign pointing left (south) to Fort Lyon, now a VA hospital. At .5 mile on SR 183 is a gray granite DAR marker on the right (west) side of the road, just past a faint intersecting dirt road leading west into a field. In summer it may be hidden by weeds.

At 1 mile from US 50 is the fort entrance gate. Driving straight in through extensive grounds turn left at C Avenue. That street leads east.

The fort parade ground is on the right. A row of two-story houses on the left comprises the original officers quarters, now much remodeled, some of them dating back to the late 1860s. The middle house, in line with the flagpole in the center of the parade ground, was the commanding officer's house. Continue straight ahead past a main building with columns on the right. Behind this building is the Kit Carson Chapel with a steeple. The small structure was originally the residence of the post surgeon. An ailing Carson was brought here from his nearby home at Boggsville and died on May 23, 1868.

The upper two-thirds of the building was dismantled in 1957 and the stones used to rebuild it in the form of a chapel, so in fact the structure has little historical integrity. An explanatory sign is on the outside wall, and an inscribed stone brought from the site of Old Fort Lyon downriver is located to the left of the entrance.

Return to the junction of C Avenue and the entrance road (called Gate Street). Turn left (south) on Gate and follow it past the west side of the parade ground until it curves left to become A Avenue. To the right (south) of A Avenue are two large buildings of cut limestone, the best preserved original structures still standing. The one on the east (or left as you face south), Building 17, housed the commissary department. It has an incised stone in the west gable reading: "Capt. E. B. Kirk, 1867." The building on the west (right) was the quartermaster warehouse.

Return to US 50 and continue toward Las Animas. At about 2 miles west of the US 50 and SR 183 junction is a paved crossroads, County Road 13, marked by a small green street sign. On the northeast corner is a DAR marker.

Continue west. Nearing the eastern limits of Las Animas and approaching the Alpine Inn Restaurant, a DAR marker can be seen on the right (north) side of the highway.

BOGGSVILLE

Just past the Alpine Inn and before the bridge over the Arkansas River, SR 194 turns off US 50 to the right and goes 15 miles west (along the north bank of the Arkansas) to Bent's Old Fort. Before taking that road, however, continue south on US 50 across the bridge and down the main street of Las Animas. At the end of the street US 50 curves right and a block later intersects with SR 101. Turn left (south) on SR 101 and go about 1.5 miles to a Y. The left fork is 101, but take the right

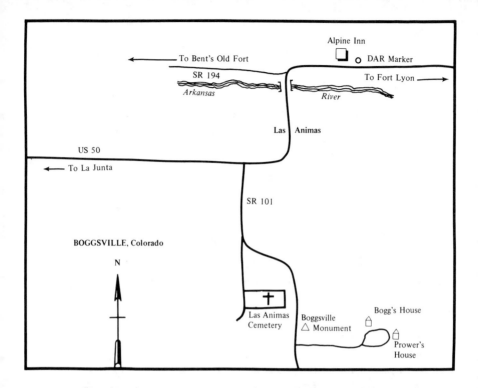

Alpine Inn

☐ ○ DAR Marker

To Bent's Old Fort ←

SR 194

Arkansas

To Fort Lyon →

River

Las | Animas

US 50

← To La Junta

SR 101

BOGGSVILLE, Colorado

N

✝

Las Animas
Cemetery

Boggsville
△ Monument

Bogg's House

Prower's
House

fork (really straight ahead), a gravel road that goes .5 mile south to the entrance of the Las Animas Cemetery on the left.

At the back righthand (southeast) corner of the cemetery, at the junction of the lanes marked 6th and South Drive and opposite the original iron-arch cemetery gate, is a stone column with an urn on top marking the grave of William Bent (May 23, 1809-May 19, 1869), one of the most prominent men associated with the SFT. From this point go north on 6th 1 block to the next intersection. On the right at the corner is the tall marble monument, also with an urn on top, for the grave of John Wesley Prowers (1837-84), who freighted for William Bent on the SFT and was later a station agent for the Barlow and Sanderson Stage Co.

From the cemetery go back .5 mile to the Y and take the other fork, continuing south on SR 101 another .6 mile to a tall concrete monument on the left (east) side of the highway. Thomas O. Boggs, long associated with the Bents and Kit Carson, settled here in the mid-1860s with local pioneer J. W. Prowers. The monument is titled "Boggsville" and gives the history of the place.

The U-shaped adobe house seen in the distance behind the monument belonged to Boggs. Behind that is the two-story house of Prowers, once a stage stop on the SFT. It is now boarded up and deteriorating badly. A road just past the monument leads to the houses.

Several hundred yards to the south, along the small Purgatoire River, Kit Carson and his family lived in a primitive house which is now gone. It was there that he became ill in 1868 and was taken to nearby Fort Lyon, where he died. Tom Boggs took the Carson children to live in his own house and was the executor of Kit's will. It is said that Boggs himself planted the huge cottonwoods that still grow around the house. At this writing (1986), the Boggsville site has been acquired by a local historical group which is making efforts to preserve it.

Return to the junction of SR 101 and US 50 on the south side of Las Animas. It is possible to turn left (west) here and follow US 50 to La Junta on the south side of the Arkansas. About midway to that place, at the Bent-Otero county line, is a roadside park on the left (south) side of the highway. It contains a wooden historical marker with extensive text on the "Big Timbers" and reference to the SFT.

However, this route will miss Bent's Old Fort, the pearl of the SFT. It is better at the above junction to turn right on US 50 and follow it to the north side of Las Animas where SR 194 can be picked up and followed west to the fort.

BENT'S OLD FORT

Bent's was the most renowned landmark on the Mountain Branch of the SFT. Many travelers wrote about it and its history has been ably presented by David Lavender in his book entitled *Bent's Fort*. The place was a private, not a military, post and served as a center for the Indian and fur trade. Faithfully reconstructed in the mid-1970s by the National Park Service, it is now a National Historic Site and one of the most exciting points of interest on the entire SFT. Here one can feel the pulse of trail days.

Approaching the grounds from the east on SR 194, the first entrance gate (now closed) is seen on the left (south). It is a large stone arch with "Bent's Old Fort" at the top. A DAR marker is at the left of the gate. Continue past it to the present entrance marked by a Park Service sign. This leads to a parking lot and another DAR marker which has a map of the fort incised on the granite surface.

At this point the imposing fort can be seen to the south in a loop of the Arkansas River. To preserve the historical atmosphere, visitors must leave cars here and walk a long path to the fort's front gate.

Inside Bent's Fort, near La Junta, Colorado.

Transportation is available for those unable to make the walk.

Approaching the main gate, the path passes the "Fort Cemetery" containing a historical marker. The only gravestone is that of Edward Dorris (d. 1865), but the plot contains twelve other unidentified burials. The cemetery was used after William Bent's abandonment of the fort and while the place was serving as a stage station.

Inside, the storerooms, shops and living quarters all have period furnishings. The Susan Magoffin room is furnished with the type of things she carried in her wagon and installed for her comfort during a brief stopover here in 1846. Two freight wagons, one an original and the other a replica, are also on display. In the summer season, persons in costume give demonstrations, and a mountain man rendezvous is held in the spring. A sales shop offers publications on the fort and the SFT.

LA JUNTA

From Bent's drive 8 miles west on SR 194 to La Junta and pick up US 50 on the east side of town. (Note: This La Junta is not to be confused with the historical La Junta at Watrous, New Mexico.) Passing through the center of town, at the railroad station (which will be on the right) turn left (south) on Colorado Street and go 2 blocks to 3rd Street. On the northwest corner is an unusual DAR marker on the Otero County Courthouse grounds.

From this marker go south to the Koshare Indian Museum located at 115 West 18th Street (at the corner of Santa Fe Street). This is the home of the famous Koshare Boy Scout dancers. The museum contains excellent exhibits of Plains Indian materials, some from the era of the SFT.

LA JUNTA TO TRINIDAD

On the west side of La Junta pick up US 350 which runs almost 80 miles to Trinidad. (No gas stations along the way.) It is a desolate stretch of road, but the country looks much as it did in trail times. The earliest wagon road stayed close to Timpas Creek, a short distance to the right (west) of the present highway. Susan Magoffin had much to say about this route.

A later stagecoach road followed parts of the highway or paralleled it on the left (east). Another, the Purgatoire Stage Road, coming from Boggsville, was 10 or more miles to the east. Some remains of stage stations are there (described by Long, *SFT*, pp. 193-200), but unfortunately much of the country east of US 350 has been condemned recently by the army for a military reservation. Thus the station ruins are no longer accessible to the public.

At a bit under 5 miles from La Junta, a DAR marker sits against the fence on the right (west) side of US 350. It is on the spot where the SFT crossed the present highway from east to west heading toward Timpas Creek. Ruts lie behind the marker. From this point on, watch for trail ruts to the west. Along here one soon gets a first view of the famed twin Spanish Peaks on the far horizon to the front right, about 70 miles away. They were a guiding landmark for trail travelers.

Approaching the ghost town of Timpas observe the Three Buttes (really three pointed hills) to the left (east) of the highway. The stage route of the SFT passed through a gap between them and the adjoining hills on the west side. Deeply eroded ruts ascend the gap. The Timpas stage station lay about ½ mile west of the present ghost town on the banks of Timpas Creek. Do not look for it, however, because no trace remains and the area is full of rattlesnakes in season.

At about 5 miles past Timpas, a DAR marker is located on the west side of US 350.

At 11 miles beyond Timpas, a section line road turns off US 350 to the left (east) and goes 1 mile to the Iron Spring Stage Station site. A metal sign in the form of a cow hangs on a red pipe post at this intersection. At .3 to .4 mile from the highway faint traces of the SFT cross the gravel road at a fence corner. Those with good eyes can see a DAR marker in the distance, about 200 yards to the southeast in the open pasture. The ruts are clearer near the monument, passing about 30 feet in front of it. It is an easy walk at a diagonal (southeast) from the fence corner to the monument and the ruts, through low grass.

Continue on the section line road and cross over a small bridge. Just past it on the left are two low stock tanks. To the right of them is a concrete box which caps the original Iron Spring. Water from the box goes underground to one of the tanks. Near it is the stone foundation of what was once the station's small fortified barn.

The adobe station itself is marked only by a very low mound of dirt around which are fragments of sun-colored glass. Stubs of fence posts to the left of the stock tank outline the original rectangular stage corral. A protective wall was built around the station soon after its establishment in 1861, but that did not prevent hostile Cheyennes from burning the place in 1864. This site is about 1 mile east of the main SFT, but an alternate route is said to have come down to the station through the saddle or gap at the end of the high bluff seen in the distance behind (north of) the Iron Spring. Please respect the property since it is on private ranch land.

Return to the highway and continue toward Trinidad to the nearly deserted town of Thatcher. It is about 45 miles from La Junta. At the only real intersection in the center of Thatcher turn right (west) on a gravel road, cross the railroad tracks and go .6 mile past a two-story deserted school. Just beyond the school is a small wooden bridge over Timpas Creek.

Stop on the bridge and look ¼ mile north down the dry creek bed to the mouth of a rocky canyon. There was located the major SFT landmark, Hole-in-the-Rock, a deep hole filled with water that was available even when the creek went dry. (This is the head water of Timpas Creek.) Susan Magoffin had much to say about it. The hole is now filled with sand. To the right of the bridge, about 30 yards behind the ranch house that is there now, is said to be the site of the Barlow and Sanderson Company's Hole-in-the-Rock Overland Stage Station. The ruined stone barn, seen rising above the corral complex adjacent to the house, is supposed to date from the 1860s which, if so, would make it part of the station facility. Margaret Long (p. 208), who interviewed old-timers in the first half of this century, speaks of a "fort" just north of the corrals which must have been for the protection of the stage personnel or possibly for use by military escorts or detachments. Could the ruined "barn" mentioned above have been part of the fort? Long also claims that the station was west of the present bridge (that is, to the left of the creek bed), which would place it, if she is right, in the vicinity of the palisade fence and old wooden barn that occupy the site at this time. Jesse Scott, Jr., tells me he has found signs of early occupation 40 to 50 yards north of that location. This SFT site, like many others, is in need of serious study.

Return to the highway and continue to Trinidad, keeping an eye on the looming Spanish Peaks just as wagon travelers once did.

TRINIDAD

From far out on the highway northeast of Trinidad can be seen flat-topped Fisher's Peak (originally called Raton Peak). It rises just to the left (east) of the entrance to Raton Pass and therefore served as a guidepost bringing wagon caravans to this important crossing of the mountains. Trinidad lies at its foot.

US 350 enters town from the east and becomes Main Street. This is the actual route of the SFT. Approaching the edge of downtown observe a two-story adobe house on the left at the southeast corner of Main and Chestnut Streets. This is the house of Don Felipe Baca, a rancher who was the principal founder of Trinidad in 1862.

Dating from 1869 (well within the trail era), the Baca House is now a museum containing furnishings recently brought from New Mexico. Directly behind it is the Pioneer Museum in an adobe building that was once the Baca servants' quarters. On exhibit is a hunting coat said to have been given to Kit Carson by a Cheyenne chief. (The Pioneer Museum is open only in the summer.)

Behind the Pioneer Museum on the southeast corner of the intersection of Chestnut and First Streets is a 1930s WPA building said to have been constructed to resemble Bent's Old Fort. If so, the resemblance is faint.

Continue west on Main Street two blocks to the intersection with Commercial. On the northwest corner is the old Columbian Hotel and on the outside wall near the door, facing Commercial, is a splendid metal plaque with an extensive text on the SFT.

Go one more block on Main and turn right (north) on Convent Street. That leads down to the railroad tracks and just beyond, after a curve, to a bridge over the Purgatoire (or Purgatory) River, which is in the vicinity of the old trail crossing. The street then passes under elevated I-25. Immediately past it turn north (right) on State Street and follow it about 6 blocks to Kansas Street. Turn right (east) 2 blocks to Kit Carson Park.

A fine archway is at the park entrance at the intersection of San Pedro and Kansas. On the hill in the center is a magnificent equestrian statue of Kit Carson showing the scout in mountain garb peering toward Raton Pass. Near the statue is the largest DAR marker on the SFT in Colorado.

SIDE TRIP TO STONEWALL

Persons who have been following the SFT journal of Marian Russell will want to make a side trip from Trinidad to her grave. Go west on SR 12 up the Purgatoire valley about 40 miles to the small community of Stonewall. Ask directions at the one store on the left.

Entrance to the local pioneer cemetery is through an unmarked wire gate (with a crosswire overhead) on the right (north) side of SR 12 about ½ mile past the Stonewall store, that is, just beyond the western limits of the community. The dirt road, which crosses an irrigation ditch just inside the gate, is merely two tire tracks leading up a hill ½ mile to a pine clearing. All the Russells are buried here and it is an inspiring place.

RATON PASS

From Trinidad take I-25 south over Raton Pass. This route, now so easy for automobiles, was a major obstacle for the wagon trains. At Exit 6 (Gallinas) is a DAR marker (just behind the Exit 6 sign). This marker is accessible only from the southbound lane of I-25.

Several miles beyond, just past the Wootton Exit watch for a little valley that opens on the right (west) side of the Interstate. A billboard-type sign facing the highway and placed by the Santa Fe Railroad reads: "Dick Wootton Ranch and Old Santa Fe Trail." In 1865 "Uncle" Dick opened a toll road for wagons over the pass. At his ranch he had an inn, stage stop and toll gate.

Remains of the ranch can be seen behind and down to the right of the sign. The large adobe barn was Uncle Dick's, but his two-story house was torn down by its owners in 1980 and a double mobile home is now on the site. Look left (south) up the valley as the Santa Fe Railroad tracks climb toward the summit and the New Mexico line. A good eye can discern traces of the SFT near the tracks.

Follow I-25 a mile or so to the summit and cross into New Mexico. Here at an exit to the right is a "Welcome Center." Drive to the parking lot at the small building of the New Mexico Motor Transportation Department. On the east side of the lot are an official New Mexico Historical Marker and a National Historic Landmark plaque, both commemorating the SFT and Raton Pass. An overlook at the west side of the lot allows a view across rough country to the west and north, the route of the SFT coming up from Wootton's Ranch. The twin Spanish Peaks are in the distance.

RATON

Upon pulling out of the Welcome Center lot at the Raton Pass summit, a wide view of the New Mexico plains opens to the south. Conspicuous in the distance is flat-topped Tinaja Peak (its name meaning "water tank" or "water jar"), a beacon for SFT caravans. The actual trail was on the other side of the ridge to the right of the highway. A little over 1 mile from the summit, a valley appears on the right (west) of I-25. The railroad tracks seen there are near the SFT route.

At 5 miles from the summit leave the Interstate at the first Raton exit (marked exit number 455) which puts you on old US 85. At 1 mile after crossing a large bridge is an official New Mexico Highway Marker, "Raton," with reference to the SFT. Entering the northern outskirts of Raton watch for a Texaco Station on the right. Opposite it on the left (east) beyond the railroad tracks is the site of Willow Springs Stage Station and ranch. There is no access across the tracks at this point.

A block past the Texaco Station (just beyond the Melody Lane Motel) is an intersection with a traffic light. The street joining from the right (unmarked) is Moulton. A black and white sign on a pole just above the traffic light reads: "Historic Old Raton Pass." The original SFT and an early auto road came down Moulton to the Willow Springs Station. (The route is described by Long, *SFT*, p. 234.)

For those wishing to follow that road back toward the summit, turn right on Moulton and go 4 blocks to the old Scenic Court where the street makes a sharp left, then bends to the right and starts up a switchback road to the top of the mesa. It is paved only about ¾ of the way up. There are no guard rails and the drive should not be attempted by the fainthearted.

The top of the mesa offers a beautiful view of Raton. The road winds on toward the Colorado line, where it ends with a fence across it. Return to the intersection of Moulton and US 85.

From this point continue south on US 85 about 3 blocks to a park and the intersection of 1st Street (which is also Highway 72). There turn left (east) and drive under a railroad overpass. Just beyond is an intersection where several streets converge. Turn left (north) and go 1 block. There the paved street curves to the right, but continue straight ahead (past a sign that reads "Dead End") on a gravel street that parallels the tracks. On the right at 545 Railroad Avenue is a white house with a sign, "Willow Springs," in the front yard.

The government established a forage station on this site about 1860. Stagecoaches began stopping here the following year when the U.S. Mail was re-routed over the Mountain Branch from the Cimarron Cut-off. By 1870 the stage station and ranch house was a four-room, flat-roofed log building. A portion of that structure is said to be incorporated in the present dwelling, which is a private residence. Behind it, the old Willow Spring, later dug out as a well, is capped and still flows.

Return to the junction of 1st Street and US 85 at the park, turning left (south) toward the downtown area. For the first block Ripley Park (named for the president of the AT&SF who donated the land adjacent to the tracks) is on the left. In the southwest corner of the park at 2nd and Savage is a DAR marker. (Although unrelated to the SFT, two other points of historical interest in this park are a pair of Civil War cannon brought from Rock Island, Illinois, in 1911 and an air porthole, installed in a stone monument, from the Battleship Maine, whose sinking in 1898 led to the Spanish-American War.)

At 1½ blocks south of the park on US 85 is the Shuler Theater on the left (east). It is two doors from the Raton Movie Theater. Entrance to the Chamber of Commerce is through the Shuler lobby, so the door is usually open. Near the ceiling of the lobby is a series of murals painted by Manville Chapman for the Public Works of Art Project in 1933-34. They depict scenes related to the SFT, including the Wootton Toll Gate, Willow Springs Ranch, Clifton Stage Station and Maxwell's Mansion in Cimarron.

Continue south through downtown and then watch for signs that will put you back on I-25.

CLIFTON HOUSE

At 8 miles southwest of Raton on I-25 take the exit at the intersection with US 64 to Cimarron and Taos. Leaving the intersection, cross a cattle guard. Just past it on the right is a turn-out containing a trash barrel. Stop here. Formerly, an official New Mexico Historical Marker, "Clifton House," was at this location. Recently, the marker was moved down the Interstate to a rest stop located 1 mile past the next (Tinaja) exit. A DAR marker is also at that location.

The site of the Clifton House is across the fence and pasture, ¾ mile to the west. It is about a 20-minute walk. Aim for the gap between the line of cottonwoods on the right and the high embankment of an abandoned railroad grade on the left. Once past the trees you have to jump across the Canadian River, which here is a narrow rushing stream. Ruins of the Clifton House are on a rise just beyond, near the railroad tracks. There are scattered foundation stones and, at last check, one piece of adobe wall rising about 10 feet.

For those not wishing to make the walk, the ruin can be seen from the highway. Go about 20 yards down US 64 from the turn-out and the Clifton wall can be seen through the gap with the AT&SF embankment directly behind it. It takes a sharp eye to pick it out, however. Binoculars are a help.

The three-story adobe Clifton House with promenade balconies around the upper levels was built between 1866 and 1870 by rancher Tom Stockton. It was located where the SFT crossed the Canadian River. The Barlow and Sanderson Stage Company soon leased most of the building for a "home station" where its passengers could get meals and stay overnight. Barns, outbuildings and a blacksmith shop were installed nearby. The food and lodging were considered the best along this section of the trail.

With advance of the railroad in 1879, the stage line was abandoned and the Clifton House closed down. In 1885 the fine mansion, whose woodwork and windows had been freighted over the SFT from Fort Leavenworth, was gutted in a fire believed to have been started by hoboes.

From the roadside pull-out look west past the Clifton House to Red River Peak, a high, rounded knob and the tallest mountain on the horizon. It was a well-known landmark for all SFT travelers.

CLIFTON HOUSE TO CIMARRON

A couple of miles beyond the Clifton pull-out, on US 64, the highway crosses the Canadian River, but there is no sign identifying it. Then the highway goes under a railroad trestle. Just beyond on the right begin the grounds of the National Rifle Association (NRA).

A sharp eye can pick out traces of the SFT paralleling the road. About ¼ mile off the highway, inside the NRA fence, is a SFT marker—a small New Mexico boulder with a bronze plaque attached. Surrounding it are four smaller stones from each of the other four trail states. The site is in the middle of the ruts of the SFT. Unfortunately, it is accessible to the public only on a single day in late June when the

NRA holds a ceremony here during its annual SFT Rendezvous. (See Appendix I.)

At high points along the highway in this vicinity watch to the left front for occasional glimpses of the silhouette of the Wagon Mound on the far horizon, 60 to 70 miles away. At 8.7 miles from the Clifton House pull-out is the Hoxie Junction, a mere Y in the highway on the bald prairie. The left fork, old US 85, continues down to Maxwell and rejoins I-25. The right fork, US 64, goes on to Cimarron. In the center of the Y is an official new Mexico Highway Marker, "Santa Fe Trail."

The Mountain Branch of the SFT divided in this area. The right fork stayed close to the foot of the ridge of mountains seen on the north and headed for Cimarron. Continuing west on US 64, ruts of this fork can be detected from time to time on the right. The left fork struck off across the rolling plain in a direct line for Rayado, a small community south of Cimarron. From the air these two forks are plainly visible as well as a number of crossovers connecting them at various points.

The next point of interest on US 64 is at the crossing of the small Vermejo River. Approaching two bridges here (the first is concrete; the second, over the Vermejo, steel), a paved road enters from the right (north). It leads to the now-closed coal mining town of Dawson. This road forks into a small Y as it joins US 64. Past the second bridge and just across the railroad tracks on the right are the remains of the ghost town of Colfax. A stage station is reported to have been at the Vermejo crossing.

Continuing west, at about 4 miles east of Cimarron good ruts of the SFT can be glimpsed on the left (south) side of the highway.

CIMARRON

Settlers, among them Kit Carson, first entered this area in the mid-1840s. Later Cimarron became the home of frontiersman Lucien Maxwell and headquarters for his 1.7 million-acre Maxwell Land Grant. He acquired the grant through his father-in-law Charles Beaubien, who had been an associate of the Bents. In 1870 Maxwell sold the grant to a group of investors. Afterward Cimarron became an outlaw hangout and the center of the bloody Colfax County War (1875-78).

As early as the 1850s, Cimarron was an important stop for wagon and stage traffic on the Mountain Branch of the SFT. A dozen buildings and sites associated with trail days can be visited. The Cimarron River divides the community into a new town and an old town. The trail sites are all in the latter, which has been declared a National Historic District.

Entering from the east on US 64 continue toward the center of

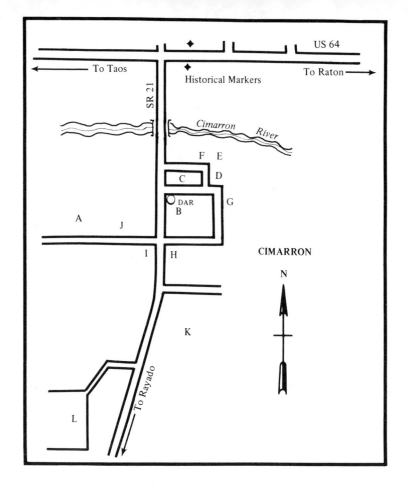

Cimarron to the junction with SR 21. Just before the junction are two official New Mexico Highway Markers, one on the right side of US 64 and the other immediately opposite on the left. Both refer to the SFT. Approaching this junction a sign reading "National Historic District" points left (south) on SR 21 to old Cimarron. Before following that route, however, turn north 1 block off US 64 and view a concrete statue of Lucien Maxwell, painted in enamel colors. It is in a park next to the small City Hall.

Go south on SR 21, crossing the rushing Cimarron River to the old part of town in the historic district. The SFT sites, all clustered within a small area, are listed below. Their locations can be noted by referring to the accompanying map.

A. Old Aztec Mill

A noted SFT landmark, it was operated as a grist mill by Lucien Maxwell between 1864 and 1870. Trail travelers bought flour here for the last push to Santa Fe, and Ute and Jicarilla Apaches were issued government flour rations, as Maxwell was their agent. The building is now owned by the CS Cattle Company, which allows the Cimarron Historical Society to operate it as a museum.

B. The St. James (Don Diego) Hotel

This two-story structure was built in the 1870s by the French immigrant Henri Lambert who once had been a chef for General Grant and President Lincoln. For a while it was a hangout for outlaws including the notorious Clay Allison. In the room that served as a saloon 29 bullet holes still show in the pressed tin ceiling. Buffalo Bill was once a guest. The hotel is now closed. A DAR marker is on the northwest corner of the block (adjacent to SR 21) behind an iron fence and hidden by bushes.

C. Site of the Maxwell Mansion

Across from the St. James to the north the entire block once held Maxwell's huge house, built about 1864 and burned in 1885. A modern brown frame dwelling now covers part of the site. It, like the original mansion, faces east toward the old plaza.

Maxwell's mansion was in two sections divided by an inner courtyard. Adobe and stone walls surrounded the rear section where the cooking was done and the many employees fed. A remnant of the original stone wall foundation can be seen at the southwest corner of the property, opposite the St. James.

Luxurious furnishings in the mansion were freighted over the SFT by Maxwell. There were two grand pianos and rooms filled with gaming tables and wheels. Maxwell's dinner table was open to all, and trail travelers took advantage of his hospitality. Many Santa Fe traders knew Maxwell or did business with him. His house has been called the "first civilized stop on the trail in New Mexico." (That was before construction of the Clifton House.)

D. Old Cimarron Plaza and Well

Maxwell's house faced the west side of the plaza. The SFT crossed the Cimarron River about 50 yards northeast of the plaza. Perhaps as early as the 1870s there was a log bridge over the river. It later burned. Wagons entered the plaza's open east end. In the center was a well, said to have been dug in 1871. It is now covered by a white well-house with a red roof. A SFT sign is nailed to an adjacent tree.

E. Dahl Brothers Trading Post and Warehouse

This long building runs along the north side of the plaza. Allegedly begun in 1847 or 1848, the structure has been extensively remodeled so that it is difficult to get any idea of its original character. However, it does contain some of the original adobe walls.

Lucien Maxwell house, Cimarron, New Mexico. (Neg. No. 102576, courtesy Museum of New Mexico.)

The history of the place is murky. Some sources claim that Maxwell first had a commissary on the site. Later it seems to have been occupied by the Dahl Brothers Company which owned 200 teams of mules and oxen. The firm made two wagon trips yearly between Cimarron and Westport. At various times sections of the warehouse served as a post office, jail, stage depot and office for the old *Cimarron News.* Fire destroyed part of the original complex toward the end of the last century.

Just behind the present building (now a private residence) is a well-preserved dugout in the river bank reputed to have been built by Maxwell's father-in-law Charles Beaubien. Local tradition credits it with being the first structure established on the site of Cimarron.

F. Grave Site

To the left (west) of the Dahl Brothers Trading Post under large trees are two graves of interest. Behind an iron fence lie Pabla Lovato Beaubien (d. 1864), wife of Charles and mother-in-law of Lucien, and Verenisa Maxwell (d. 1864), little daughter of Lucien. Before the lane now leading from the plaza west to the highway was created, the grave site was part of the Lucien Maxwell property on the south.

G. National Hotel

Located to the south of the plaza and behind the St. James, this building is reputed to date from 1854. It is thought to have become a hotel sometime after 1871. If so, it would have entertained trail travelers. Little is known of its history. Now it is a well-kept white building with bright blue trim. (Private residence.)

H. Meagers & Sanderson Stagecoach Line Office

This building recently served as a store but is now closed. I can find no historical reference to Meagers, but Jared Sanderson was of the stagecoaching firm of Barlow, Sanderson and Company which operated the Southern Overland Mail line on the SFT. In 1870 the firm is known to have maintained a station with a stocktender at Cimarron. Then it was the last major stagecoach company in the country.

I. Swink's Gambling Hall

Swink's was the most notorious gambling hall and saloon in northern New Mexico. It was originally built as a brewery in 1854. It saw service as a gas station in recent years but is now closed. An interesting bronze plaque giving a brief history is attached to the front of the building.

J. Original Colfax County Courthouse

Built in 1872, this one-story building now houses a Masonic Hall. It is on the right as one approaches the Aztec Mill.

K. Original Colfax County Jail

Also built in 1872. Past the Stagecoach Office on SR 21 is a trailer park on the left. Behind the park is the jail, a stone building with a pitched tin roof.

L. Mountain View Cemetery

Take the last gravel road to the right (west) on leaving the southern limits of Cimarron on SR 21. The cemetery was established in 1870. Of historical interest is the grave of Rev. F. J. Tolby, assassinated in 1875 during the Colfax County War.

From Cimarron a side trip can be made 55 miles across the Sangre de Cristo Mountains via US 64 to Taos and its SFT sites. Since the excursion requires an entire day, the trip is better made from Santa Fe, after completion of your main tour.

From the Cimarron Historic District go south on SR 21 toward the Philmont Boy Scout Ranch. Watch to the left of the road for ruts of the Cimarron to Rayado section of the SFT. In the open pasture to the right (west) of the road one may catch a glimpse of the Philmont's large buffalo herd. Most of the time it is hidden in swales near the foot of the mountains.

SR 21 goes through the center of the ranch headquarters. The huge Mediterranean mansion, Villa Philmonte, once owned by Waite Phillips who donated the ranch to the Scouts, can be seen on the left (east). Just past it, also on the left, is the library and museum named in honor of famed naturalist Ernest Thompson Seton (a founder of the

Boy Scouts of America), whose collections are housed here. The exhibits are open to the public. A DAR marker is in front of the facility near the road.

Just beyond Philmont, SR 21 climbs a hill and makes a curve to the left. In the hollow on the inside of this curve (that is, to the left) are deeply eroded SFT ruts that now form an arroyo. Continue on to the hamlet of Rayado, which is about 10 miles from Cimarron.

RAYADO

This small community was begun in 1848 by Lucien Maxwell and others on land belonging to his father-in-law Charles Beaubien. Kit Carson also had a farm and house here. In 1850 a small military post was established at Rayado (using Maxwell's buildings) to escort SFT caravans between Raton Pass and Las Vegas. Later the community was designated a "home station" by the Barlow and Sanderson Stage Line.

Deeply eroded SFT ruts sweep into Rayado from the northeast, joining the present SR 21 as it makes a right-angle turn on a hill and drops down to the town. Watch for the trail on the left at that point. This is the reunion of the two branches of the SFT that split back at the Hoxie Junction. When early stagecoaches came over this hill or ridge, the driver blew a bugle signalling the station ahead as to the number of passengers on board so that enough places could be set at the table.

Entering Rayado from the north, note the small, private Santo Niño chapel on the left (east). Directly across the road on the west is Lucien Maxwell's long adobe house with white wooden posts and railing on the veranda. It was begun in the early 1850s. Originally it had a flat roof. Late in the decade Maxwell moved north to Cimarron, where he built his larger mansion on the plaza. The Rayado house afterward came into the possession of Jesus Abreu, another son-in-law of Beaubien.

Just past the Maxwell house on the right and facing the road is a boarded-up building of brown stucco which has a red pitched roof. This was the combination stage station and store operated by Jesus Abreu.

Several hundred yards beyond, also on the right (west) side of the road, is the "restored" house of Kit Carson. The large building with interior courtyard incorporates some of the walls of the original, but the plan and design bear little resemblance to what Kit built. The place is operated as a museum by the Philmont Scout Ranch. Usually it is open during the summer only. Inquire at the Seton Museum and Library back at the ranch. A DAR marker is located in front of the Carson house. Inside are a stagecoach and covered wagon as well as other exhibits relating to the SFT. The wagon is reputed to have been used on the SFT by Cerán St. Vrain, a partner of the Bents.

About 1 mile south of the Carson house, SR 21 crosses Moras Creek. Looking to the right (west) note that a wide canyon forms a bay in the mountains. This is the gap mentioned by Commissioner George Sibley in 1825 as the one through which a "trace" or rough trail passed, then ascended Grulla Mesa and crossed the mountains to Taos. Pack trains heading for Taos rather than Santa Fe left the Cimarron Cut-off of the SFT at the Rock Crossing of the Canadian River, about 30 miles to the east, and steered for the Moras gap, visible in the distance.

Continuing on several miles, the main road makes a sharp turn to the left (east) and becomes SR 199. SR 21 goes south through a ranch gate and becomes a primitive jeep road. That is the route of the SFT as it threads its way around mesas to the Ocaté Crossing and eventually on to Fort Union. The jeep road, however, does not go as far as Ocaté. Stay on the main road, now SR 199, about 20 miles to Springer, back on I-25.

SPRINGER

Near the center of Springer on US 85, 2 blocks north of its junction with US 56, is the Santa Fe Trail Museum, lodged in the historic old Colfax County Courthouse. Few if any of the exhibits actually pertain to the trail, and the facility is only open in the summer.

To continue on toward Wagon Mound go south on US 85 to the outskirts of Springer and pick up I-25. The convergence of US 85 and US 56 at Springer brings together the Mountain Branch and the Cimarron Cut-off, at least for modern highway travelers. Originally the trail's arms at this point were still some miles apart, moving across country toward a union at La Junta (modern Watrous).

Here we drop back to the parting of the trail in western Kansas and describe a motor tour of the Cimarron Cut-off from Lakin through the Oklahoma Panhandle to Springer.

THE CIMARRON CUT-OFF

WAGON BED SPRING

From Lakin, Kansas, on the Arkansas River go south 28 miles on SR
25 to Ulysses. At the intersection of SR 25 and US 160 turn left (east)
about 3 blocks to the Grant County Museum, a large white building set
back on the left. It has excellent SFT exhibits with special reference to
the nearby Wagon Bed Spring site. From Ulysses continue south on
SR 25 another 11 miles or so to the highway bridge over the Cimarron
River.

The stretch between Lakin and the Cimarron represents part of
the infamous *Jornada* of trail days. This was the waterless section of the
SFT that caused so much trouble for the early caravans. Most travelers
mentioned it in their journals in doleful terms. Today with all the farms
supported by deep-well irrigation, it is difficult to visualize the country
when it was considered an uninhabitable desert, a place to be gotten

through quickly.

Just over 1 mile beyond (south of) the Cimarron bridge is a roadside pull-out on the right. It is at a high point on the highway giving a view of the twisting, tree-lined Cimarron River in the valley below. The Wagon Bed Spring, surrounded by trail ruts, is in this valley 2 miles west of the pull-out. There is a DAR marker near it, but the site is on private land and accessible only by a primitive road, not recommended for passenger cars. (Note: Those determined to search for the site should consult the USGS Kansas map, "Wagon Bed Spring Quadrangle.")

At the pull-out are three historical markers: an official Kansas Highway Marker, "Wagon Bed Spring," with extensive text; one of the new Mormon Battalion markers; and a bronze plaque on a small monument commemorating Jedediah Smith. It was at or near Wagon Bed Spring in 1831 that Smith, famed mountain man and explorer, was killed by Comanches. He was scouting for a wagon train and had ranged out ahead to find the Cimarron and water.

The name Wagon Bed Spring came into use in 1847 when someone sank a wooden wagon bed in the spring to collect the water and serve as a holding tank. Before that it was commonly referred to as the Lower Spring and was the first in a series of three that lay in the valley of the Cimarron. The next, the Middle Spring, was on the SFT upriver about 36 miles, and the Upper Spring beyond that another 18 miles. These springs were crucial because the river itself seldom had water in summer, at least along this section, and when it did the water was bitter with alkali.

MIDDLE SPRING

For those following the SFT on foot, it is possible to continue up the north bank of the Cimarron directly to the Middle Spring. By car, it will be necessary to take a roundabout course to arrive at the same spot.

From the Wagon Bed Spring pull-out drive south about 15 miles to the town of Hugoton and rejoin US 56, which was left in Dodge City. Go southwest on US 56 to Elkhart, almost on the Oklahoma border. The highway passes along the east side of Elkhart and at the one flashing traffic light intersects with Morton, the main commercial street. Turning right here will take you through downtown on the way to Middle Spring.

Before proceeding to Middle Spring, however, go beyond the intersection on US 56 for another couple of blocks past the white grain

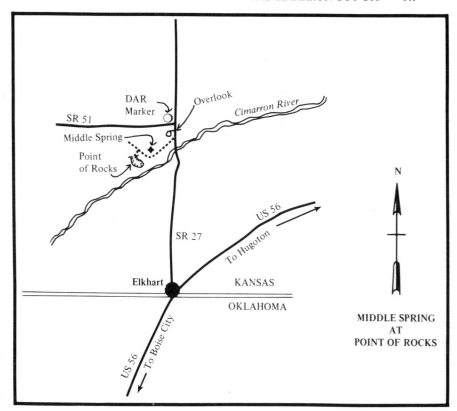

SR 51 · DAR Marker · Overlook · Cimarron River · Middle Spring · Point of Rocks · US 56 · To Hugoton · SR 27 · Elkhart · KANSAS · OKLAHOMA · US 56 · To Boise City · N

MIDDLE SPRING
AT
POINT OF ROCKS

elevator to a turn-out on the right. Here is the last official Kansas Historical Marker, "Point of Rocks & La Jornada," whose text deals entirely with the SFT. The Point of Rocks was a conspicuous landmark near the Middle Spring.

From the turn-out return to the intersection with Morton and take that street through the several blocks of the business district. Just past a park on the right, Morton ends in a T at Baca Street. Turn right on Baca and join SR 27 headed north toward Middle Spring at Point of Rocks. At 8 miles cross the Cimarron River. At .5 mile beyond the bridge a dirt road intersects from the left (west). It has a yellow cattle guard and leads to Middle Spring.

Before taking this dirt road, however, continue straight ahead on SR 27 another ½ mile to the crest of the ridge that is the edge of the Cimarron valley. There on the left (west) is a dirt road leading to a pull-out and overlook. At the site are a DAR marker and a "Cimarron

National Grassland" marker with extensive text on the SFT and Point of Rocks. From this spot one has a good view of the valley, the open grassland beyond on the south and the Point of Rocks, a prominent thumb of mesa that juts into the valley several miles to the west.

Return to SR 27 and go another .5 mile north to SR 51 which intersects from the left (west). A DAR marker, its inscription much weathered, is on the northwest corner. Now go back 1 mile to the yellow cattle guard and the road leading to Middle Spring.

At about 2 miles after leaving the paved highway and cattle guard a small road intersects from the right (north). Immediately after turning on it is another yellow cattle guard and just past it is the Middle Spring historical sign with excellent text. Just behind the sign the spring forms a pond surrounded by a grove of trees. There are several picnic tables.

Go back out on the main dirt road and turn west again toward Point of Rocks. At .3 mile from the Middle Spring intersection (or 2.3 miles from the highway) a small white metal sign on a wooden post can be seen about 50 yards to the left (south) of the road toward the river. The sign reads, "Santa Fe Trail," and has a picture of a covered wagon. It stands in the center of a wide band of ruts. At about 1.5 miles beyond this point, the road divides at a Y.

Take the lefthand fork a short distance to the top of Point of Rocks. At the parking area is an interpretive marker. The SFT passed between the foot of the bluff and the river. An excellent view is had of the Cimarron snaking its way southwestward about 5 miles where it clips the extreme corner of Colorado before dropping into Oklahoma.

Return to Elkhart and rejoin US 56 leading to Boise City (pronounced Boyce), Oklahoma.

THE OKLAHOMA PANHANDLE

Soon after entering the present state of Oklahoma, the SFT crossed to the south bank of the Cimarron River at a well-known site called Willow Bar. It took its name from a stand of willow trees growing on a sandbar in midstream. At that point the trail left the river, but for the next 20 miles or so it remained in the Cimarron "breaks," that is, the rough country composed of hills and mesas lying in the wide valley of the river.

The next campsite after Willow Bar was the Upper (or Flag) Spring, followed by Cold Spring and then the site of Fort Nichols. About 5 miles beyond the last place, the trail entered what is today the state of New Mexico. Unfortunately, all of these sites are on private

Dry bed of the Cimarron River in the Oklahoma Panhandle.

ranch land and none are easily accessible. However, several good markers and some fine trail ruts can be seen.

In the center of Boise City is the Cimarron County Courthouse. On the grounds on the north side is a new Mormon Battalion marker dedicated in the summer of 1983. At this location a highway with the combined numbers of US 286 and US 385 goes north. Follow it about 9 miles to a roadside pull-out on the left (west). There is a historical marker here commemorating J. C. Brown, the surveyor for the Sibley party of 1825.

The SFT crossed the highway at this point and ruts can be found on both sides of the road. Look northeast, across the highway, and observe prominent Wolf Mountain. Branches of the SFT passed around both sides of it, angling up from Willow Bar on the way to the Upper Spring. That spring lies about 1.5 miles due west of this location. Excellent ruts begin directly behind the pull-out, head west toward the railroad tracks, and continue beyond them. Even though the fine site at Upper Spring (or Flag Spring) is only a 30- to 45-minute walk away, persons not familiar with the country are apt to miss it.

Return to Boise City. On the west side of the courthouse square pick up a paved state road that leads to Kenton. At 15 miles, the paved road to Wheeless intersects from the left (south). That is the road which goes to New Mexico, but for the moment continue straight ahead another mile where the highway makes a sharp-angle turn to the right (north). At about 3.5 miles from the turn is a pull-out on the left (west).

Here is one of the choicest spots on this section of the SFT. There are no fences and the unspoiled prairie stretches toward the western horizon. The trail crosses the highway coming from Upper Spring and Cold Spring and heading for Fort Nichols, 7 miles to the southwest. An official Oklahoma Highway Marker refers to the founding of the fort in 1865 by Kit Carson. During its few brief months of existence it guarded this section of the trail from hostile Indians. A second handsome marker refers to Sibley's surveyor J. C. Brown. Behind the markers, heavy vegetation in the trail ruts appears as a discoloration in the prairie.

Return 4.5 miles to the Wheeless junction. There go south 1 mile where the paved road turns right and leads 12 miles west to the New Mexico border.

McNEES CROSSING

At 2 miles inside New Mexico from the Oklahoma border, the road reaches an intersection and stop sign. Here go west toward Clayton on SR 18. Because of the nature of this junction that means a lefthand turn.

At this point the SFT can be seen in the fenced pasture on the east (right). It is represented by a wide swale, or cut, that makes a conspicuous indentation on the horizon. In late summer, because of the extra moisture it collects, the trail depression is marked by a thick stand of bright green rabbit weed.

From the high ground at this intersection the Rabbit Ears, a renowned trail landmark, can be seen in the distance to the southwest. They are a mountain and a butte of unequal size lying close together, but from certain places on the trail they do vaguely resemble a pair of rabbit ears. One story, however, claims that they took their name not from their appearance but from Chief Rabbit Ears of the Cheyennes, who was killed in the vicinity by the Spaniards. In any case all travelers on the Cimarron Cut-off were familiar with the twin peaks which remained in sight for many days. The main SFT passed along their north flank, while a less-used alternate branch skirted them on the south.

From the intersection and stop sign go west on SR 18 for 2.4 miles to the highway bridge over the usually dry North Canadian River (called locally Corrumpa Creek). By this time the road has curved to the left and is heading south. At .8 mile past the bridge is a wire gate on the left (east) side of the highway. It is right on the SFT and by looking toward the western horizon traces of the trail can be seen disappearing in the distance.

The gate gives access to a two-track ranch road leading east across an open cow pasture .5 mile to McNees Crossing. This is private land, but the current owner allows entry, provided you CLOSE THE GATE BEHIND YOU! There are livestock inside. From the gate a windmill can be seen near the end of the ranch road and to the right of it is the white monument marking the crossing.

Go to the end of the ranch road past the windmill and right up to the large square monument. The road is okay for passenger cars in dry weather, but in the summer the center is high with weeds. Immediately to the southeast of the monument, a dirt ramp (the original trail) leads down to the crossing of the North Canadian.

Both upstream and downstream the bed is loose sand, but at this one spot is a rock shelf in the bottom of the river bed, making a natural and firm crossing for wagons. On the east and west banks can be found traces of caravan campgrounds.

From the monument or ramp look east across the North Canadian where tracks of two SFT branches can be seen coming down to the crossing, where they converge. The beginning of this short split was 8 miles or so back in the vicinity of Fort Nichols, Oklahoma.

In the autumn of 1828 two young traders named McNees and Monroe rode ahead of their eastbound caravan and stopped to take a nap at this crossing. Indians came up and shot them. When the caravan arrived, McNees was dead and was promptly buried on the spot. The wounded Monroe was carried on to the Cimarron where he died.

Josiah Gregg records an Independence Day celebration here on July 4, 1831, the first such observance in New Mexico. The white monument was placed by the American Legion in 1921 to commemorate that event. Return to SR 18 and continue south toward Clayton, keeping the Rabbit Ears in sight on the southwest.

THE CLAYTON COMPLEX

In 1964 New Mexico State Senator William Wheatley of Clayton was instrumental in having the "Clayton Complex" designated as a Registered National Historic Landmark. The Complex includes an assembly of SFT campsites and geographical features beginning at McNees Crossing and extending for about 35 miles southwest along the trail to the Round Mound. (A description of the various sites in the Complex is supplied by Brown, *SFT*, 1963, pp. 32-II to 35-II. Several, like the Turkey Creek Camp and the Rabbit Ears Creek Camp, are on private land and not easily accessible to the public.)

From McNees Crossing follow SR 18 south to its junction with US 56 at 4 miles east of Clayton. There turn right (west) on US 56. At .1 mile on the right (north) is a pull-out with an official New Mexico Highway Marker, "Rabbit Ear Mountain."

At .1 mile beyond the pull-out, also on the right, is a roadside park. It contains the Clayton Complex Registered Landmark plaque (set in a monument of lava rocks at the flagpole); an official New Mexico Highway Marker, "Trail Landmarks," at the entrance to the restrooms; and two old wagons. Continue west into Clayton.

In the center of town is the old Eklund Hotel, founded in post trail days by a Swedish-born Clayton pioneer, Carl Eklund. Although it is closed as a hostelry, the dining room has been restored in grand Victorian style and serves splendid meals.

At ½ block east of the Eklund take US 64 and US 87 that lead northwest toward Raton. At the city limits just beyond the Holiday Motel (one of only three in town) is an official New Mexico Highway Marker, "Clayton," with reference to the Cimarron Cut-off. It is in a pull-out on the left (south) side of the highway.

At 1 mile beyond is the Union County Feed Lot (on the right) with plenty of cows. Just past it is another official New Mexico Highway Marker, "Rabbit Ear Mountain," with an SFT text that is different from the one on the marker of the same title seen earlier east of Clayton. From this point is a good view of the Rabbit Ears just to the north.

At 18 miles from Clayton, US 64 & 87 goes through the small community of Mt. Dora. The large, rounded mountain from which the town takes its name lies to the right (north) of the highway. The SFT coming from McNees Crossing passed along its north side and then headed southwest to intersect the highway straight ahead.

At 5 miles beyond Mt. Dora is a roadside park on the right (north). Here, alongside its tracks, the Colorado and Southern Railway has erected a SFT marker (a bronze plaque set in a white monument) to mark the trail's crossing the tracks and the highway. Directly to the south and slightly west is the dome of Round Mound (today often called Mt. Clayton), a major trail landmark recognized by all wagoners. Travelers often scaled the summit for a view of the surrounding country. In his *Commerce of the Prairies*, Gregg has a lithograph showing the

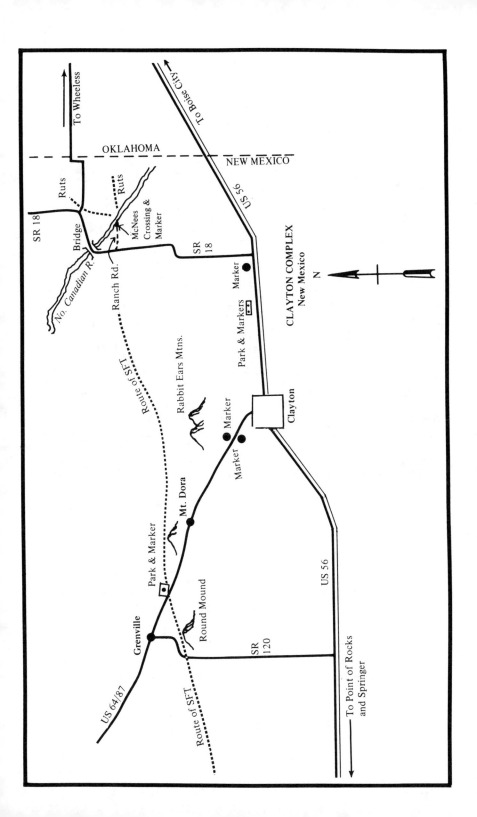

Round Mound, famous trail landmark west of Clayton, New Mexico.

view from the top with a wagon train passing below.

From the park and railway marker you want to rejoin US 56 which is some 20 miles to the south. The safest but longest way is to return to Clayton and pick up US 56 on the west side of town. If the weather is bad or threatening that course is recommended. In good weather you can continue ahead on US 64 & 87 another 3.5 miles to the nearly deserted community of Grenville. There dirt SR 120 intersects on the left (south) and leads 22 miles down to US 56. After a period of rain or snow the road, although dried out, may remain badly rutted. After turning onto SR 120 Round Mound is straight ahead.

At 2.5 miles from Grenville the road turns sharply to the right (west). At this point the SFT is off to the left of the road between you and Round Mound. The trail can be seen from the top of the Mound. Those wishing to make the climb park here. Allow at least half a day as the distance across the flat prairie to the base and the height of the Mound are deceiving.

At 2 miles from the first turn is a second one to the left (south), which takes the road along the west side of Round Mound. Soon after the second turn the SFT crosses SR 120 headed west, southwest toward the next major landmark, Point of Rocks. The crossing of the road is unmarked, however, and I have not located ruts. Continue south to the junction of US 56 (which is 29 miles west of Clayton) and turn right (west) toward Springer.

TO POINT OF ROCKS

At about 18 miles west of the above junction, US 56 crosses the western boundary of Union County into Colfax County. The line is marked. From this point look north to a long sloping mountain in the far distance. This is the 8,720-foot Sierra Grande which first became visible to wagon travelers as they crossed the Oklahoma Panhandle and remained a prominent landmark for many days thereafter.

From the same point also look north and west (to the front right of the highway) at the corner of a mesa jutting onto the plains. That is the dark outline of New Mexico's Point of Rocks. Caravans used it as a guide westward after passing the Round Mound. There was a fine spring at the site, but it was also a place Indians used for ambushes.

At 31.5 miles from the aforementioned junction is a roadside park with trees on the right (north). Here is an official New Mexico Highway Marker, "Point of Rocks."

A gravel county road, C 52, intersects with US 56 at the east end of the park. A power transmitter is on the northeast corner of this junction. Look north and a bit east of C 52 to a cluster of ranch buildings and trees seen about 5 miles away on the plain. The rounded mountain (behind and to the right of the ranch) with the outspreading mesa at its base marks the Point of Rocks.

For a closer look drive (in dry weather only) north on C 52 about 7 miles. Between 6 and 7 miles the deep swale of the SFT crosses the road. The Soil Conservation Service has placed low earth dams across the swale to check erosion. At 7 miles turn right (east) at the intersection onto C 53, go 2 miles, then turn left (north) 1 mile toward a ranch house near the base of the Point of Rocks. Anywhere in this area provides a closeup view of the site. The main SFT stuck to the flat plain about 1 mile to the south. Return to the park and continue west on US 56.

ROCK CROSSING OF THE CANADIAN

At 14.5 miles from the Point of Rocks roadside park look for an old, abandoned stone house that is a partial dugout with a weathered shingle roof. It is on the left (south) side of US 56, and a telephone pole is directly behind it. In this vicinity, the SFT coming from Point of Rocks crosses from the right to the left side of the highway although the ruts are not in evidence close to the road. (They can be seen, however, at another ¼ mile down the highway to the left.)

Stop here and look southwest past the house and down a natural trough between the mesas about 2 miles away. The mesas form the edge of the Canadian River valley which lies just beyond them. The river itself is at the bottom of the trough, marked by a line of trees. Here was the famed Rock Crossing of the Canadian (El Vado de las Piedras). A natural rock bottom at the ford (similar to the one seen at McNees Crossing on the North Canadian) aided the passage of wagons. The trail led down the trough to the river.

Once past the crossing the SFT forked. The main trail (the left branch) continued in a southwesterly direction to the Wagon Mound. The right branch, merely a pack trail, went due west to the vicinity of modern Rayado where it crossed the mountains to Taos.

The actual Rock Crossing is on a private ranch, accessible only by a jeep road. Thus visitors will have to settle for this distant view. (Stocking, *Road to Santa Fe*, pp. 210-13, gives a historical sketch of the site.)

Continue 8 miles on US 56 to Springer, where today's Cimarron Cut-off via the paved highway rejoins the Mountain Branch of the SFT.

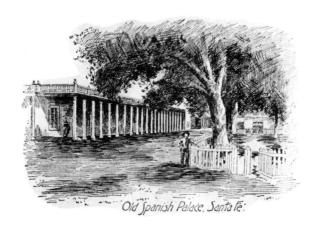

Old Spanish Palace, Santa Fe.

NEW MEXICO

WAGON MOUND

From Springer I-25 goes almost due south 26 miles to Wagon Mound. About halfway there, at the Colmor exit, the silhouette of the Wagon Mound becomes clearly visible on the horizon to the front-left of the Interstate.

Early Santa Fe traders thought the mountain's shape resembled a high-top shoe. Later someone decided the profile better resembled a covered wagon pulled by oxen, so the feature became known as the Wagon Mound. It was the last great landmark on the westward journey across the plains, in renown ranking alongside Pawnee Rock and the Rabbit Ears.

To the right (west) of the Wagon Mound are two elevations known to trail guides as the Pilot Knobs. The one on the left is a narrow flat-topped butte; the right one is a wider mesa. In former days the term "pilot knob" was applied rather indiscriminately to any natural feature serving wagonmasters as a point of reference. The Rabbit Ears and Round Mound, for example, were both referred to by some diarists as "pilot knobs." The SFT (like today's I-25) threaded a narrow, open pass between the foot of the Wagon Mound and the Pilot Knobs.

From a distance the Wagon Mound appears to rise alone and untrammeled from the plains, but drawing nearer one sees the small town by the same name that hugs its base. Approaching the community's one interchange look right (west) from the highway up Santa Clara Canyon, a deep indentation in the edge of the plains that stretch westward. At the head of this canyon, about 2 miles away, is Santa Clara Spring, now covered over and serving as the source of the town's water supply. Formerly the open spring was a rest stop for caravans and stagecoaches, its environs a favorite ambush site used by hostile Indians.

Upon taking the exit at the interchange, note the cluster of ranch buildings, including a large barn, to the right of the highway. Incorporated into the fabric of this complex are believed to be the walls of a later stage station that lay close upon the main trail, unlike the original station at Santa Clara Spring.

Coming off the exit turn left (east) and drive under the I-25 overpass. Immediately beyond note the marshy pond with reeds on the left behind the Texaco Station. It shows that water was fairly close to the surface in the immediate area and probably accounts for the placing of the stage station at the ranch site just across the Interstate.

Continue straight ahead ½ block (on SR 120 that leads to Roy) to the junction of old US 85. The same Texaco Station is on the northwest corner, facing US 85. In front of it in a tiny park area is an old wagon and two plaques set in a low red sandstone monument. One is the bronze marker designating the Wagon Mound as a National Registered Historic Landmark. The other shows William Becknell's first pack train over the SFT with the Wagon Mound in relief in the background. Made by the same sculptor who prepared a similar plaque for Pawnee Rock, this one was installed in 1971 on the 150th anniversary of the opening of the trail.

Cross US 85 and continue ahead on SR 120 through the town of Wagon Mound. After a couple of blocks turn right on Catron Street and go a short distance to the junction of Long Street. Here the municipal building is on the right. On its porch (we assume for safekeeping) is the displaced DAR marker for Wagon Mound. Return to SR 120 and turn right toward Roy.

Watch for the Wagon Mound school complex on the right at the

Wagon Mound, New Mexico.

edge of town. One of the oval SFT signs of the American Pioneer Trails Association used to be attached to the large school sign in the yard, but it has long since been stolen. Continue past the school out of town. Very quickly is a dirt road that leads to the right to two cemeteries at the base of the Wagon Mound. The cemeteries are easily seen from the highway.

Follow the dirt road to the entrances. The Protestant Hillside Cemetery is on the left. The Catholic Santa Clara Cemetery is on the right. In it is an extraordinary white marble tombstone of the SFT freighter Charles Fraker. Of mixed German and Cherokee ancestry, Fraker was closely involved with the Santa Fe trade during its last days. He married María de Luz (Lucy), a daughter of Manuel LeFevre, a French Canadian trapper who settled in Taos in the 1820s. (Another of LeFevre's daughters, Dolores, married Uncle Dick Wootton of Raton Pass fame.) The tombstone, somewhat damaged by time or vandals, shows a magnificent ox team and covered wagon in bold relief.

At this location the Wagon Mound towers overhead behind the

cemetery. From the high ground here, one can also look north and a bit east to observe the route (though not the ruts) of the Cimarron Cut-off coming from the Rock Crossing of the Canadian toward the Wagon Mound.

In May 1850 a war party of Utes and Jicarilla Apaches used this same vantage point to watch the approach of the Santa Fe-bound stage carrying ten men and the U.S. Mail. They concealed themselves behind the low rounded hill (an outlier of the Wagon Mound) which is just to the southwest of the cemetery. Then they dashed out suddenly for an attack. After a furious battle all the whites were killed and the stage destroyed. Days later a military patrol from Las Vegas found the human remains, scattered by wolves, and buried them. The Santa Clara Cemetery, established many years later, may well have been placed on the site of that earlier burial.

Return to SR 120 and turn left back toward the town. At a high point in the road before reaching the school complex look in the distance to the west (straight ahead) for a good view of the Santa Clara Canyon, the site of its spring surrounded by trees. At the interchange rejoin I-25 headed toward Fort Union and Watrous.

Just beyond Wagon Mound ruts of the SFT lie to the left between the highway and the railroad tracks. From the air they stand out boldly but at ground level from the Interstate they are more difficult to see.

About 13 miles from Wagon Mound, exit at the Fort Union Rest Stop on high ground to the right. In this little roadside park are an official New Mexico Highway Marker, "The Santa Fe Trail," and a DAR marker, the latter moved here a few years ago from the vicinity of Colmor. In the lobby of the visitors' building is a small SFT exhibit containing a map and historical photographs.

About a mile beyond this rest stop is another one in the eastbound lane of the Interstate. There is no crossover, so it is not accessible to westbound travelers. At that stop is another DAR marker (moved here from its original location west of Watrous) and an official New Mexico Highway Marker, "The Mormon Battalion.".

About 1 mile beyond that rest stop the main SFT crosses from the left to the right side of the Interstate. For the next 8 miles, paralleling the highway on the right is one of the longest stretches of ruts to be seen anywhere. They are unsurpassed.

At a high point about 2 miles beyond the last rest stop the country falls away in a vast sweep providing a spectacular vista rimmed by mountains in the distance. The eye can follow the trail as it leads down to Watrous (marked by a far clump of trees) to the front, left. It is possible to pick out a secondary trail that breaks off and heads to the right toward Fort Union. For the past few miles the wooded Turkey Mountains have been visible to the right of the highway. Beyond them the Mountain Branch of the SFT follows their western flank on its way to Fort Union and to its original junction with the Cimarron Cut-off just beyond at Watrous.

FORT UNION

Approaching the interchange on the north side of Watrous, SFT ruts can be seen on both sides of I-25. Exit here for Fort Union. At the end of the off-ramp turn right onto SR 477 for the 8-mile drive to Fort Union.

At about .5 mile after entering this road, a small grassed lane intersecting from the left leads down to the small Tiptonville cemetery. Stay on the highway and at .7 mile a narrow gravel road intersects from the left. Follow it .5 mile where the road bends sharply to the right. The ghost town of Tiptonville begins here.

At the bend in the road, a residence, which may be occupied, lies straight ahead. To the left of it is a large adobe and rock quadrangle, once the Tiptonville store and reputedly a stage stop. The structures in the quadrangle are well-preserved. It is private property, but a good view of two sides of the complex can be had from the road.

Just as the road makes its bend, the ruined walls of a house are close by on the left. This was the residence of William Tipton (1825-88) who came over the SFT and was prominent in the territory during the Civil War and after. He was a son-in-law and business partner of trail figure Samuel Watrous. Settling 2 miles north of his in-laws, he founded Tiptonville on the trail leading down from Fort Union. His large two-story house burned in 1957.

After making the bend to the right continue a short distance just past a large cottonwood on the right. Immediately inside the fence is a dirt bank and behind it are the ruins of the old Tiptonville Masonic Lodge, whose membership included soldiers from Fort Union. Just past the lodge on the left side of the road but almost hidden back in the trees are the remains of the Rev. Thomas Harwood's Methodist mission school, built in 1869. After his arrival on the SFT, Harwood became a circuit preacher using Tiptonville as his headquarters.

Continue straight ahead past other deserted buildings until the road ends in a T. Turn right and go ¼ mile to rejoin SR 477. There turn left toward Fort Union once again. Very quickly notice a deep cut

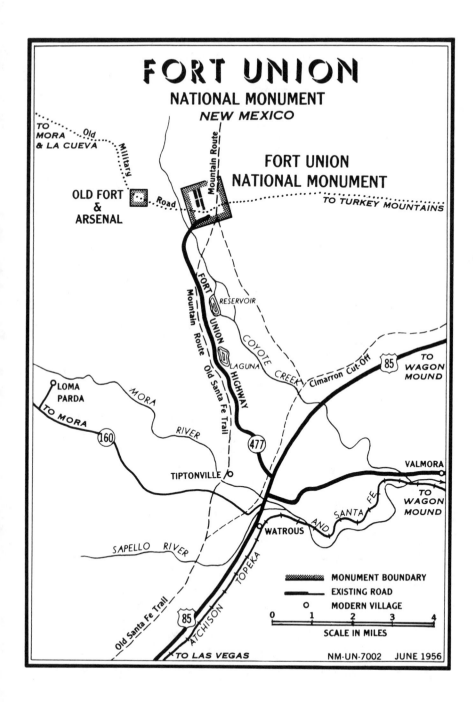

in a low ridge to the right of the highway representing some of the many SFT ruts in this area. A network of alternate trails led from Fort Union to Tiptonville and Watrous and from here on traces can be observed on both sides of the road.

SR 477 ends in the parking lot of Fort Union National Monument. The approach to the fort and the site itself offer superlative views of a landscape that has experienced only minor changes since the days of the wagon caravans. The Monument is one of the most exciting places along today's trail. Herds of antelope can often be seen grazing on the surrounding plains, and rangers warn visitors, at least in the summer, to watch for rattlesnakes. There is so much to be seen that several hours should be allotted for a tour.

A small but excellent visitors' center and museum provide an introduction to the fort and its history. Publications relating to the site and to the SFT are also offered for sale. The National Park Service personnel are extremely helpful.

The long self-guided tour around the parade ground and through the ruins is furnished with interpretive signs and audio speakers. At the rear of the fort, a marker calls attention to the ruts of the Mountain Branch of the SFT coming down from the northwest side of the Turkey Mountains.

Fort Union was established in 1851 to replace Santa Fe as military department headquarters because the New Mexico territorial capital was regarded as "a sink of vice and extravagance." Soldiers from the new post patrolled the western end of the SFT to protect it from the kind of Indian raids that had led to the stagecoach massacre at Wagon Mound in 1850. The army also maintained a large quartermaster depot from which military supplies, freighted over the SFT, were dispersed to forts all across the Southwestern frontier.

Over the years three separate forts were constructed. The first was located about a mile west of the visitors' center. Look across the open plain and its few scattered ruins can be seen near the foot of a long wooded ridge. A ranch road leads to that site, but permission to visit it should be obtained at the Monument headquarters. That first fort was the one described by Marian Russell in her trail memoirs as in part having palisade walls. For those traveling with her book in hand reread her vivid account of life at Fort Union.

A second installation, the "Star Fort," was begun on the plain east of the original post in August 1861. An earthwork in the form of an eight-pointed star, it was built to repel a Confederate attack which never materialized. The location is west of the visitors' center and is well-marked on the walking tour.

The third and last site of Fort Union, begun in 1863, adjoined the Star Fort on the north. The ruins of its large adobe and stone buildings form the central feature of today's Monument. Arrival of the railroad in Watrous in 1879 lessened the fort's importance, but it was not closed until 1891. This is one trail stop worth visiting again, particularly to catch some of the fort's special summer events when reenactment groups in period uniforms put on exhibitions.

Return via SR 477 to the interchange at I-25.

WATROUS (LA JUNTA)

Cross I-25 on the overpass, following the sign pointing to Watrous, and enter upon old US 85. Soon after note that the highway is lined with huge black willow trees. Homer Hastings, former superintendent at Fort Union, informs me that the original cuttings were brought in wagons over the SFT by Samuel B. Watrous, who arrived in this area in 1849 and built a large adobe store and residence.

That structure is incorporated now in the beautiful white building with a pitched roof that serves as the Doolittle Ranch headquarters. It faces US 85 on the left about ¾ mile from the I-25 interchange. Watrous traded with soldiers from Fort Union and travelers on the SFT. One of his daughters, as noted, was married to William Tipton, founder of nearby Tiptonville, and another wed George Gregg, manager of the Sapello Stage Station (described below). Watrous and his son died mysteriously in the mid-1880s, probably murder victims.

Just beyond the Watrous/Doolittle house, US 85 crosses bridges first over the Mora and then almost immediately over the Sapello River. To the left of the highway, the two small streams come together at what the Spaniards called La Junta, meaning The Junction. That name became doubly applicable later when the Mountain Branch and the Cimarron Cut-off of the SFT united nearby to form once more a single trail on the final stretch to Santa Fe.

About 1 mile north and west up the Mora, British-born Alexander Barclay, a former employee of the Bents, built an adobe fort that served as a major stopping place on the SFT and a relay station for the Independence-to-Santa Fe mail. The ruins were washed away in a flood in 1904, and the site, now on a private ranch, is not open to the public.

By the late 1840s persons eastbound for Missouri had begun using the La Junta area as a rendezvous site where travelers camped until a caravan large enough to insure protection could be formed. Here officers were elected and regulations adopted that would govern the

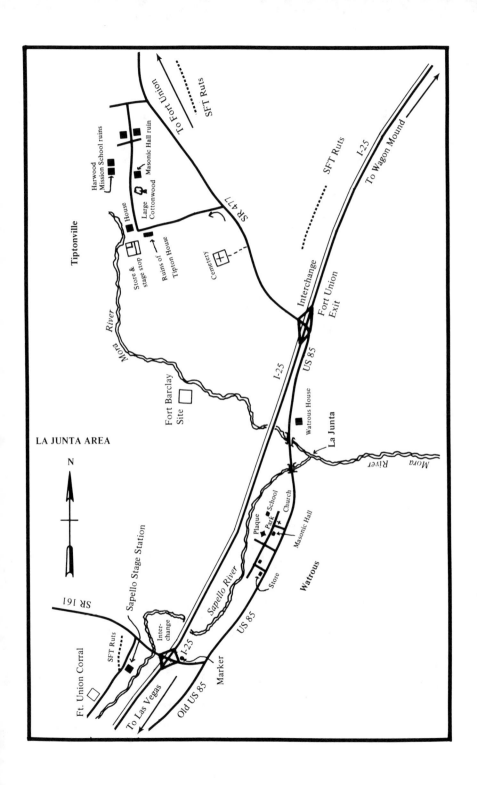

LA JUNTA AREA

N

Tiptonville

Harwood Mission School ruins
Masonic Hall ruin
Large Cottonwood
House
Store & stage stop
Ruins of Tipton House
Cemetery

Mora River

To Fort Union

SFT Ruts

SR 477

I-25

SFT Ruts

To Wagon Mound

Interchange

Fort Union Exit

US 85

Fort Barclay Site

Watrous House

La Junta

Mora River

Sapello Stage Station

SR 161

SFT Ruts

Ft. Union Corral

Inter-change

I-25

Sapello River

US 85

Plaque
Park
School
Church
Masonic Hall
Store

Watrous

Marker

Old US 85

To Las Vegas

wagon train on its trip to Independence. In this respect La Junta was the counterpart of Council Grove, the main rendezvous point on the eastern end of the trail. When the AT&SF tracks reached this vicinity in 1879, the railroad changed the name of the small community that had grown up from La Junta to Watrous. It did so mainly to honor Samuel B. Watrous, who is said to have donated land for the right-of-way, but also because there was already another place called La Junta on the main line in southeastern Colorado.

Continue on US 85 a short distance to the tiny community of Watrous. The few businesses and residences are all on the right side of the road. Turn onto the second dirt lane that intersects the highway from the right. Go 1 block toward the park. On the right pass a tiny church built by Reverend Harwood from Tiptonville and said to be the oldest Protestant church still standing in New Mexico.

The lane ends in a T at the untidy park. To the right see the deserted WPA-built Watrous school. It once had an American Pioneer Trails Association SFT marker on the front, but it has been stolen.

Turn left on the gravel street. To the right in the park is the Registered National Historic Landmark plaque for La Junta. Across the street from the plaque is the abandoned Masonic hall with a beautiful stone front containing an arched doorway and windows. Like the one in Tiptonville, it included among its original members soldiers from Fort Union.

Continue straight ahead on the street running in front of the park for another 2 blocks to the old livery stable. It is at the corner on the left. The fading word "Horseshoeing" can be seen across the front. According to one report, the building also once contained a saloon. Now deserted, it is deteriorating badly and may soon collapse.

Turn left along the south side of the livery building and go 1 block to rejoin US 85. At that intersection on the right is the old Schmidt and Reinkens General Store, now an antique shop. It postdates the SFT but is a nice stone structure worthy of a look.

Turn right (south) on US 85 and go a mile or so out of town to the second Watrous interchange on I-25. (The first was back at the Fort Union exit.) A new official New Mexico Highway Marker, "Watrous," is on the right. There go under the overpass and enter SR 161 to Las Golondrinas. Go ½ mile or so to the first gravel road that intersects the paved road from the left. Turn onto it. Ahead and to the left see a newly stuccoed house with a pitched roof and stone chimney.

This is the Sapello Stage Station once operated by the Barlow and Sanderson Stage Company as a "home station" where coaches made half-hour meal stops. The manager, George Gregg, must have sold alcohol as well because the place was known locally as Gregg's Tavern. In 1868 a stage driver got into a fight with the station employees and was stabbed to death. A private residence now, the station is well-preserved.

Across the road on the right beyond the fence good trail ruts lead close to the station. The actual union of the Mountain Branch and Cimarron Cut-off is believed to have been at the Sapello Crossing in the valley behind the station.

Drive straight ahead on the gravel road .3 mile past the stage station to the Fort Union Corral on the right. It is a large enclosure of native stone. The corral is reported to have been built after the arrival of the railroad in Watrous. Army horses were off-loaded from stock cars and were held here briefly before being driven the 8 miles or so to the fort.

Return to the interchange and continue on I-25 south toward Las Vegas. For the first several miles after rejoining the Interstate watch for SFT ruts along the high ground to the right.

LAS VEGAS

About halfway between Watrous and Las Vegas, Hermit's Peak can be noted in the range of mountains that fill the horizon on the west. It is the tallest peak in the chain, hump-shaped with a sheer face of exposed pink granite. The color is evident only in the early morning hours when the slanting sun strikes it.

The peak is named in honor of Giovanni Maria Augustini (or Agostini), the hermit whose cave at Council Grove has already been described. He arrived in Las Vegas in 1863 with a freight caravan of the Romeros, who with the Bacas were one of the two leading merchant families of the town. Augustini reputedly performed a number of cures and miracles, but the crowds he was attracting caused him to flee to the flat-topped mountain 14 miles east of Las Vegas and take up the hermit's life once more. He remained there three years and then headed for southern New Mexico where he was murdered in the Organ Mountains near Las Cruces in 1867. A few pilgrims from the Las Vegas area still climb Hermit's Peak to visit a shrine honoring Augustini.

About 4 miles from Las Vegas, I-25 curves to the left so that it is heading almost due south. Along here the wide valley of the little Gallinas River begins to parallel your route on the right (west), forming a trough between the highway and the foothills of the mountains beyond. In the valley were the well-watered meadows (*las vegas* in

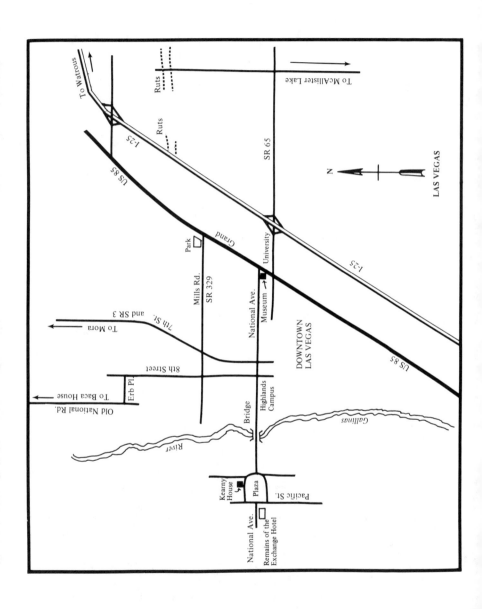

Spanish) that gave the area its name. Here SFT caravans camped to give their stock a good feed and rest before braving the pass through the mountains on the last leg of the trip to Santa Fe.

Until 1835 there were no permanent settlers in the area, the first New Mexican town encountered by the wagoners being San Miguel on the Pecos, 20 miles farther on. But about 1835 a group of San Miguel residents took up residence in the grassy valley and Las Vegas was on its way.

There were actually two small communities, or plazas. The first, Upper Plaza, was on an eastside bench above the Gallinas, while 2 or 3 miles downstream on the west bank was the Lower Plaza, the one that now lies near the center of the modern city of Las Vegas. Sometimes, wagon trains that had no business in either plaza skirted the valley on the east (to the left of I-25) and swung west through Kearny Gap south of the present city.

Entering the northern limits of Las Vegas, take the first exit off I-25 and continue toward the city on old US 85, which parallels the Interstate. At the first major intersection, Mills Road (which is also SR 329) joins US 85 from the right (west). There is a park here on the right with a locomotive on display.

Turn right (west) on Mills, go .8 miles to the intersection of 8th Street (the first street past McDonalds), and turn right (north). After 1.9 miles on 8th a small street called Erb Place intersects from the left (west). Go west on Erb 1 block to Old National Road (a dirt street) and turn right (north) 1.1 miles to the José Albino Baca house.

It is located on the left (west) side of Old National Road. At the entrance a mailbox reads: Bottorff, Rt. 1, Box 505. Visitors will have to view the building from this entrance because it is a private residence not open to the public. Baca, a prominent SFT trader, built a large three-story adobe mansion in the 1850s for his family and for the headquarters of his freighting and mercantile business. Only about half of the second story remains. The house has been much remodeled in recent years. Along the road and around the rear of the house is a beautiful stone wall, inside of which SFT wagons once parked.

From this site it is possible to look north up Old National Road .2 mile to a church that faces on the Upper Plaza. That area is now neglected and decaying. Return to 8th by driving east from this plaza on a poor dirt road and turning right (south). Thereafter, take any of the main cross-streets turning left (east) that lead from 8th over to 7th Street.

At 7th Street (which is also SR 3) you may elect to turn left (north) and make a 60-mile roundtrip to SFT sites at La Cueva and Mora. If

Don José Albino Baca residence near Las Vegas, New Mexico, 1937. Photo by Ina Sizer Cassidy. (Neg. No. 11254, courtesy Museum of New Mexico.)

not, then turn right (south) on 7th toward the center of Las Vegas. After describing the trip to Mora, our narrative will pick up again at this point.

SIDE TRIP TO LA CUEVA AND MORA

Several miles north of Las Vegas, SR 3 crosses the small dam that impounds Storrie Lake. At about 5 miles after leaving the dam is a pull-out on the east (right) side of the highway. It contains an official New Mexico Highway Marker, "Hermit's Peak." From this spot there is a good view of Hermit's Peak directly to the west.

Behind the pull-out immediately to the east are superb ruts of the old Mora-to-Las Vegas wagon road. This trace may be regarded as a branch of the SFT. Some caravans coming from the states left the main SFT in the vicinity of Fort Union and struck almost due west 15 miles to the town of Mora, located in a bay or valley of the Mora River at the

José Albino Baca House, Las Vegas, New Mexico, after extensive alterations.

eastern foot of the Sangre de Cristo Mountains. Mora was then an important place, a distribution center for communities lying in the high country beyond and a producer of surplus farm products, particularly wheat. From Mora the caravans would turn south to Las Vegas, their route completing two sides of a triangle with the main SFT from Fort Union to Las Vegas forming the third side.

Just beyond the Hermit's Peak pull-out, SR 3 tops a ridge and starts down into a small valley. A wide swath of fine trail ruts, some deeply eroded, stretch along the east side of the road. Watch for them along the highway from this point on. At about 10 miles from the Hermit's Peak pull-out the ruts are exceptional, first on the right side of the highway and then crossing to the left.

After another 2 miles, SR 160 to Watrous intersects SR 3 from the right (east). The eye can follow SR 160 as it leads through a gap in a ridge of hills about a mile away. The Mora River also flows east through this gap. Fort Union at this point is approximately 12 miles due east. The road from there traversed the gap, following the north bank of the

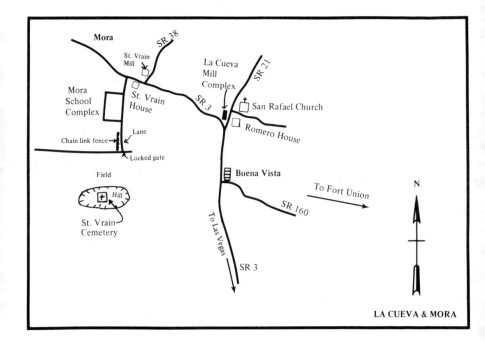

LA CUEVA & MORA

river, on its way to La Cueva and Mora. From SR 3 can be seen the deserted adobe buildings of the ghost town of Buena Vista strung along the river bank for quite a distance. All remain private property.

At 3 miles beyond, SR 3 forks to the left as it enters the Mora Canyon. The righthand fork is SR 21 to Ocaté. At this junction, in the center of the Y, are the magnificent ruins of La Cueva Mill.

An extensive stone-and-adobe complex includes the well-preserved mill with its wheel and race, store building, storage structures and a large stone-walled corral behind. The site is part of the William Salman Ranch. It is private property and access is prohibited. However, a great deal can be seen from the road and the complex is a photographer's dream. A sign facing SR 21 gives a brief history.

Shortly after the opening of Fort Union in 1851, Vicente Romero established a ranch at La Cueva to grow grain and forage for the new post. At one time Romero controlled some 33,000 acres, much of it in the bottomlands along the Mora River. He developed an intricate system of irrigation to water his vast fields of wheat and corn, and it is said that engineers came from Europe to study his techniques. His mill, using machinery freighted over the SFT, supplied a huge quantity of

St. Vrain's Mill, Mora, New Mexico.

flour to Fort Union, from which it was distributed to other military posts in the Southwest. Although the sign says the mill began in the 1870s, it probably was in operation by the 1850s or at the latest the 1860s. Today this is one of the most interesting and scenic places on the entire SFT.

Directly across the road from the mill, that is, on the east side of SR 21, it is possible to see through the trees the rear of Vicente Romero's large two-story adobe house. Now authentically restored, it is a private residence and the headquarters of the Salman Ranch. A long double veranda with white trim runs across the front of the building, but it is not visible from the highway. (By continuing up SR 21 a short distance past the mill and taking the road intersecting from the right that leads down toward the abandoned San Rafael Church—an adobe structure with pitched roof and arched windows now open to the elements—it is possible to look to the right before getting to the church and catch a glimpse through the trees of the front of the Romero house.) Soldiers from Fort Union were frequent guests at the many parties given by the Romeros when the house was a center of social activity.

From La Cueva continue west on SR 3 about 5 miles to the town of Mora. A revolt against the newly-established American rule that began in Taos and resulted in the death of Charles Bent there, spread across the mountains to Mora early in 1847. Eight members of a SFT caravan were killed here, including L. L. Waldo, a younger brother of traders William and David Waldo. In retribution, the American army leveled the town with artillery.

In 1855 Cerán St. Vrain, noted SFT figure and longtime associate of the Bents, moved to Mora from Taos and started a store and mill. The only three points of SFT interest in town relate to him:

A. St. Vrain Mill

Drive to the center of Mora on SR 3. Just past the new post office, which is on the left side of the road, SR 38 to Guadalupita intersects from the right (north). Turn onto 38 and go 1 block to cross the Mora River. Just beyond the bridge the highway curves and on the left is the large three-story stone St. Vrain mill. It is boarded up but still roofed and from the front looks to be in fair condition. Major cracks seen at the rear, however, indicate that the beautiful building is in a precarious state.

The mill is thought to have been started in 1855. At least one account suggests that the initial mill was a frame structure that afterward burned, the present stone building, which replaced it, being built in 1864. In any case, the St. Vrain mill as it now stands is an impressive sight. Like the La Cueva mill downriver, it furnished flour to the quartermaster at Fort Union.

B. St. Vrain Residence

Return 1 block to the intersection of SR 38 and SR 3. Turn right and stop immediately. On the left (south) side of SR 3 is the St. Vrain residence, unmarked. It is a long adobe building with lavender stucco. The room in the extreme east end is a store. Next to it on the left is a bar and beyond that on the east the post office. A wing extends back along the west side so that the building now appears to be in an L-shape. Probably when St. Vrain lived there (he died in 1870), the other two sides were enclosed in good New Mexican style to form an open courtyard or *placita* in the center.

C. St. Vrain Family Cemetery

Continue on SR 3 west for 2 blocks to the entrance of the Mora Schools on the left (south). Enter and follow the road that leads down the east side of the school complex. Behind the last building a primitive lane continues south along a chain link fence about 100 yards. It ends at a locked wire gate. From this point the St. Vrain family cemetery can be seen to the south ¼ mile beyond a field and atop a knoll.

Shrub oak surrounds the plot, which is enclosed by a waist-high chain link fence. Two of the tall white monuments are visible from the wire gate. You will have to climb through or over the gate and walk to the site. Cerán's grave is in the center of the little cemetery surrounded by those of his family. Just outside the fence on the north side is a marker for Colonel George W. Cole, 2nd US Cavalry.

Return to Las Vegas via SR 3.

LAS VEGAS TOUR CONTINUED

Follow SR 3 (7th Street) into the center of Las Vegas. At the intersection of National Avenue turn left and go east on National several blocks to the intersection of Grand (US 85). On the southwest corner (to the right) in the stone municipal building is the Rough Riders Memorial and City Museum. In front is a green and white "SFT Point of Interest" sign.

Although not directly related to the SFT, the museum is worth a visit. Teddy Roosevelt recruited members of his famous Rough Riders unit from this area to fight in the Spanish-American War. For many years Las Vegas held an annual Rough Riders Reunion. The collection contains mementos of the unit as well as other historical artifacts.

From the museum a swing can be made east of Las Vegas to view excellent ruts approaching the town. Go south on Grand 1 block to a main intersection with University Avenue. Turn left (east) on University, which becomes SR 65, and after crossing over I-25 go another 1.2 miles to a crossroads with sign that points south (right) to McAllister Lake. But turn north (left) on a dirt road (dry weather only). Between .8 and 1 mile, a wide band of SFT ruts winding across the plains from the east crosses the road. Return just over 2 miles to the junction of SR 65 and I-25. Turn right at the first on-ramp and join I-25 going north. At just over 1 mile are two sets of ruts intersecting the Interstate on the right. The first set is a shallow depression, and the second, about 25 yards beyond it, has been eroded to become a gully. The trail here is an extension of that just seen 2 miles to the east. The view at this point overlooks the Gallinas valley and Las Vegas.

Continue north another .6 mile to the off-ramp at exit 347. At the bottom turn left and go west to rejoin US 85. Follow it south once more to the City Museum at Grand (US 85) and National.

Go west on National to the intersection of 8th Street and the beginning of New Mexico Highlands University campus. Continue straight ahead through the campus 3 blocks to the bridge over the small Gallinas River (often containing little or no water). Here National Avenue is on the exact route of the SFT as it heads for the river crossing and the old Lower Plaza just beyond. On the northeast bridge abutment at about knee-level is an inscription commemorating stagecoaching on the SFT. The northwest abutment is dedicated to the Coronado Expedition, which crossed the Gallinas River in this vicinity in 1541. The southeast abutment has an inscription honoring General Kearny and his march over the SFT.

Cross the bridge and continue 1 block west to the historic Las Vegas plaza. A DAR marker is in the park facing you as you enter the plaza area. To its right in the northeast corner of the plaza is a tall petrified log to which is attached a wooden marker with historical text containing reference to the SFT. That marker is the replacement for a fine bronze plaque honoring General Kearny that was stolen several years ago and, according to reports, thrown into Storrie Lake by vandals.

The most historic building on the plaza is the cream-color, flat-roofed adobe with white trim located in the row of units along the north side at numbers 210 to 218. It is now known as the Dice Apartments. This house is believed to be the one used by General Kearny on August 15, 1846, as a platform from which he read a proclamation annexing New Mexico. After his march over the SFT from Bent's Fort, he camped on the ridge to the east where the Highlands campus is now and from there he went to the plaza for the ceremony. He and the alcalde (town mayor) used a ladder to climb to the flat roof from which Kearny spoke to the townsfolk assembled in the plaza below.

West of the Dice Apartments, almost in the middle of the block, is the renowned Los Artesanos Book Shop. Specializing in fine Western Americana, it always carries a good stock of SFT books. Past the bookshop on the northwest corner of the plaza is the newly-refurbished and reopened Plaza Hotel. Begun in 1880 soon after the arrival of the railroad and closing of the SFT, it played host to numerous dignitaries in the past.

On the west side of the plaza, National Avenue exits in the middle of the block. Entering National, empty buildings are on the left. This is the site of the Exchange Hotel, built in 1850 by Dr. Henry Connelly and a partner named Mitchell. Connelly was heavily involved in the Santa Fe trade. In the first year of the Civil War he was appointed territorial governor. With the advance of the Confederates in early March 1862, Connelly and other officials fled Santa Fe for Las Vegas, where they set up a temporary capital in the Exchange Hotel. After the Battle of Glorieta later in the month the seat of government was returned to Santa Fe.

Behind the hotel on the west a large corral served SFT travelers. Stagecoaches also stopped here and used the livery facilities. A narrow wing of the hotel ran along the north side of the corral, its rooms facing on present National. The Exchange survived until 1959 when a fire destroyed the main building facing the plaza. However, part of the wing behind escaped damage and is now used for storage. It is a small building with pink stucco and brown trim, bordering the street.

Take Pacific, which leaves the southwest corner of the plaza and drive south through a residential area 1 mile to the intersection of US 85 (Grand Street). Turn right and go south to an official New Mexico Highway Marker, "Las Vegas," with reference to the SFT on the right. From there follow US 85 to its junction with I-25. An on-ramp straight ahead leads to the Interstate. However, instead of taking the Interstate at this point veer left under the overpass and beyond it turn right (south) at the sign pointing to Mineral Hill.

This is SR 283 which for the next mile parallels the Interstate on the right. During this mile look across the Interstate to the west and ruts of the SFT can be seen close to the base of the hills heading down toward Kearny Gap from Las Vegas. SR 283 makes a loop and passes over the Interstate pointing west toward Kearny Gap, a natural pass in the high ridge ahead.

Approaching the gap, ruts of the SFT curve toward it from the right. Through it went the main route of the SFT, used by General Kearny and his troops in August 1846. Before Kearny's time, the gap was called Puerto del Norte (North Pass) to distinguish it from the Puerto del Sur (South Pass), which is about 2 miles farther south and is now threaded by I-25.

Once through the gap note an abandoned iron bridge to the left (south) of the highway. Just over the bridge the old road climbs a low ridge. At its top Spanish or Mexican settlers once had a *torreon*, a round defensive tower, to defend access through the pass. Kearny left a detachment of troops here to protect his rear, and later a small

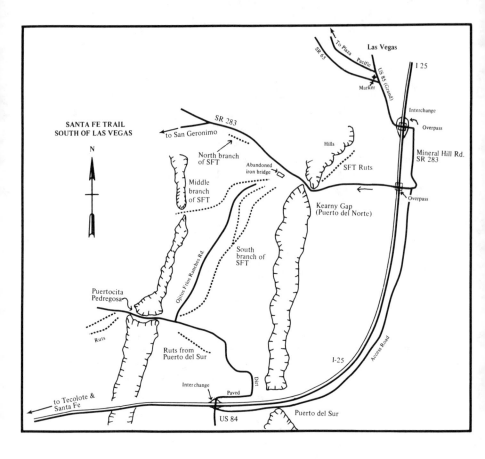

permanent military post was placed somewhere in the immediate vicinity. It remained to guard the gap until Fort Union was established in 1851.

From the iron bridge look to the left rear (southeast) and a small section of a stone wall can be seen in the grassy field several hundred yards from the road. It marks all that remains of the Kearny Gap stage station. Traces of a stone corral said to run up the sloping hillside behind the station were reported to have existed a few years ago, but I am unable to find them. Why this station was needed so close to Las Vegas is something of a puzzle, although one early account claims it was used by coaches and express riders who wished to skirt the town by taking a shorter trail passing a mile or so to the east of it, a route that entailed crossing the Gallinas River just opposite the mouth of Kearny Gap.

Just inside Kearny Gap, the SFT split into three branches, which are clearly shown on Lieutenant George Wheeler's geographical survey map of the mid-1870s:

A northern branch followed the present road to the little village of San Geronimo, where it struck off over the mountains almost due west. After passing through the community of Las Colonias it emerged on the Pecos River at the modern town of Pecos, there to rejoin the main trail. Even though it was much shorter, this must have been a very difficult route for wagons, and I suspect it was a trail favored mainly by pack trains. Traces can still be seen from the highway as far as San Geronimo.

The middle branch led from Kearny Gap in a southwesterly direction up a long valley but very quickly veered to the right, crossing through a small pass in the long wooded ridge on the west. From the pass it circled around the north side of distant Tecolote Mesa on its way to the village of Tecolote.

The south branch, probably the main route of the SFT, started by paralleling the middle branch. Where that trail turned west through the pass, the south branch continued on up the valley another mile or so to the Puertocita Pedregosa (Little Rocky Gate), a better pass leading to Tecolote.

Ruts of the middle and south branches can be seen in profusion by looking to the southwest from inside Kearny Gap. From the air these ruts are visible as a wide fan leading from the Gap. Because of fences they are not accessible by car at this point, but they can be approached by an access road farther up I-25. From Kearny Gap return and rejoin I-25 going to Santa Fe.

PUERTOCITA PEDREGOSA

South of Las Vegas I-25 makes a sweeping curve to the west and passes through the Puerto del Sur along with the AT&SF tracks, which can be seen to the left. This was a secondary route for still another branch of the SFT. It was used by a portion of Kearny's army in 1846, although as indicated the main force went through the gap 2 miles north that now bears his name. Once inside the Puerto del Sur, the SFT branch moved off in a northwesterly direction to join the main trail at the Puertocita Pedregosa.

To reach the Puertocita, exit at the Santa Rosa interchange just beyond the Puerto del Sur. Turn right on a paved road that starts back toward the east, parallel to the Interstate. Shortly it turns to the left (north) and becomes a bumpy dirt road that may give trouble to some low-slung autos. This road makes a couple of curves before pointing west toward the Puertocita.

Approaching the mouth of the gap, a road intersects from the right (north). This junction is about 2 miles from I-25, and there is a sign here reading "Ojitos Frios Ranches." This is a new subdivision road in good condition, and it can be followed north almost two miles to the vicinity of Kearny Gap. Along the way excellent ruts of the middle and south branches of the SFT can be viewed.

Back at the junction continue west into the Puertocita, which is a winding canyon for about ½ mile or so. As you exit on the west side well-defined ruts are on the left, leading off in a southwesterly direction toward the flat-topped Tecolote Mesa, which is clearly visible in the distance. From this point return to I-25 and continue on toward Tecolote and Santa Fe.

TECOLOTE

From the re-entry onto I-25 to Tecolote is about 5.5 miles. Near the beginning of this stretch at a high point in the highway a break in the trees and an open valley on the right provide a panoramic view of the distant mountains to the north. Hermit's Peak appears as the most prominent elevation in the chain. From this perspective it presents the outline of two huge tilted and connected blocks, quite unlike the shape observed from the plains approaching Las Vegas.

For the next several miles Tecolote Mesa looms closer at hand on the right. The main SFT coming from the Puertocita passes around its southern end and draws near the route of the Interstate in the last mile or two before reaching the village of Tecolote.

Leave I-25 at the Tecolote interchange, turn right at the end of the exit ramp, cross a cattle guard and turn left to follow a dirt road that leads 2 blocks to the plaza. An interesting white adobe church faces the plaza. Opposite it an old, unpaved highway goes toward Tecolote Creek. On the corner of the plaza and this road is a DAR marker, behind a wire fence and inside the yard of a deserted adobe house.

Tecolote (which means "owl" in Spanish) retains the historical flavor of an earlier day. Readers of Marian Russell's journal will recall her account of the trading post she and her husband operated here after he left service at Fort Union. (Hobart Stocking says he saw their building being demolished in the late 1960s.) In the latter trail days, Tecolote was maintained as a U.S. Army forage station. It is said that large stables and a headquarters building were in evidence as late as the 1930s.

BERNAL

Another 5 miles on I-25 leads to the Bernal interchange. Exit, then turn left and cross the overpass. Just beyond, the road ends in a T. Turn left (east) and go 50 yards or so to a clump of junipers on the right (south) side of the road. Here is a DAR marker, easily missed.

To the right rear in the distance is Starvation Peak, properly called Bernal Hill. It is actually a flat-topped butte. Legend claims that a band of travelers, either colonial Spaniards or Santa Fe traders depending upon which version you accept, was attacked by Indians and fled to the summit where they starved to death after a long siege. The tale is probably pure fiction.

A SFT stage station was in the vicinity of nearby Ojo de Bernal (Bernal Spring), but its exact location is open to debate. By continuing east past the DAR marker, the village's interesting church can be visited.

SAN MIGUEL DEL VADO

Continuing toward Santa Fe on I-25, at about 5 miles from Bernal are a pair of rest stops on either side of the Interstate. The one for eastbound travelers contains an official New Mexico Highway Marker, "Starvation Peak," with a brief text. It is not accessible to westbound travelers.

At the next interchange (Exit no. 323) leave I-25 and turn left (south) on paved SR 3 to San Miguel, which is about 3 miles south of the Interstate. Entering the village, the large adobe church with its twin towers is on the right (west).

The community was begun in the mid-1790s and the church started in 1805. Although the church has been remodeled many times, the outline of the facade remains basically the same as it was in 1846 when SFT traveler Lieutenant J. W. Abert captured it in a watercolor. Near the church door at ground level is a bell whose casting indicates that it was made in Ohio in 1861. It was freighted over the SFT to San Miguel del Vado. According to popular belief, it was one of the last bells cast in the East before foundries were converted to the making of cannon at the outbreak of the Civil War. (A bell with a similar inscription, now in the Catholic Church at Belen south of Albuquerque, apparently was brought over the SFT at the same time.) Also on the bell note the name of the priest, Don Juan Guerin, and the names of the two *padrinos*, literally, the godparents, who were sponsors of the bell.

In the initial years of the Santa Fe trade, San Miguel del Vado was the first New Mexican community encountered by caravans arriving from the States. William Becknell received a warm welcome here in 1821 on his inaugural journey. During the Mexican period, San Miguel was a port of entry where the Missouri merchants had their first dealings with Mexican customs officials.

The SFT forded the Pecos River just east of the main plaza. (*Vado* means "ford" in Spanish.) The village with its several hundred inhabitants had a defensive plaza, that is, contiguous adobe houses forming a large rectangle with an open area in the center. A single gate could be closed during Indian attack. Just past the church SR 3 cuts through the center of the old plaza. Many of the houses have disappeared but enough remain to outline the original rectangle.

Behind the church area are the ruins of a number of stone and adobe houses (outside the plaza area) which date from trail days. Standing at the entrance of the church look straight ahead (due east) across SR 3 to a small lane that leads down to the Pecos a block away. Traces of the ford can still be seen.

Return to I-25.

SAN JOSE DEL VADO

Several miles up the Pecos River was an alternate ford for the SFT at San José del Vado. It was on a small cut-off that was shorter, but the approach was rougher. San José began to assume more importance as San Miguel declined after 1835. In that year, it will be remembered, Las Vegas was founded farther east so San Miguel was no longer the first community encountered by incoming wagon trains.

At about 1.7 miles from the I-25/SR 3 interchange the Interstate crosses a bridge over the Pecos River. On a bluff overlooking the west bank of the river to the left (south) of the highway is scenic San José, a tight cluster of red rock buildings. Gaining access requires a bit of doing.

Continue on another .7 mile and take the San Juan/San José exit no. 319. Then take a right on the old highway to go .5 mile back toward the river to find the entrance road to San José. On the way pass the Pecos River Campground on the left (north) side of the road. Behind the campground are ruts which may be the SFT.

San José was built around a fortified plaza like San Miguel, but more of the houses survive here and the arrangement is clearer. A large church, post-dating the SFT, is in the center of the plaza.

Follow a road that leaves the southeast corner of the plaza. About a block later, a DAR marker can be found on the right side of the road. When Margaret Long published her guidebook in 1954, this was the main highway. Continue on several more blocks to the abandoned steel-girder bridge over the Pecos. This may have been the site of the original wagon ford, but I have not been able to determine that with certainty.

Return to I-25.

Ruins of Church at Pecos in 1846

PECOS

At San José begins the Glorieta Mesa (sometimes called Rowe Mesa), whose towering escarpment will remain close by on the left for the next 20 or 25 miles. Maps of the 1870s show that the SFT (by that date often labeled the Fort Leavenworth Road) roughly followed the route of present I-25 and the AT&SF tracks which are to the left. The earlier SFT probably took this same path since the country to the right is very rough, broken by arroyos leading down to the deep canyon of the Pecos.

At just over 11 miles from the San Juan/San José interchange leave I-25 at the Rowe/Pecos exit no. 307. Take SR 63 leading toward Pecos National Monument. Within a mile or two, SFT ruts can be seen to the left of the highway, where the cutting and clearing of piñon timber has left a grassy pasture.

At about 3.4 miles from the exit ramp of I-25, SR 63 passes the headquarters of Greer Garson's Forked Lightning Ranch. It is on the right (east) side of the road, a salmon-colored adobe building with bright blue trim. Near the corner of the front porch, next to a blue wagon wheel, is a DAR marker. An ox yoke hangs from the top of the porch. Since this is a private residence, the marker must be viewed from the highway.

The modern headquarters is on the site of and incorporates some of the original walls of Kozlowski's Ranch and Stage Station. Martin Kozlowski, a Polish immigrant, entered New Mexico after 1846. Later he acquired this site on the SFT and put up a ranch and barn using materials scavenged from the ruined Pecos mission and Indian pueblo one mile away. Meals provided to stage passengers by his wife, including fresh trout from the Pecos River, were said to be the best on the western end of the trail.

Just past the ranch house SR 63, crosses a bridge. Kozlowski's Spring, the reason for his locating here, can be seen on the right, down in the creek bed against the north bank. (We should note too that Kozlowski's was also site of the Union headquarters in late March 1862, when the Blue and the Gray fought the Battle of Glorieta several miles to the west.)

At .6 mile ahead is the entrance to Pecos National Monument on the left (west) side of SR 63. Extensive Indian ruins are to be seen and the remains of a huge Spanish colonial mission church. Pecos was located on the east side of Glorieta Pass and stood at the gateway to the plains. It has a long and fascinating history, beginning with a visit by members of the Coronado Expedition in 1541. It was a major landmark on the SFT, mentioned in practically all trail journals, including those of Josiah Gregg and Susan Magoffin.

Excellent publications on Pecos are available at the visitors' center. One such is a book by Alden C. Hayes, *The Four Churches of Pecos.* Therein on page 62 is an aerial photo of the site showing ruts of the SFT leading up to the mission. The ruts are across a field behind the Ranger headquarters. Special permission must be obtained to visit them as that area is normally off-limits to the public. A film shown in the visitors' center deals, in part, with the SFT.

Continue north on SR 63 to the center of the modern community of Pecos. At a Mobil station on the right, SR 50 intersects from the west. Turn left onto it and immediately on the right is an official New Mexico Highway Marker, "Pecos," with reference to the SFT. Follow winding SR 50 toward Pigeon's Ranch and stage station.

PIGEON'S RANCH

At 4.3 miles from the junction of SR 63 and SR 50 is a roadside pull-out on the right. Close to the pavement is an official New Mexico Highway Marker, "Glorieta Battlefield," with text on the Civil War battle that occurred in this vicinity on March 28, 1862. The conflict is often described as the Gettysburg of the West.

Union troops advancing from Fort Union on the east and Confederates coming from Santa Fe on the west both followed the SFT. The battlefield lay athwart the trail. Set in a boulder behind the marker is a red marble plaque placed on the centennial of the battle by the Texas Daughters of the Confederacy. To the left of the marble plaque is a bare inset square where the National Park Service on the same anniversary bolted a bronze plaque designating the battlefield as a Registered National Historic Landmark. Like so many other markers on the trail, it has been stolen by mindless vandals.

At .5 mile beyond, on the right side of SR 50, are the remains of Pigeon's Ranch. Only three adobe rooms (adjacent to the highway and behind a steel guard rail) survive of what was once a 23-room complex. In 1985 the State Highway Department announced plans to move the road 50 yards to the south, away from the historic building. Mounded ruins are behind the building and the stone footings of a corral are attached on the west end. A porch across the front, now gone, bordered the SFT. Weathering caused the north wall of the structure to fall in April 1983, but emergency repairs have assured survival, at least for the time being.

In the 1850s Alexander Valle, of French background from St. Louis, established a combination ranch and SFT hostelry on the site. According to an often-repeated story, he was nicknamed Pigeon because of his fondness for "cutting the pigeon wing" at fandangos. That explanation has recently been called into question. In any event, the place was universally referred to as Pigeon's.

During the Battle of Glorieta, the ranch alternately changed hands between Union and Confederate forces. Briefly it served as a makeshift hospital and bodies of dead soldiers were stacked to the ceiling in one room. Most of the fighting occurred in the open area to the west, beyond the present highway bridge and on both sides of the road.

In June 1864 Kit Carson spent a night here telling stories of his exploits to members of the Doolittle Commission, a United States Senate investigative body sent West to study the condition of the Indians. However, for reasons not readily apparent few latter-day SFT travelers mentioned stopping at Pigeon's.

Pigeon's Ranch, Glorieta, New Mexico, June 1880. Photo by Ben Wittick. (Neg. No. 15782, School of American Research Collections in the Museum of New Mexico.)

TO JOHNSON'S RANCH SITE

At 1 mile beyond Pigeon's, SR 50 reaches an interchange that leads back onto I-25 to Santa Fe. The high point on the Interstate directly ahead is the unmarked summit of Glorieta Pass. There the highway curves to the left. Traces of the SFT are hidden in the trees on the left.

At 5 miles from entry onto the Interstate is Cañoncito at Apache Canyon. Here blasting for the AT&SF and I-25 has widened what was once a narrow wagon gap on the SFT. Governor Manuel Armijo fortified the gap in August 1846 with the intention of opposing Kearny's advance on Santa Fe, but he abandoned the position before any hostilities could take place.

As I-25 passes out of the gap take the off-ramp at exit 294. Turn right and drive past the small, quaint Cañoncito church with its bright red roof. You are now heading back toward the mouth of the gap, parallel to the Interstate.

Continue past a green stucco house down to the bottom of the hill where a dirt road intersects from the left. At this intersection on the left is an old corral which is adjacent to the site of the Johnson's ranch house and stage station. Large gray logs inside the corral are the vigas, or roof beams, from the old station. The building was leveled in the 1950s by the owner.

Anthony P. Johnson of St. Louis came to New Mexico in the late 1840s. Afterward he worked as a teamster out of Fort Union. From an officer there he borrowed $400 to purchase this ranch in 1858. His adobe-and-rock residence with a porch across the front became a stop for stagecoaches on the last stretch of trail before Santa Fe. Johnson was absent in March 1862, when Confederate troops occupied his ranch and used it as a headquarters and supply depot for several days prior to the Battle of Glorieta. He sold the ranch in 1869 and was murdered by outlaws in 1879.

Return to I-25 and continue to the end of the trail in Santa Fe.

SANTA FE

At approximately 12 miles from Cañoncito is the first of three exits leading to the right off I-25 to Santa Fe. Take the first one, Rodeo Road/ Old Pecos Trail exit 284. At the end of the off-ramp several roads intersect. Pick up Old Pecos Trail leading toward the downtown area.

Approaching the eastern edge of the old residential section, pass a Phillips 66 Station on the right. At 1 block beyond, the street called Old

Arrival of the Caravan at Santa Fe.

Santa Fe Trail merges from the right to join Old Pecos Trail. From this point on, the street is called Old Santa Fe Trail for the remaining 10 blocks to the central plaza. It is, of course, the original route followed by the overland caravans.

Santa Fe's maze of streets requires that you obtain and follow a city map. Many hotels, shops, galleries and restaurants have maps and historical brochures sitting on counters, free for the taking. In summer months, a tourist information booth is usually maintained on the porch (in Santa Fe called a *portal*, with the accent on the second syllable) of the First National Bank (Banquest) on the west side of the plaza. A bundle of useful printed material can also be assembled at the offices of the Chamber of Commerce, 200 Marcy Street, two blocks northwest of the plaza.

In addition, the many local bookstores sell a variety of city guides that provide directions to numerous points of historical interest not associated with the SFT. Especially recommended is the magazine shop in the lobby of La Fonda Hotel on the plaza, or the Museum Shop of the Palace of the Governors. The latter carries a good stock of SFT books as well.

Some words of warning are in order for those making a first visit to Santa Fe. This is a tourist town and during the height of the season, mid-June to Labor Day weekend, the place is apt to be jammed. The Santa Fe Opera draws thousands at this time, and many weekends are taken up with special events—fiestas, craft shows, the Santa Fe Rodeo and the famed Indian Market in August. Accommodations may not be available for persons arriving without reservations. In summer, parking

Street Scene in Santa Fe

is always scarce...and expensive.

Downtown hotels and the finer restaurants charge big city prices. In fact, they are exorbitant! More modestly priced motels and restaurants are concentrated for several miles along Cerrillos Road, which begins 4 blocks south of the plaza and eventually joins I-25 going to Albuquerque. Best times to visit are in May, and September through mid-October.

Any tour of SFT sites should begin at the plaza. Points of interest A through P, described below, fall within a 3 to 4-block radius of the plaza and are best reached by walking. The remaining sites are a little farther out, and all but experienced walkers will probably prefer to reach them by car. Consult a map or inquire locally for directions.

The Plaza Area

A. The Santa Fe Plaza

This plaza marks the official end of the 1000-mile-long SFT. As one of the oldest historic sites in America, dating back to the founding of the city by the Spaniards in 1610, it has been designated a Registered National Historic Landmark. A bronze plaque to that effect is mounted near the center of the plaza.

In the earliest days of the Santa Fe trade, Missouri merchants unloaded and sold their wares here in the open air. But soon they began to rent space for stores in the rambling adobe buildings surrounding the plaza. Before 1846, one end of the historic Palace of the Governors was

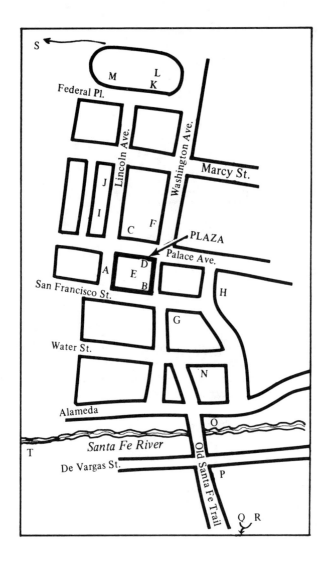

SANTA FE, Plaza Area

A. The Santa Fe Plaza
B. The End of the Trail Monument
C. The Palace of the Governors
D. The Kearny Monument
E. The Soldiers Monument
F. Cowbelle's Plaque
G. La Fonda Hotel
H. Statue of Archbishop John B. Lamy
I. Hewett House / Ft. Marcy Officers Quarters
J. Ft Marcy Plaque

K. Kit Carson Monument
L. Mural of the Old Santa Fe Trail
M. U' S' Post Office
N. Loretto Chapel (Chapel of Our Lady of Light)
O. Santa Fe River State Park Historical Sign
P. San Miguel Chapel
Q. The Mystery Monument
R. Trail Ruts
S. Bent's Grave
T. Escalante - Dominguez Marker

even given over to the traders.

B. End of the Trail Monument

Located on the southeast corner of the plaza, this historic granite stone is the last of the 160 or so DAR markers that travelers have been finding along the trail since Franklin. It signals the completion of a journey that commenced at the Beginning of the Trail Monument, a stone's throw from the Missouri River. The Santa Fe marker was dedicated in special ceremonies on August 21, 1911. A map of the trail incised on its face has an error. Can you find it?

C. Palace of the Governors

This building, dating from the early Spanish colonial period, had a close association with the SFT. For many years prior to 1846, it was the residence of Governor Manuel Armijo who was deeply involved in the overland trade. General Kearny, after crossing the Mountain Branch of the SFT and occupying New Mexico for the United States, raised the American flag over the palace and took up temporary quarters inside.

The Palace of the Governors is a part of the Museum of New Mexico. Although the current exhibits change, some relating to the SFT can usually be seen. On display is a stagecoach that was held up in Raton Pass in the latter days of the trail and New Mexico's bicentennial covered wagon (in the patio), which traveled part of the SFT in 1976.

D. The Kearny Monument

A small stone monument on the plaza facing the entrance to the Palace of the Governors honors General Kearny and his famous march over the trail in 1846.

E. The Soldiers Monument

This 33-foot column, surrounded by an iron fence in the center of the plaza, was dedicated in 1867. It honors Union soldiers who died at the Battle of Glorieta (March 28, 1862) on the SFT near Pigeon's Ranch. Another inscription honors pioneers (among them many trail travelers) who died in battles with hostile Indians. The monument can be seen in early-day photographs showing ox caravans arriving in the plaza.

F. Cowbelle's Trail Plaque

This bronze plaque honors the early trail drivers. At ground level under an iron hitch rail, it is located on Washington Avenue at the east end of the Palace of the Governors.

G. La Fonda Hotel

This historic hostelry, entirely rebuilt in the 1920s, was known as the Inn at the End of the Trail. Its fame extended back to Missouri and beyond. The original adobe building played host to some of the best known persons who came over the trail. The present structure, on the site of the first La Fonda, is on the outer corner of the plaza, opposite the

The Ellsberg-Amberg wagon train on the Santa Fe Plaza, October 1861. (Neg. no. 11254, courtesy Museum of New Mexico.)

End of the Trail Monument.

Facing the La Fonda, across Old Santa Fe Trail and about 12 yards east of that street's junction with San Francisco Street, is one of the DAR's special bronze trail plaques. It is set into the wall of a commercial building.

H. Statue of Archbishop John B. Lamy

This fine statue, which inspired Willa Cather to write her famous novel *Death Comes for the Archbishop*, is located at the entrance to the cathedral he built, at the east end of San Francisco Street just past La Fonda Hotel. Lamy made numerous trips over the SFT by wagon train and stagecoach. In a famous crossing of 1867, his caravan was attacked by Comanches. An erroneous report went out that he, together with priests and nuns accompanying him, had been massacred. All eventually reached Santa Fe safely.

Points North of the Plaza

Leave the plaza by the Art Museum (on the site where Marian Russell's mother ran a boarding house in the 1850s) and walk north on Lincoln Avenue.

I. Hewett House/Fort Marcy Officers Quarters

Located behind the Art Museum at 116 Lincoln, this much remodeled building is one of two surviving officers quarters of old Fort Marcy. (The other is a block northwest of this building at 135 Grant Avenue, next to Safeway.) General Kearny ordered construction to begin on Fort Marcy in August 1846. A blockhouse was built on a prominent hill about 600 yards northeast of the plaza, but it was never garrisoned or used. (Inquire locally if you want to visit that site.) Instead, decaying Spanish military installations behind the Palace of the Governors were used for barracks and warehouses.

In the 1870s, during the last decade of the SFT, seven two-story gabled officers quarters were built along Lincoln and Grant Avenues. When Fort Marcy was abandoned in 1894 these quarters passed into private hands and five were demolished. The one now on Lincoln was purchased in 1916 by Frank Springer (publisher of the *Cimarron News* and attorney for the Maxwell Land Grant Company, both closely identified with the trail), who remodeled the structure in the Spanish Pueblo architectural style. Springer gave the building as a residence for Museum of New Mexico Director Edgar L. Hewett, who occupied it until his death in 1946.

J. Fort Marcy Plaques

These plaques, giving a summary of the history of the Fort, are attached to the front wall of Sears on Lincoln Avenue. (Note: Sears will move from the site after 1986.)

K. Kit Carson Monument

This tall stone column is located at the end of Lincoln Avenue in front of the main entrance to the U. S. Courthouse. Carson (1809-68), a mountain man, scout and soldier, was perhaps the most famous person associated with the SFT. He traveled it many times and, although his home was in Taos, he was a frequent visitor to Santa Fe. He was a member of this city's Masonic Lodge, which still preserves his rifle.

L. Mural of the Old Santa Fe Trail

Located immediately on the left just inside the main door of the U.S. Courthouse behind the Kit Carson Monument, the mural was painted by Santa Fe artist William Penhallow Henderson as part of the New Deal federal art projects in the early 1930s. It shows a wagon train from Missouri approaching Santa Fe through the eastern hills. Other historical and scenic murals of interest are also in the building.

M. Coronado Mural

Located in the lobby of the U.S. Post Office just west of the Carson Monument and Courthouse. Really two murals showing explorer Coronado and the Pueblo Indians in 1540, they were painted by local artist Gerald Cassidy in 1921.

Points South of the Plaza

Return to the plaza and follow the street signs that say Old Santa Fe Trail, beginning on the west side of La Fonda. (This is the route that first brought you to the plaza.)

N. Loretto Chapel (Chapel of Our Lady of Light)

The building faces Old Santa Fe Trail behind La Fonda. Lamy brought six nuns of the Order of Loretto over the SFT in the early 1850s to establish a girls' academy surrounding this site. The Gothic chapel was begun in 1874 and completed in 1878, while freight wagons still rumbled past. Inside is the famed miraculous staircase.

O. Official New Mexico Highway Marker, "Santa Fe River Park"

This marker stands in the park on Alameda Street, just east of the Old Santa Fe Trail river bridge. Santa Fe traders camped here after unloading in the plaza.

P. San Miguel Chapel

On Old Santa Fe Trail, 1 block beyond the Santa Fe River bridge. This chapel, destroyed in the Pueblo Revolt of 1680, was rebuilt in 1710 and is sometimes referred to as "the oldest church in the USA." In 1859 Lamy brought the Christian Brothers over the trail to manage the chapel and found a school for boys on adjacent lands. Both this structure and the so-called "Oldest House" next door were familiar sights to travelers on the SFT.

Q. Mystery Monument

This plain, waist-high monument on the corner of East Buenavista and Old Santa Fe Trail has a fading inscription of which only the first words, "Santa Fe Trail," can be read. It is not known who placed this monument or when. It stands in front of a low log stockade fence.

R. Trail Ruts

The last ruts remaining in Santa Fe can be seen in the front yards of residences on the west (right) side of Old Santa Fe Trail beginning at Camino Corrales and continuing toward the entrance to the museums on Camino Lejo. The trail angled across what is today the parking lot of the Museum of International Folk Art. In the field to the west (just to the right of the point where Camino Lejo changes from pavement to dirt) are long, grassed ridges of earth representing trail remains. They are unmarked and difficult to see.

Other Points of Interest in Santa Fe

S. Grave of Charles Bent

Celebrated SFT trader Charles Bent was appointed first civil governor of New Mexico after the conquest by General Kearny in 1846. The following January he was killed in an uprising while at his home in Taos. Later his body was brought to Santa Fe for burial in what became the National Cemetery. About 10 blocks northwest of the plaza, this cemetery is opposite the De Vargas Shopping Mall on the Taos Highway. Inquire locally for directions.

Entering the main gate of the National Cemetery, drive straight ahead to an adobe service building at the rear. There turn right and go about 50 yards. Bent's over-sized white marble stone is on the left toward the back of the cemetery. Next to it is a tall brown sandstone marker for Major Lawrence Murphy, one of the figures in the notorious Lincoln County War in which Billy the Kid was a participant. Behind Bent's is the grave of William F. Arny who came over the SFT by stagecoach in 1861 to become Indian agent for the Utes and Jicarilla Apaches at Cimarron. He succeeded Kit Carson as the agent for those tribes and while at Cimarron became closely associated with Lucien Maxwell. Arny also served a term as the Secretary for the New Mexico Territory.

T. Escalante-Domínguez Marker

This marker is located in the river park on the southwest corner of Alameda and Galisteo Streets. It commemorates the expedition of the Franciscan fathers Vélez de Escalante and Atanasio Domínguez, who in 1776 attempted unsuccessfully to find a trail from Santa Fe to Spanish California. The so-called "Old Spanish Trail," opened in 1828, finally joined the two provinces. Its route in part followed that of the friars. Horses and mules brought over that trail after 1830 were driven on to Missouri via the SFT.

SIDE TRIP TO TAOS

In 1825 Commissioner George C. Sibley and his trail survey party reached Taos, as earlier noted. He had intended that this town serve as the official end of the SFT, even though it was locked in by mountains and virtually inaccessible by wagon from either the east or south. But its attractions were several. Taos was becoming a resort for American trappers operating in the Southern Rockies and a center of the fur

Kit Carson

trade. The Mexican government maintained a port of entry there. And because of its location in the northeast part of the province Taos was the closest settlement to both Raton Pass on the Mountain Branch and the Rock Crossing of the Canadian on the Cimarron Cut-off. Notwithstanding, Taos failed to become a major trail terminus.

From Santa Fe drive north on US 84 and US 285 to Española, about 20 miles. From there the highway north to Taos is listed on older maps as US 64 and on newer ones as SR 68. The distance from Santa Fe to Taos is approximately 75 miles. At Velarde, the highway enters the scenic canyon of the Rio Grande and some 10 miles south of Taos emerges onto a high plateau that extends to the foot of the Sangre de Cristo Mountains.

Boasting 80 art galleries, Taos is a smaller and more charming version of Santa Fe. Its Chamber of Commerce is also helpful to visitors. (The mailing address: Drawer 1, Taos, New Mexico 87571.) Historic Taos plaza in the center of town is the site where formerly all mountain trails converged. Nearby are at least four points of SFT interest:

A. Kit Carson Home and Museum

On US 64 East, 1 block east of the plaza on Kit Carson Road. Built about 1825, this structure was owned by Carson from 1843 to 1868 and served as residence and as office during the years he was agent for the

Pueblo de Taos

Utes and Jicarilla Apaches. In addition to fine exhibits, there are several furnished period rooms that impart the flavor of trail days. Admission fee.

Note: Across the street from the Kit Carson home is the renowned Taos Book Shop, specializing in volumes on the Southwest.

B. Governor Bent House and Museum

North of the plaza 1 block on Bent Street. SFT trader Charles Bent spent more of his time at the Taos home during his last years than he did at Bent's Fort on the Arkansas River. As noted, he was assassinated here in January 1847 while serving as the first appointed civil governor under American rule. Admission fee.

C. Kit Carson Park and Cemetery

On Pueblo del Norte Road, also SR 3, at 1 block north of the plaza. The graves of Kit Carson, his wife Josefa and other notables are enclosed within a fence at the rear of the park. Padre Antonio José Martínez, who married Kit and Josefa and who was a foe of the Bents, has a fine carved headstone made in the East and freighted over the SFT. A number of excellent historical markers have recently been added to the cemetery.

D. Taos Pueblo

From the entrance of Kit Carson Park continue north several blocks on SR 3 to a Y. In the center of the Y is an official New Mexico Historical Marker, "Taos Pueblo." Take the righthand fork 2 miles to the pueblo. Parking fee.

This spectacular adobe pueblo played a prominent role in the history of the Southwest, but its association with the SFT is only marginal. In 1843 Governor Manuel Armijo took a large force from

Santa Fe over the Cimarron Cut-off to meet and escort westward the annual SFT caravan. At Cold Spring in the present Oklahoma Panhandle, he sent ahead a party of 100 Taos militiamen under Captain Ventura Lobato. Many were Taos Pueblo Indians. In southwestern Kansas, Lobato was attacked by raiders from the Texas Republic who killed or captured almost all his command. The severe losses sustained in the incident embittered Taos Indians against Americans as well as Texans.

This enmity is believed to have led them to participate in the murder of Charles Bent and others four years later. At the edge of the pueblo can still be seen ruins of the church that became a refuge for the rebels and was battered down by Colonel Sterling Price's artillery during the U.S. Army's assault in February 1847.

SIDE TRIP TO ALBUQUERQUE

While Albuquerque, on the Rio Grande 60 miles southwest of Santa Fe, was not situated on the SFT, many Missouri traders passed through it on their way south to El Paso and Chihuahua City. This route, beginning at Santa Fe, became known to the SFT merchants as the Chihuahua Trail. It was really the old Camino Real of colonial days. Several persons prominent in the Santa Fe trade settled in Albuquerque and opened stores on or near the plaza. Chief among them was German-born Franz Huning whose trail journal has been published.

From Santa Fe take I-25 south to Albuquerque. About halfway (3½ miles or so beyond exit 259 for Santo Domingo Pueblo) is a large stone monument with a plaque dedicated to the Mormon Battalion. It is located along an access road on the right (west) side of the Interstate. (Note: As this book was going to press highway expansion resulted in demolition of the Mormon Battalion Marker. Latest word is that it will be reconstructed nearby in a roadside park.) After arriving in Santa Fe, the Battalion followed this route south to pick up what was to become the Gila Trail leading to California.

Continue on to the main interchange in Albuquerque where I-25 intersects with I-40. Exit to I-40 heading west to Grants. A mile or so beyond take the Rio Grande Boulevard exit and once off the Interstate turn left (south) on Rio Grande to the Old Town Plaza, the former center of Albuquerque. There are numerous historical markers in the center of the plaza, some of which relate to the period of the SFT. On the northeast edge of Old Town, at 2000 Mountain Road N.W., is the Albuquerque Museum, whose splendid historical exhibits include sections on Coronado and the Chihuahua and Santa Fe Trails. Admission fee.

The fourth and last Madonna of the Trail statue (or Pioneer Mother) on the SFT is located in McClellan Park in the 800 block of North Fourth Street. (Inquire locally for directions to the park.) It was supposed to have been placed in Santa Fe in 1927, but artists and writers there rejected it as being ugly and not representative of the region's Spanish pioneer women. In a huff the DAR moved the statue to Albuquerque.

APPENDIX I

SPECIAL EVENTS

There are a number of special events held annually that have a direct relation to the Santa Fe Trail and its history. It is often worth the effort to coordinate a tour of the SFT to take advantage of the opportunities such events offer, always keeping in mind that local accommodations will probably be at a premium.

The schedule of many activities may vary from year to year. Addresses are provided below so that travelers can write to confirm the exact dates and obtain a program.

ARROW ROCK

Various events are held during the year that are of historical interest. For example, on June 18-19, 1983, there was a "Militia Muster." On Labor Day weekend of that year a "Santa Fe Trail Re-enactment" was staged, and it is now a yearly event. Write: Historic Site Administrator, Arrow Rock State Historic Site, Arrow Rock, Missouri 65320.

FORT OSAGE

A River Days Celebration and Mountain Man Rendezvous is held on a weekend late in May. Write: Chamber of Commerce, Box 147, Independence, Missouri 64051.

INDEPENDENCE

The Santa-Cali-Gon Celebration takes place annually on Labor Day weekend. The term is an acronym for Santa Fe, California and Oregon, the names of the three trails that began here. Write: Chamber of Commerce, Box 147, Independence, Missouri 64051.

WESTPORT

Several events of interest to trail buffs occur during the summer months, including a living history program. For a calendar of activities write: Westport Tomorrow, 4000 Baltimore, Kansas City, Missouri 64111.

KANSAS

In recent summers, the Kansas Chapter of the Arthritis Foundation has sponsored a Santa Fe Trail ride across the state as a fund raising activity. It includes horseback riders, wagons and hikers. For those who are hardy, participation in this event is a good way to get in the spirit of the trail. Write: Arthritis Foundation, 1602 East Waterman, Wichita, Kansas 67211.

COUNCIL GROVE

On June 10-12, 1983, Council Grove held its first Washunga Days Celebration, named in honor of the last Kaw Indian chief. It has become an annual event. Kaws come from Oklahoma to participate and there is a historical pageant. Like everything else that happens here, the celebration gives strong emphasis to the SFT. Write: Chamber of Commerce, Council Grove, Kansas 66846.

LARNED

In late March of even-numbered years, the Santa Fe Trail Center sponsors a SFT Rendezvous extending over three days. Events include presentation of popular and scholarly papers on trail history and tours to nearby sites. Write: Santa Fe Trail Center, Rural Route 3, Larned, Kansas 67550.

Nearby, Fort Larned National Historic Site from time to time offers special historical programs and re-enactments. Write: Superintendent, Fort Larned National Historic Site, Box 69, Larned, Kansas 67559.

BENT'S FORT

A primitive rendezvous for "buckskinners" in period dress is held for four days in March and/or September. There is registration and strict historical requirements for participants, but fort visitors are allowed to join in some of the events. Other special activities are offered during the year. Write: Bent's Old Fort National Historic Site, 35110 Highway, 194 East, La Junta, Colorado 81050.

LAS ANIMAS

Santa Fe Trail Day, an event held for more than fifty years, takes place in late April. Write: Chamber of Commerce, Las Animas, Colorado 81054.

LA JUNTA

The famous Koshare [Boy Scout] Indian dancers here are world famous. Try and catch one of their summer programs. Write: Koshare Indian Museum, 115 West 18th Street, La Junta, Colorado 81050.

BOISE CITY

"Santa Fe Trail Daze" is held during the first weekend in June. A free, all-day bus tour offered by the Chamber of Commerce takes visitors to Autograph Rock near Cold Spring on the SFT (among other places). The local *Boise City News* puts out a special edition containing much on local history and trail-related items. Write: Chamber of Commerce, Boise City, Oklahoma 73933.

RATON

The National Rifle Association sponsors an annual Santa Fe Trail Rendezvous at its facility west of Raton. It includes a mountain man encampment and trappers' trade fair plus a re-enactment of frontiersmen and families traveling in the ruts of the SFT. Observers are welcome. For a brochure write: NRA Whittington Center, Box 1086, Raton, New Mexico 87740.

CIMARRON

Cimarron Days, including events of historical interest, takes place on Labor Day weekend. Write: Cimarron Chamber of Commerce, Cimarron, New Mexico 87714.

FORT UNION

In the summer months excellent historical events, including military encampments and re-enactments, are presented to the public. The dates vary, but Founders' Day Weekend is in late July. Write: Unit Manager, Fort Union National Monument, Watrous, New Mexico 87753.

LAS VEGAS

Rails-N-Trails Days, launched in 1984, takes place annually on the first full weekend in June. Write: Chamber of Commerce, P. O. Box 148, Las Vegas, New Mexico 87701.

SANTA FE

Santa Fe offers many history-related activities, among them a July rodeo, a late July Spanish market and a mid-August Indian market and trade fair. The Santa Fe Fiesta takes place in mid-September. For a schedule of events write: Chamber of Commerce, 200 West Marcy Street, Santa Fe, New Mexico 87501.

APPENDIX II

NATIONAL HISTORIC LANDMARKS
ON THE SANTA FE TRAIL

The Registered National Historic Landmark Program, which grew out of the National Survey of Historic Sites and Buildings (begun in 1957), was designed to identify and encourage preservation of significant sites. Those places receiving Registry designation have been plaqued by the National Park Service.

At least nineteen sites along the Santa Fe Trail have been selected for inclusion in the National Registry. For convenience in identifying them they are listed below as a group:

Arrow Rock, Missouri
Fort Osage, Missouri
Fort Leavenworth, Kansas
Mahaffie House and Farmstead at Olathe, Kansas
Council Grove, Kansas
Fort Larned, Kansas
Trail Remains West of Dodge City, Kansas
Lower or Wagon Bed Springs, Kansas
Pawnee Rock, Kansas
Fort (Camp) Nichols, Oklahoma
Rabbit Ears-Clayton Complex, New Mexico
Raton Pass, New Mexico
Wagon Mound, New Mexico
Fort Union, New Mexico
Watrous (La Junta), New Mexico
Pecos Pueblo and Mission, New Mexico
Glorieta Pass, New Mexico
Plaza and Palace of the Governors, Santa Fe, New Mexico
Kit Carson House, Taos, New Mexico

INDEX